JONAS OF KIIVIJARVI

Jonas of Kiivijarvi

Finnish Freedom Fighter

LESLIE W. WISURI

NORTH STAR PRESS OF ST. CLOUD, INC.

Library of Congress Cataloging-in-Publication Data

Wisuri, Leslie W., 1925-
    Jonas of Kiivijarvi : Finnish freedom fighter / Leslie W. Wisuri.
    240 p. 23 cm.
    ISBN 0-87839-104-5 (alk. paper)
    1. Finland—History—Revolution. 1917-1918—Fiction.
  2. Finland—History—1909-1917—Fiction. I. Title.
PS3573.I885J65 1996
813′.54—dc20   96-14416
                                                 CIP

Cover Illustration: Bob Linden

ISBN: 0-87839-104-5

Printed in the United States of America by Versa Press, Inc., of East Peoria, Illinois.

Published by: North Star Press of St. Cloud, Inc.
                  P.O. Box 451
                  St. Cloud, Minnesota 56302

Dedication

I dedicate this book to my wife, Jackie, for her patience and help all through the writing, and to Linda Frye and the rest of the Jefferson City Literary group for their help and critique.

I also dedicate this book to the memory of my grandfather, Jonas, who told me these stories and was my inspiration.

Contents

Preface

JONAS WISURI WAS MY GRANDFATHER and the narrator of these stories. I suspect that my grandfather and the hero in these tales were one and the same. At this late date, I have no way to confirm this, but many things point in this direction. I believe it to be true.

My grandfather and I were very close from the time I was eleven until his death when I was sixteen. Grandfather owned a farm but did very little work, as he had two grown sons living there (my uncles), who did most of the work. He'd give orders in the morning, and then he was free to do whatever he wanted the rest of the day.

My own father, busy working for the Forest Service in connection with the Civilian Conservation Corp, came home only on weekends. I spent as much time as possible with my grandfather. Perhaps I searched for that connection I had failed to make with my father.

After morning orders, grandfather and I would go fishing or hunting or just loafing. At a lake on the back side of the farm, we spent many hours fishing and talking. The stories he told were always in the third person. At the time, I thought them interesting, and I had no reason to question their source or authenticity. Now, in retrospect, I see clues that point strongly to my grandfather.

As a teenager, I didn't think to ask him how he knew so much detail about the person in the story and his relationship with others. Nor did I think to ask him point blank if he was the hero. Now I wish I could have him here to ask these questions.

Clues came to mind as I started to put these stories to paper. Over the many years, I assumed that all my aunts and uncles knew these same stories. We had a family reunion, and I recounted some of the stories, and all my relatives were amazed. None of them had heard them. They knew he had served in the Russian army; he did the manual of arms in Russian on occasion as a kind of joke. That was the extent of their knowledge of his early days.

Other clues surfaced as I started to write. Grandfather never used a name for the hero other than the ghost. He used other names of Finnish people and Russians but never the name of the hero. One name that did crop up continually was Vilho, the ghost's best friend. I didn't think about it until I started writing, but my father, the first born, had been named Vilho. Coincidence? I think not.

Another interesting point was that my grandfather also used the third person when he told stories of his life in America after coming over from Finland, making them sound like an extension of the ghost stories. These same stories were verified by my father, aunts, and uncles as real events that happened to my grandfather.

Some of the stories I had him repeat over and over because I especially liked them. He never varied the details of the stories from one telling to the next. To me now, this sounds like memory not memorization.

Of course, it's just possible that my grandfather was a great storyteller or that he knew the person in the stories described as the ghost. These also could be a collection of happenings of different people. But, to me, none of these theories makes as much sense as the ghost being my grandfather. His absolute wizardry with a knife and being a deadly shot conjured up visions of him doing the same things in Finland against the Russians. He had the ability to tell when something was wrong in the forest—a large animal or a person approaching. Several times when I was with him, he predicted deer coming long before we could see or hear them. One time he told me to get ready to swim because he suspected a bear was coming. Sure enough, a few minutes later, one appeared. He could tell the difference between an animal approaching and a person just by some imperceptible change in the sounds in the woods. I thought that ability was wonderful; now I also think it was developed because he was a fugitive from the Russians.

He always carried a salt shaker and matches with him wherever we went, and he could light a fire in no time and cook fish, grouse, or rabbit on a stick. We seldom took food from home when we went hunting or fishing. He said we could live off the land. Again, I think this ability came during those fugitive days when he was forced to survive in the wilderness.

He seldom went shirtless, but one hot summer day at the lake, he took off his shirt and soaked it in the lake to cool off. I noticed some vivid white scars on his back and asked him about them. He just shrugged off my question and said, "It was a long time ago." When I think about the ghost being whipped for the ice rink prank, I can see the scars on my grandfather's back.

I had a hard time translating these stories, which my grandfather told to me in Finnish. I wrote them down as my imagination perceived them, but

I'm not sure if all my interpretations would meet my grandfather's approval. The stories are in as near a sequence as I could put them, although they weren't told to me in any particular order. I chose a sequence that seemed to make logical sense. As I wrote them down, I began to feel as if my grandfather had singled me out to tell these stories so they would not die. It took many years to write the stories and be satisfied with my work, but now I have a record of the wondrous events of my grandfather's life in Finland.

Leslie W. Wisuri
1996

Introduction

FOR SIX HUNDRED YEARS, Sweden used Finland as part of its own country and a defensive buffer against Russia and its enemies to the east.

In 1808, under a flag of truce, the Russians overran Finland. Sweden was busy elsewhere and could not come to Finland's aid. The Finns, numbering twelve thousand, held off a Russian force of eighty-five thousand. After a year and a half, they surrendered. Sweden ignored their valiant defense of Finland and Sweden. In the resulting treaty of 1809, Sweden gave all of Finland to Russia.

The Russian rulers decided Finland would made a good buffer between them and their western enemies. Starting in 1809, under the reign of Alexander I, the least oppressive of all the tsars, Finland became a Grand Duchy of Russia. Little regard was given to the people of Finland.

Terrorists assassinated Alexander I, and Alexander II took the throne. More oppression resulted from his trying to keep down terrorist activity and stay alive.

The accession of Nicholas II to the throne in 1894 began like the rule of his predecessors, promising the Finnish people respect for their constitution. The Russians, they were told, only needed Finland as a buffer state. The Finnish people hoped for no more oppressive, autocratic measures of the latter years of Alexander III. Nicholas II's rule proved more oppressive.

Tsars had little experience with the behavior of men except as traditional slaves to the autocratic rule. When they saw cooperative endeavor as well as individualism developing in Finland, they feared the results.

Nicholas sent General Nickolai Ivanovich Bobrikov, his most ruthless commander, to Finland. Bobrikov immediately pushed hard to gain full control of Finland and make it an integral part of the Russian empire. This included serious restrictions of the freedom of the Finnish people. All able-bodied young men were immediately drafted, and they had to serve at least two years in the Russian army, commanded, of course, by Russian officers.

Resentment mounted. Even under Sweden, who ruled Finland with an amount of fairness, resentment had existed, but, under the Russian yoke, life had become oppressive.

Jonas and Nicholas II were tied together even though they had not met . . . would never meet. In the winter of 1897, an incident occurred in the small Finnish town of Kiivijarvi, an important outpost and training center for Finnish men conscripted into the Russian army. Kiivijarvi was also a supply depot and warehouse center for smaller outposts in the region.

The incident itself was of relatively minor importance. Had the man been executed as planned, nothing likely would have come from it so crushing was the hold the Russians held on the Finnish people. But, as it turned out, the man escaped. So began a different course of events, a path that sparked the torch of freedom in Finnish hearts that eventually overthrew the Russian domination. Because of a sense of humor, an accident, and the workings of a clever mind, history in Finland changed forever.

JONAS OF KIIVIJARVI

Chapter 1

The Ice Rink Incident

In the winter of 1897, at a Russian outpost in Kiivijarvi, Finland, an incident occurred that ignited the smoldering torch of Finnish freedom to full flame. Of itself, the incident was of little consequence, except that it pushed one Jonas Kekola to the forefront as a leader of the Finnish people's fight for freedom.

"THIS WILL TEACH YOU TO TRY to make a fool of me, Jonas," snarled Karloff. "Proceed with the punishment, Lieutenant!"

The first blow looked tentative as the black snake of a whip whistled through the air. *Crack!* Before the whip snapped back for another stroke, a diamond pattern rose on Jonas' back, then small pin points of blood oozed to the surface of his skin. He never made a sound as the lash strokes fell. His back knotted up, as if he could tense his muscles enough to block out the pain. The blood drained from his face, bringing on a dizziness. With the dizziness came a flash of remembrance of the events that brought him here. The severity of the "discipline" far outweighed the so-called crime. It had all started earlier as a mischievous prank.

A week earlier, the Russians dumped ashes on the skating rink used by the Finns in a vain attempt to attract Finnish women to use their rink. Finnish men were not allowed to use the Russian rink and the Finnish women ignored the invitation, much to the chagrin of the Russians.

Rancor built rapidly when the Russians announced a demonstration of their skating prowess, and the Finnish enlisted men were forced to work overtime to get the Russian rink ready for the event.

"I saw those damn Russians spread ashes on our rink, and now we have to fix theirs," grumbled Aimo Hakala.

Jonas turned his head in surprise, "You mean you saw them do it and are just now getting around to telling us? All this time, I thought some young pranksters did it!"

"I thought everyone knew it was the Russkies," said Aimo.

1

"I wish we could get back at those Russian bastards for ruining our rink," said Jonas' best friend Vilho.

"We can't stand around and argue about how it happened," said Sergeant Makela. "We've got to get the team hooked to the water sleigh. Those officers will be on our backs if we don't get that rink flooded."

Jonas and Vilho harnessed the team and hooked up the water sleigh. Makela sent for more men to help haul water. The men boarded the barrel-loaded sleigh and headed for the lake.

The lake sat in a rocky depression giving the town its name, Kiivijarvi, meaning rocky shore. Jagged, jumbled rocks with spruce trees growing among them surrounded three-fourths of the shore, but the east end of the lake, nearest to town, had a gradual sandy beach. Eons of rain and snow melt had carried sand down the long, gradual sluiceway to the lake making a smooth beach for summer fun.

"Jonas, you take the ice saw," Makela ordered. "Vilho, use the ax to chop the first hole, so we can get the saw through."

The task was going well when Jonas said, "I have an idea that might work to get back at those damn Russkies for ruining our rink."

"What is it? Let's hear it." clamored the crew.

"I'll do anything to make life miserable for the Russians," Vilho said.

Jonas briefly outlined a plan to turn the upcoming skating demonstration into a fiasco.

"Are you sure it'll work?" asked Vilho.

"I'm not sure," Jonas replied, "But what have we got to lose? If it works, the Russians will make fools of themselves. If it doesn't work, so what? We have to flood the rink anyway."

"You take over, Jonas," Makela said, "You have some idea how this should be done."

"We'll have clear going," Jonas said. "The Russians are back in their quarters toasting their feet by the fire with glasses of vodka in their hands. They're probably laughing at us dumb Finns for working late into the night. We'll see who has the last laugh." He chuckled.

The idea of pulling a prank on the Russians put everyone in high spirits. Everyone except Aimo, who voiced opposition to doing anything against the Russians for fear of reprisal. Despite his objections, off they went, singing and having a high good time, arms around each other's shoulders in camaraderie.

The rink stood outside the main gate of the post. The officers would have preferred it closer to their quarters, but there wasn't a level place big enough inside the post. The only flat place inside was the training field and parade ground, which was out of the question for a rink. The Russian compound consisted of administration buildings, barracks, warehouses, stables, and the prison.

"If this works, it'll be worth all the extra effort," Vilho laughed. The rest of the crew chuckled in anticipation. They worked with a will until late in the night.

Saturday morning the sun came up like a big bronze disc shining in a cloudless, azure sky. The bright sun reflecting off the white snow hurt the eyes. Jonas and Vilho were at the rink early to check the condition of the ice, which, frozen slate grey, showed no trace of the treachery beneath.

The Russians in their quarters prepared for the skating show and the party afterwards. "We'll show those dumb Finns a real Russian gala affair," said Captain Karloff to his men.

Tall, wiry, Captain Karloff was the best skater of the group. With his black, wavy hair and light olive complexion, he might have been considered good-looking were it not for the cruel slit of a mouth partially hidden behind a heavy moustache. His excessive liking for alcohol was responsible for his exile to this remote post. He meted out heavy punishment to the men for slight offenses.

The civilian population also suffered under Karloff's tyrannical rule. His troops confiscated cows, pigs, chickens, and produce, and gave nearly worthless scrip in return. Karloff made the heavy Russian yoke even harder to bear.

The Finns reluctantly attended the skating demonstration because they would be conspicuous by their absence. They hated Karloff and the Russian rule intensely but didn't know how to change matters.

"Men, I'll go first with a small warm-up and a few maneuvers," Karloff said. "Ivan, you and John will go next with that duo you execute so well. The group maneuvers come after, like those we do on land only with more grace and finesse. Then we'll have a short intermission and invite the ladies to skate. After that, each man does his specialty. Ivan and John will go next to last, and I'll do the finale. We'll break and start the party with plenty of vodka. There's strong wine for the ladies who think vodka might be too much for them. Before you know it, we'll have a real Russian party. After that, it's going to be every man for himself. I'm going after that beautiful blond, Emma Lehtinen, the girl I saw with Jonas Kekola. I'm sure she'll give up that clod for a Russian officer, especially after she sees me skate."

Earlier the Russians had set up a red-and-black-striped tent with pennants flying from the outrigger poles and top. That morning they pulled up in a sleigh, painted red and black and drawn by a pair of pure black horses set with white harness. Even the Finns had to admire their style. The black horses contrasted just right with the white snow.

With great fanfare, Lieutenant Gerchenoff announced, "Here, ladies and gentlemen, is the greatest skater in all of Russia, Captain Peter Ilonovich Karloff!"

Captain Karloff glided out on the ice, resplendent in his scarlet-and-blue uniform. A white silk scarf, tied loosely around his neck, billowed out behind him as he skated.

Karloff made a few fast laps around the rink to test it. Speeding up, he did a double-reverse turn and backward jump. The jump and cut-in backwards was his undoing. His skates appeared to snag on the ice and stop but he did not. The backward momentum kept him going to make a spectacular three point landing that brought roars of laughter from the crowd.

"I can't be that out of shape to take a fall like that," Karloff muttered to himself. "What's the matter with me?"

Utterly mortified, Karloff got up quickly and brushed himself off, trying to hide his anger. He tried several more times to get through the move he knew so well. Each attempt resulted in the same hilarious disaster. The entire assemblage was in tears from laughter. The captain retired to the changing tent in a rage, his red face advertising his embarrassment. His chance for glory before the townspeople and his men had turned to bitter humiliation.

Noticing several smirks on the faces of the men, Karloff said, "The first remark will result in that man doing lonesome duty with the Laplanders and reindeer. Up there even the reindeer start looking good."

"Captain, is there something wrong with your skates or the sharpening job on them?" Ivan asked.

"No, damn it, I sharpen my own skates, and I don't make mistakes. There's something wrong with the ice. I just can't see what."

"Do you think we ought to cancel until we find out what's wrong?"

"No, you and John go out and do your routine. I hope your performance is better than mine."

Their routine was primarily precision skating, and they had no problems, which enraged Karloff even more. This was to be the day he showed the Finnish clods how a gentleman Russian officer performed.

Next came the close order drill, a routine maneuver. No mishaps.

Karloff went back out to redeem himself. "I'll show them this time," he told himself. If anything, his falls were better—or worse, depending on the point of view. In his last fall, he made a complete somersault, which knocked the wind out of him. He had to be helped to the changing tent.

"Damn, I know there's something wrong with that ice. I'll have the person responsible whipped on the town square."

The party with the town women fizzled. The Finns walked off in a group, laughing about the spectacle Karloff had made of himself. Karloff went back to his quarters, mumbling to himself about the ice problems.

The rest of the officers proceeded to get roaring drunk on the vodka

4

and wine intended for the party. Lieutenant Barloff chuckled saying, "I can't keep from laughing about the old man falling on his ass so many times."

"You better not laugh too loud," cautioned Lieutenant Brezinski, "or he'll have you whipped or sent up north with the Laplanders. You know how mean he can get."

Two days passed, and everything appeared normal. Only a few remarks floated about concerning great Russian skaters and their graceful falls. Karloff ignored the snide remarks but resolved to find out if someone had tampered with the rink.

On the third day, Karloff called in the rink crew one by one and questioned them about the ice. Everyone, except Aimo Hakala adamantly denied any knowledge of rink tampering. Aimo's nervousness confirmed Karloff's suspicions of something amiss. He continued the interrogation until Aimo broke down and confessed, "Jonas came up with the idea of putting a layer of that fine white beach sand on the ice and flooding over it. Your skates cut through the thin layer of ice to the sand."

To protect Aimo from the other men and use him as an informant later, Karloff acted as though he was checking the rink himself. He took a crew to the rink and had them chop out a square of ice. Everyone could see the problem after he melted it down. One piece of ice was saved to show the sand imbedded in it. He told the officers Jonas was the ring leader of the prank.

After the weekly Saturday morning inspection of the troops, Captain Karloff said, "Corporal Jonas Kekola, report to the orderly room right after formation. Dismissed."

Jonas relaxed from his position of attention and wondered why the Captain wanted to see him. He was slightly angry because it would delay his getting off to see his fiance, Emma Lehtinen.

In the orderly room the First Sergeant sent Jonas directly to Karloff's office. Jonas was surprised to find Lieutenants Gerchenoff, Barloff and Brezinski present. He snapped to attention, saluted and said, "Corporal Kekola reporting as ordered, sir."

Karloff did not give him permission to stand at ease, which Jonas expected. He was also surprised at the formality of the meeting.

Karloff sat at his desk idly toying with a pencil for a few minutes trying to create an effect. He could not help but admire Jonas as he stood at attention. His well-built body contrasted sharply with the Russian officers present who looked slovenly by comparison. Jonas was tall, fair skinned and blond, and all the Russians in the room were dark haired and much shorter.

Karloff looked at the lieutenants and back at Jonas, cleared his throat and said, "Corporal, it has been brought to my attention that you were the ring leader in sabotaging our ice rink and causing me great embarrassment. What do you have to say about the charges?"

Jonas stood for a moment flushing red and trying to find the right words. Finally he just stood mute in surprise at the charge.

Karloff came out of his seat and around his desk like a tiger. He put his face next to Jonas' and growled in a low voice, "Jonas, I am the law of the land, and I have the right to say or do anything I want. You are about to see what happens when you defy my rules. Tie him up and take him to the town square.

Lieutenants Gerchenoff, Barloff, and Brezinski seized him, bound him tightly and marched him off.

The church bells rang to summon the townspeople to the square. The Finns knew this meant a punishment or another decree reducing their freedom even further. They gathered in small groups, murmuring to each other and speculating about the reason for the gathering. When they saw the Russians leading Jonas out, they were surprised. They knew him to be a model soldier.

The Russian officers removed Jonas' greatcoat, stripped his shirt and undershirt off, leaving him naked to the waist. Jonas shivered from cold and anticipation of what was to come. He had seen this done before.

When Karloff was sure everyone was there, he had them tie Jonas' legs spread eagle to a sleigh brought for the purpose. Gerchenoff jerked his left hand around and tied it to the sleigh seat while Barloff tied his right hand to the tail gate.

"Damn," said Reino Makela, "they could have picked someone else for the job of whip wielder. That damn Gerchenoff really enjoys his work. He isn't going to let up on Jonas at all."

The next whip stroke was a little harder, opening the flesh in several places. The next ones were even harder, Gerchenoff laying them on with a will. Each cut exposed pink flesh a moment before it started to bleed. Gerchenoff was sweating heavily despite the cold day.

Emma Lehtinen, Jonas' sweetheart, and her brother Matt, came to the town square by sleigh when the church bells rang. They didn't know it was Jonas they were going to see punished. Emma was aghast. She buried her head in her brother's shoulder, sobbing uncontrollably. She was angry with herself for being unable to control her emotions, angrier still at the helplessness of the situation.

The crowd waited for Jonas to cry out in pain or beg for mercy. Not one sound did he utter. The only visible effect was his jaw muscles getting tighter and tighter as he clenched his teeth in pain. After twenty-two lashes, his mind slipped into a black void, and he passed out from the pain, his body sagging on the ropes.

"That's enough, Gerchenoff," Karloff said. "He can't feel it anymore. We don't want to cripple him so bad he can't soldier."

Karloff didn't notice or didn't care about the extreme hostility exhibited by the Finnish enlisted men and townspeople. His face showed great pleasure in finding the rink culprit and meting out punishment for the same. He walked off with an arrogant swagger, "That will teach those dumb Finns who really runs this territory."

Little did he know this was the spark that would start the flame of freedom in Finland. The man he had whipped would become the torch to ignite the conflagration.

Chapter 2

Pain

SERGEANT REINO MAKELA AND VILHO cut the unconscious Jonas loose from the sleigh. Vilho caught him when he started to slide to the ground. Jonas partially came to and groaned.

"They can't kill an old 'sisu' Finn like you, Jonas," Vilho said.

Matt pulled their sleigh close so that Reino and Vilho could load Jonas. Emma spread her lap robe. They laid Jonas face down on it and gently covered his back with his coat. Jonas winced when the cold coat touched his raw back. Reino and Vilho jumped into the sleigh, and Matt whipped the horse and headed for the Lehtinen house.

Emma rode up front, ashen faced, afraid to think of the carnage inflicted on Jonas' strong body. She looked at Matt, tears streaming down her face, "Is he going to all right? Will he live and be crippled or maybe die?"

"He'll be all right. He's tough. Lots of men have survived worse. He's going to be sore for a while though, and he'll have some scars."

They arrived at the Lehtinen's large farm house on the edge of town. Originally two brothers had built adjoining houses for company and mutual help. The Lehtinens and the Hakalas now owned the farms.

Emma ran into the house to get her father to help. The four men picked up the lap robe by the corners to carry Jonas into the house.

"I can walk," Jonas objected.

"Lie still. We can handle you," said Vilho.

Anna, Emma's mother, cleared the huge oak kitchen table so they would have a place to put Jonas down. They lifted the coat off him.

Anna gasped as she saw Jonas' back, "Oh my, why did they have to do that?"

The kitchen was the biggest room in the house, serving also as dining room. A big wood cook stove dominated one wall of the room. Gleaming copper pans hung on racks, and everything was spotless. The kitchen spoke of love as well as the love of cooking.

Jonas was shivering when they laid him on the kitchen table. "He needs to be kept good and warm," Toivo said. "He could go into shock."

Emma heated water and got clean rags to cleanse the wounds.

Gerchenoff's whip had left a curious pattern on Jonas' back, alternating diagonals from left to right resulted in a pattern of large diamonds. The small scars made by the whip's braiding would eventually disappear. The large pattern would remain with him for the rest of his life.

After an hour of tender, loving care, Emma had the wounds cleansed and anointed. Emma didn't dare put any other dressing on his back for fear of it sticking to the wounds. Jonas sat up, slowly swung his legs down off the table, and thanked everyone for their help. Moving his arms up a little, he grimaced with pain.

"What I can't understand is how Karloff found out about the sand and that I was behind it. Someone had to have told him."

"I have an idea it was Aimo," said Vilho. "He was against the idea in the first place. And he was in the captain's office too long to deny any knowledge."

"Maybe," said Jonas, "but I don't want anyone to get into trouble over this affair until I know for sure. I'll find out who's responsible in time."

"We don't need our people going over to the side of those damn Russians," said Vilho angrily.

"You don't know that for sure, so let it drop," said Jonas.

"Jonas, are you going to stay in the army or skip out because of this whipping?" Reino asked. "I wouldn't blame you if you decided to leave."

Jonas replied, "I have six months to go until I'll be through with this Russian army. I can do that kind of duty standing on my head, Karloff or no Karloff."

"You may have to do just that, as mean as Karloff is to us Finns. Now he'll really have it in for you," Vilho added.

"I know it's going to be tough, but I have Emma to think about."

With that he drew Emma to him giving her a quick kiss. Emma blushed and cuddled closer.

Jonas, looking at Emma but talking to the group said, "Emma and I plan to get married and settle down on a small farm. We've been looking at one in particular for some time. With my army mustering-out pay, some savings, and a small loan from Emma's father, I think we can make it. The farm isn't big, but it has a beautiful spring-fed lake with plenty of trout. We have enough cleared land to raise a few cows and some crops for cash. It's isolated, but then we won't have to deal with the Russkies."

"Jonas, I didn't think you had it in you," said Vilho, "All you've ever done is hunt, fish and trap. You like being a hermit for weeks on end."

Jonas smiled. "With Emma it'll be worth settling down. I'm getting older all the time. Besides, I can still hunt and fish. I know I can get Emma to take a few trips into the back woods now and then."

"I like the outdoors almost as much as Jonas," said Emma. "That's another reason we like this farm. We can get back to nature."

Jonas looked off in the distance as if seeing the future and said, "If I stay in this area, I know I'm going to get mad enough to do something about the other Russian indignities. The whipping is of minor importance to me. It's our loss of freedom that bothers me. Every day the Russians curtail our freedom even more."

"I've been saying that for a long time," retorted Vilho, "We need to do something about it, or we'll never get out from under them."

"Snellman and others have preached passive resistance," said Jonas. It doesn't seem to work. The assassination of Bobrikov by Shauman scared them for a while, and they gave us a little breathing room, but now they're back to their old ways. We need a leader to take the people by the hand. I don't know who it will be, but there has to be someone."

"Why not us?" Vilho asked.

Jonas moved his shoulders and winced in pain. "I'll have to give it some thought. Maybe we could do something to start a little resistance around here. I'll think about it. You think, too."

"I can think of a lot of things to do," Vilho said.

Jonas smiled. "I know you can, but I feel that, if we do anything, it must be slow and well planned. I know you, Vilho. You can be quite headstrong."

"But those damn Russkies make me mad all the time!"

They decided Jonas best spend the night in the living room rather than go back to the barracks. The next day was Sunday, and he would need all the time possible to recuperate for duty on Monday.

Emma helped him lie down on a big sheepskin pad by the fireplace. Everyone except Emma said good night and left. She laid down along side him being careful not to touch his back.

"Are you feeling any better?" she asked gently.

"Some, but I still hurt."

"I'm sorry, I was really scared for you. When I saw it was you they were going to punish . . . . I love you so much. Conflicts like this really scare me. I know you can let your temper get the best of you. Please don't let this ruin everything."

"I'm over it, it will be all right."

They kissed and touched softly, their faces lit by the flickering of the dying fire. Every little while the fire gave a new spurt of energy giving their faces a soft, ruddy glow. A log fell, creating a shower of sparks, startling them.

"You know as bad as I hurt," Jonas whispered, "I still want you very much right this minute."

10

"I want you, too," Emma said shyly, "but it will be better if we wait. Besides, mother or father could walk down the stairs any minute."

Jonas chuckled, "You worry too much. They wouldn't come down here without making some noise to let us know they're coming."

"I know you're right, but I still want to wait."

"I know, I can wait, but I do get impatient. There are times when I think it's all a dream, and I'll wake up and find you gone. I feel I'm the luckiest man in the world just getting to know you."

"Do you feel lucky after what you went through today?"

Jonas laughed a little and said, "That has nothing to do with you."

They lay together, enjoying the closeness of each other's company, the warmth of fire creating a feeling of lethargy.

Emma said sleepily, "I'd better get to bed. Father is going to come down to see what's going on, whiplashes or no whiplashes."

"All right, sweetheart. Give me a good-night kiss."

She gave him a long, lingering kiss, reluctant to say good night. She started for the stairs but came back to give him another quick kiss.

"This is almost worth taking the whipping."

"Good night, I love you."

The next morning, Jonas woke up stiff and sore with his back still on fire. Moving made him painfully aware of the previous day's events.

He mumbled to himself, "Somehow I have to survive. I have to go back to duty in the morning, and I know I'm not going to get any sympathy from the Russian officers."

Emma came downstairs. She kissed him good morning, which helped take his mind off his pain. Jonas lay there taking in all her fresh beauty, his face lighting up in love and awe. He felt glad just being near her.

She's the most beautiful, wonderful person I have ever known, he thought. *I couldn't stand being away from her for very long. I don't have the words to tell her how much I love her. I wish I was better with words. I never felt as if I needed to talk better until I met her. I want to tell her my innermost thoughts and feelings, but I don't know how. I hope she knows without me giving her any big, flowery speeches.*

Emma inspected and admired his well-muscled but marred back carefully. She warmed the ointment so it wouldn't be a shock to the raw nerve endings when she applied it.

"Oh, that feels good," Jonas said. "You have such a gentle touch."

"I'm trying not to hurt you. Do you think these whip marks will ever go away?"

"I doubt it, but who cares. I don't."

"I hate to see you carry these scars for the rest of your life."

Emma and Jonas lolled around, waiting for the rest of the family.

11

Jonas was sitting on the edge of a chair with a shirt draped over his shoulders to keep off the early morning chill when Anna came downstairs to start breakfast.

Anna, Emma's mother, was an extremely good-looking woman. She didn't show her age at all. Anna and Emma could pass for sisters. Always neat and pert, she wore a starched white apron because she loved to cook for her family. She wore her long, blonde hair braided and done up in a bun on the back of her head. Her sky-blue eyes twinkled with merriment. The only sign of age was a few laugh wrinkles around her mouth and eyes. She and Emma were close, again almost like sisters. Anna was deeply religious and devoted to her husband, Toivo. Toivo worked as a bookkeeper for several stores. Anna ran the household.

"Good morning, you two love birds. I suppose you want some breakfast," Anna said cheerily.

"I'm not hungry," Emma said, "but you know Jonas, he's hungry all the time.

"Oh, Anna, you know it's your good cooking that gets to me every time," said Jonas, laughing.

Anna blushed slightly, pleased that Jonas liked her cooking and was good enough to tell her.

"You have a choice this morning," she said, "fresh pork with eggs, smoked fish and eggs, or hot oatmeal and cream. What's your pleasure?"

Emma said, turning to Jonas, "You know how father likes his smoked fish and eggs on Sunday. Would that be all right with you, Jonas?"

"Fine. You know me. I can eat anything that doesn't eat me first."

Anna busied herself around the stove with kindling and birch bark. She put the small pieces of birch bark against the coals, fanning them slightly. As the bark sputtered into flame, she added cedar kindling. Soon the fire was crackling merrily. She replaced the lid on the stove, letting the fire take hold before adding more wood. She moved around the kitchen efficiently, getting ready to cook breakfast.

Emma asked, "Mother, can I help?"

"No, right now you would just be in my way. Later you can set the table. You might as well stay close to that man of yours."

Emma sighed. She had hoped her mother would say that. She marvelled at Anna's insight, forgetting that her mother was once her age.

Toivo and Matt tromped downstairs. Anna started breakfast preparations in earnest.

Toivo and Matt looked at Jonas' back, and Matt said, "I'm glad that's not me. I know I'd try to get even with that damn Karloff."

Matt was a year younger than Emma but looked two or three years younger. He had the same fine blond hair and fair skin, so he hadn't started to shave yet and took some ribbing from his friends about his peach-fuzz, baby face. Quizzical blue eyes inherited from his mother looked out at the world in a lazy sort of way. He exasperated Anna by his lack of ambition.

"Well," said Jonas, "I'm going to try to forget about it if he will. I'll finish my tour of duty and let it go at that. It was almost worth the whipping to see that arrogant Karloff get some of the wind knocked out of him. Those were beautiful falls he made in front of everyone."

Everyone laughed, remembering the incidents at the ice rink.

Anna said, "You must be feeling better this morning if you can laugh about it."

"I am feeling better, but I still hurt. I know I'll heal eventually."

With breakfast over, they sat around the kitchen table, drinking coffee and talking. It was still dark outside as the sun was far in the southern hemisphere.

They got ready for church. Jonas draped a shirt over himself and then his coat, trying to let as little as possible touch his tender back.

The minister gave a typical Lutheran sermon, leaning heavily on the fire-and-brimstone approach. Several people squirmed in their seats as though he talked directly to them. Maybe he did; not much escaped a preacher in a small town. The minister may have thought he had Jonas' rapt attention because he sat at the edge of the pew. Jonas was only trying to keep his whip-ravaged back from touching anything.

After church, everyone complimented the minister on his fine sermon. Emma and Jonas talked with some of their friends. They were anxious to catch up on news. A few hadn't heard about Jonas' whipping, but all who had, were aghast.

Toivo, Anna, and Matt headed for home with Emma and Jonas bringing up the rear, talking about the "little nothings" lovers talk about. Emma forgot and put her arm around Jonas. He winced.

"I'm sorry," she said, instantly almost in tears. "I just forgot."

"That's all right," he said, careful not to let the pain show too much in his voice. "You just happened to touch an extra-tender spot."

They walked arm in arm the rest of the way home.

Once home, Emma and Jonas pulled the sheepskin pad close to the living room hearth so Jonas could take his shirt off and still keep warm.

Anna busied herself with dinner, while Matt and Toivo went upstairs to change into comfortable clothes.

Toivo was slow and methodical about everything he did. He wasn't quick to make decisions, but, once made, he stuck to them. He tended to be a little fat due to Anna's good cooking and lack of physical exercise. His hair, turning a silver gray, was still full. His heavy moustache also had shaded salt and pepper. A long, jagged scar on the left side of his face, received in a fall from a horse, stayed white even in summer when his face tanned leather brown.

Emma called, "Mother, do you need any help with dinner?"

"No, you and Jonas visit. Who knows when you'll get another chance."

Little did she know how true that statement was.

Most everything for the dinner had been raised on their farm. A wonderful aroma arose as Anna lifted the roaster lid, revealing roast pork, carrots, and potatoes all turned a golden brown. Then there was Anna's bread and her apple pie topped with a slice of good sharp cheese. Strong coffee and the apple pie made the grand finale.

After dinner, Jonas said, "Emma, I'd better get back to the barracks so I can get my gear ready for tomorrow."

"Surely, they won't make you soldier with your back like that?" asked Emma in horror.

"Other men have had to. I'm sure I won't be an exception."

"I'll go with you to keep you company." Emma said.

"No, you would just have to walk back by yourself."

"Let me harness up old Bessie," said Matt, "and I'll give you two lovebirds a sleigh ride. Besides, I think Jonas needs all the rest he can get. He shouldn't walk back to camp."

"Sounds like fun to me," Emma said.

Matt went on out to get Bessie harnessed and hooked up to the sleigh. Jonas eased into his shirt as he was still quite sore, but he thought, *I have to get used to this sometime because tomorrow it's back to duty. They won't take any pity on me, not that I would want any.*

Matt drove around to the front of the house with sleigh bells ringing merrily. Bessie's nostrils blew steam into the cold, winter air. The mare was getting on in years, so they used her only for short jaunts.

The three crowded into the front seat of the sleigh and wrapped up in the sheepskin robes. They snuggled up and were off for the camp. Bessie was feeling frisky, so Matt let her have her head for a little while, but then slowed her down. He was afraid she might overtax herself, and Anna would never forgive them if something happened to her favorite horse.

They drove up near the skating rink. Jonas said, "You better let me out here. They don't want civilians inside the post."

Matt stopped the sleigh. Emma and Jonas got out, skirted the rink, and headed toward the gate house. As they passed the rink, Emma said, "This is where it all started with such a small incident. I don't understand."

Jonas kissed her lightly and said. "It's all over now, just forget it."

Emma held him, not wanting to let him go. "I hate it that you have to go back to duty in your condition," she said. "I'll worry all week about you and how you're doing."

"Don't worry your pretty little head. Anyway, I may be able to get away one night during the week to see you."

Around the corner of the gate house came Captain Karloff and Lieutenants Gerchenoff, Barloff, and Brezinski. All three of the lieutenants were slightly tipsy, but Karloff was roaring drunk.

Karloff was upbraiding his junior officers unmercifully and was fuming inwardly because they weren't kowtowing to him. They were laughing at him in his drunkenness. All were drinking vodka and wine left over from the aborted skating party.

When Karloff saw Emma and Jonas embracing, he flew into a rage, shouting, "What kind of mischief are you up to now, you dumb Finlander? Don't you know when you've had enough?"

Karloff reeled over to Emma and Jonas, holding a bottle in one hand. Spittle ran out the corner of his mouth, and his eyes were bleary and bloodshot. The alcohol on his breath overpowered the senses.

Karloff grabbed Emma by the arm and pulled her toward him, saying, "You don't deserve anything this pretty. I'll have to take over for you."

"Get your filthy hands off her, or I'll break every bone in your body!" hissed Jonas through clenched teeth.

Karloff shouted, "Soldier, don't talk to me that way, or I'll have you tied down and flogged again. This time I won't stop until we have flogged the very life out of you. You damn Finns can't get it through your thick heads that we Russians are your masters."

They were standing toe to toe glaring at each other. Jonas' rage built up from the whipping and this affront to Emma. And this scum, who represented everything he hated, had the audacity to touch the person he loved. Jonas' fist came up from his side with sledge hammer force, connecting with the point of Karloff's chin. Karloff's sable hat flew off as he went over the snow ridge surrounding the ice rink. He sailed over the snow bank in a strung-bow arched position, hitting the back of his head on the ice with a sickening crack. Everyone knew instantly he was dead.

Gerchenoff clambered over the bank and knelt by him. He shouted, "I don't feel any pulse! Brezinski, run for the doctor and get some more help to carry the captain!"

Brezinski took off at a dead run to get the doctor.

"Run for it, Jonas!" Matt yelled.

Jonas tried to get his mind and body to function together. Dazed, he felt as though he watched events from a great distance. He said to himself, "I just killed a man. I just killed a man. May God forgive me."

He knew he should run; he heard Matt yelling at him and Emma crying. His body wouldn't answer the demands his brain made.

15

Brezinski came back with the doctor, who listened vainly for a heart-beat. The men stood around, not knowing what to do. Their leader was dead.

Then the lieutenants grabbed Jonas. Gerchenoff said, "You're in for it now, Jonas. They'll kill you over this deed."

Still in a daze, Jonas was led off without resistance. He looked back to see Matt helping the still crying Emma into the sleigh. He thought, *Well, at least Matt will see her safely home. I'm glad he was here.*

The Russian soldiers took Jonas directly to the prison. They took away his knife and literally threw him into a cell. Jonas picked himself up, looked around at his meager surroundings. A straw-filled box formed his bed, and a bucket provided for his sanitary needs. Jonas looked out the barred window and saw Matt and Emma disappearing down the road.

"I'm doomed, I should have run while I had the chance," he said aloud to himself.

Chapter 3

Barloff

FIRST LIEUTENANT GERCHENOFF, second in command, was now com-mander of his unit, and it scared him to death. He was over three hundred miles from headquarters in Helsinki and three times that from St. Peters-burg. All his adult life someone had given him orders. Now decisions had to be his, right or wrong. How to deal with Jonas eluded him. The sudden rise to command with the many problems and responsibility thrust upon him kept him awake all night.

Gerchenoff once prided himself on being a trim and neat soldier but his liking for alcohol had taken its toll. His face had a myriad of red spider web veins; his eyes were brown, bleary and blood shot. His body had taken on the slack, slovenly look of soft fat, and his clothes looked rumpled most of the time. As he slouched through that first day of command, his speech became more slurred as the day passed, keeping pace with his alcohol intake. What to do with Jonas was the major problem. Execute him for murder immediately and report the event to headquarters in Helsinki? Transport him to Helsinki and let them deal with him as they saw fit? Send a messenger to Helsinki post haste, informing them of the problem and wait for their advice on the situation? No Finn had ever killed a Russian officer before, and it was very upsetting.

All the indecision on his part began to wear on him. He knew he must decide on some course of action. The Russian high command expect-ed its officers to make firm, hard decisions. In this case, the murder created other kinds of problems. The local people were not friendly toward the Russians. Any provocation would be tough as the unit was at a low ebb and would not be able to resist even a small skirmish. Further, the bulk of the garrison was Finnish cadre that wouldn't fight their own kind. Worse, they might defect and fight the Russians.

Gerchenoff tried to anticipate ways to combat overt action on the part of the Finns; everytime he came up short. Only four officers and twelve enlisted men were Russian. Out of these sixteen men, four he discounted—two cooks and two orderlies—as practically useless in a fight. The rest of the

17

garrison were Finnish enlisted men and non-commissioned officers. By morning he made up his mind to let headquarters in Helsinki handle the whole nasty situation.

Lieutenant Barloff, seeing the light on in Gerchenoff's office stopped in on his way to his morning shave and sauna. "Good morning, Captain-to-be," greeted Barloff.

"Don't count on it." Gerchenoff replied sourly, "I'm still in disgrace back in St. Petersburg."

"That's probably all blown over by now. You'll get the promotion, I'm sure," Barloff said as he ducked out the door.

Gerchenoff shouted after him, "Come back before you go to breakfast. I need to talk to you."

"All right. I'll stop," Barloff hurled back over his shoulder.

Barloff sulked that he would have to delay breakfast. He wondered what Gerchenoff wanted to talk about.

As Barloff went out the door, Gerchenoff leaned back in his chair, sighing, and thinking about the circumstances in St. Petersburg that that had brought him to Kiivijarvi. Gerchenoff looked out the window at the still-dark morning as if his eyes could penetrate the darkness and distance to his beloved St. Petersburg.

The memories came back in a flood. He had been a young and up-coming officer, a member of the elite palace guard with many privileges not enjoyed by field officers until they reached the rank of major or higher.

He remembered the lavish parties at the palace, the pomp and ceremony that he so dearly loved. Mountains of food, wine of all kinds, and the beautiful women. The women had been his undoing. Most of the time his duty was to be a charming and entertaining escort for the older women of the court. He had to keep them happy and out of their husbands' way while they romped with younger women. This was an unwritten law of Nicholas II's court. The older men had the younger ladies. But he and a young, beautiful cousin of the Tsar fell in love. This was bad enough, but she was also the paramour of powerful General Pribiloff.

"Well, here I am, all bathed and shaved at your command, Captain-to-be," announced Barloff. Gerchenoff started from his reverie. "You know one good item that the Finns have is the sauna. I'm glad we decided to build one for us. I feel so good after that steam I can't believe it. That was your idea wasn't it?"

"Yes," Gerchenoff replied somewhat testily. He found Barloff's good humor grating in the light of his own problems.

Barloff was easy going and very nonchalant about everything but women, his main drive in life. His rugged good looks made his drive for feminine affections very easy. He had a sense of humor that stood him in good

18

stead in adverse circumstances.

"What was it you wanted to talk to me about?" asked Barloff.

"I finally decided what to do about Jonas."

"What's that?"

"I'm sending you to Helsinki with a full report of the incident," said Gerchenoff. "You're to leave today."

"Why me?" asked Barloff in dismay.

"I could send one of the enlisted men, but this is an important matter. The commander is probably going to want more details than I can put into a report, and you were an eye witness. Besides, you wouldn't mind spending a few days in Helsinki, would you? I wouldn't mind getting away for a few days myself, but I have to stay here until headquarters decides if I'm going to command this post."

"Helsinki? I would much rather be in St. Petersburg," said Barloff.

"That goes double for me."

Barloff took his leave to have breakfast and pack for the trip. He had been secretly courting Liza Hakala. She was no great beauty, but in a far-flung outpost not that many women were available. The progress he had made with her over the past few weeks would be lost if he was gone for any length of time. She would find some one else. Gerchenoff's orders to pack and leave immediately wouldn't give him time to get a message to her. They had planned to meet in a hay loft, where he had hidden some sheepskin robes. It would have been a cozy love nest under all those sheepskins. Now his planning was all for naught.

He wondered how much Liza's brother Aimo know about them. Maybe he could tip Aimo, and he would tell Liza of the change in plans.

He needed someone to get his horse ready, so he asked one of the orderlies to bring Aimo to his quarters. When the young man arrived, he told him to get his horse saddled and ready to go to Helsinki.

Aimo was surly in his reply. He had been getting favored treatment since the ice rink incident. "Why don't you have your orderly do it? After all, that's his job."

"I know," replied Barloff. "But he has to help me pack. I need to get going to Helsinki without delay. I also need you to head another detail of men to pick up supplies from one of the warehouses. If you get through early, you can have the rest of the day off."

Barloff knew full well that they would finish early. He was sure Aimo would mention the Helsinki trip to Liza.

Barloff, packed and ready to go, reported to Gerchenoff, who handed him the dispatch case. He said, "Just tell the commandant what happened. Don't elaborate on Karloff's being drunk and out to steal Jonas' girl friend. I *would* emphasize that Jonas is from this town along with a lot of other enlisted men who are lifelong friends. If they can help him, they will."

"Ivan, do you think you're going to have some problems here?"

"No," replied Gerchenoff. "As long as Jonas is alive and here with no disposition of his case, we're safe. Hint that we could use more Russian troops in case of an emergency."

"Do you want me to come right out and ask him for more help?"

Gerchenoff considered. "No. He'll think we're over-reacting. If the opportunity arises so you can make him think it's his idea, go ahead."

Aimo and two other enlisted men drove up with a team and sleigh leading Barloff's horse.

"John," pleaded Gerchenoff, "get there as soon as you can and get back here. You're going to be my right hand man if I wind up with the promotion and command of this post."

"That suits me, Ivan. There's no one I would rather soldier with than you, but you already know that."

"John, you're a hell of a good soldier. If we ever get in a tight spot, I would want you there, protecting my back side. But, enough of this. Get on your way. Pat a few bottoms and have a few drinks for me."

Barloff grinned. "That I will. Good-bye."

Five days of hard riding and seven horses later, Barloff rode into headquarters in Helsinki. An orderly ushered him into the presence of Colonel Golovin, commander for the area. Golovin took the dispatch case without comment and started reading. He looked up surprised to see Barloff still standing at attention.

"Sit down, Lieutenant. I'll be through shortly."

Barloff sat down, surveying the colonel's office. Fairly sumptuous for a colonel on outpost duty, but there were some things that didn't fit.

Golovin had a pot bellied stove that clearly didn't have enough pipe above the roof. Every time the wind blew a little gust, a puff of smoke erupted from the stove, mixing with the strong turkish tobacco coming from Golovin's soggy pipe. As the colonel read the dispatch, he sucked on his pipe, making gurgling sounds in the bottom. The room was quiet except for Golovin's pipe and an occasional crackle from the fire. The room was warm and Barloff was still in heavy clothes. He began to perspire heavily.

Damn, why didn't I take an extra hour when I hit town to find a sauna, thought Barloff. *I'll bet I smell like horse dung and billy goats after five days of hard riding. I hope that colonel has a cold or a bad nose.*

Golovin finished reading the dispatch and paused for a moment to digest the matter before turning to Barloff.

"What's the situation with the townspeople? What is their reaction to the incident?"

"Colonel, sir, I don't believe they had much time to react before I left, but I would imagine they're upset."

"Upset, hell, I don't give a damn about the townspeople unless it's going to escalate into something bigger. It's St. Petersburg I care about."

Golovin jumped up from his desk, knocking his pipe to the floor in the process. He bent over smartly to pick it up, surprising Barloff with his agility despite a rather prominent bay window. Pacing the floor and emphasizing his statements by punctuating the air with his pipe stem he said, "No question about it, we'll have to kill him. The tsar will agree. We can't have peasants going around murdering Russian officers."

"In all fairness sir, Captain Karloff was quite drunk, and he grabbed Jonas' girlfriend. Jonas struck with no intention of killing him. It was an accident."

"Lieutenant," roared Golovin, "I'll have no mention of any of my officers being drunk, disorderly, or not in full control of their faculties. It will end here and now with no further mention of his being drunk. You will inform the other officers, discreetly of course, of the same. Carry out this order to the fullest and without fail, or I will tatter your hide worse than Karloff tattered Jonas'."

"Yes sir," said Barloff, paling under the unexpected onslaught.

Barloff was beginning to squirm with copious perspiration, wishing he could get out in the cold and to a sauna.

As if reading his mind, Golovin said, "Lieutenant, why don't you get cleaned up. I'm sure you could use a bite to eat plus a drink or two after your long ride. Dismissed!"

"Thank you, sir. Will I be taking any messages back to Kiivijarvi?"

"Yes, but get a good night's sleep. Report to me right after lunch tomorrow. My orderly will show you to your quarters. If you like, there's a good sauna down the street. My orderly will point it out from your room. Thanks again. See you tomorrow afternoon."

"Yes sir. I'll be here promptly at 1:00 P.M."

The orderly showed Barloff to his quarters, pointing out the sauna most of the officers used and left.

Barloff opened his saddle bags, shaking out his spare uniform along with clean socks and underwear. From the other side, he took out his traveling flask, taking two big swallows of straight vodka. The fire burned all the way to his toes, relaxing him immediately. The fire died down quickly, but the feeling of euphoria lingered on. He wanted to take another drink, but knew better than to do that on an empty stomach.

Folding his clean clothes over his arm he headed for the sauna. An old woman greeted him, collected his money, handed him a towel, wash cloth, and soap, and the traditional *vihta*, a bunch of cedar or birch branches used to beat oneself in the sauna to stimulate circulation. Some people liked it, some not. Barloff liked it, using it with vigor, finding it both stimulating and somewhat chastising for his past misdeeds.

He had hoped for a young woman at the sauna, so he could flirt with her. Surely the other officers had women, but he didn't want to ask the old woman. His asking might be misunderstood by her.

He stripped off his dirty clothes in the changing room. The dry heat hit him full in the face as he opened the heat room door. He liked his sauna very hot. He noted with pleasure that the room was spotless. Three benches, like wide stairs, ran the length of the back wall. Four wooden buckets sat on the floor, each with its own wooden dipper. He filled one of the buckets with cold water from the main barrel and sloshed a dipperful of water along the top bench to cool its surface. Climbing to the top bench to get the most heat, he took the bucket of water and dipper with him.

"Whenever I retire, no matter where it is, I'm going to have a sauna to indulge myself. This is one of the great, simple pleasures of life."

He flung a dipperful of water on the hot rocks making them hiss and erupt in a short column of steam. This dissipated quickly in the super heated air. The hot air rolled around him, enveloping him completely as though a warm woman held him. Another dipper of water on the rocks jumped the temperature twenty degrees. He had difficulty breathing the hot air directly, so he breathed through a clenched fist to cool the air entering his lungs. The hot sauna and the vodka acted like a strong sedative, relaxing his saddle-weary body. Sweat began oozing from every pore, making larger and larger rivulets rolling down his body. After a half an hour in the steam heat, he prepared a bucket of hot soapy water, scrubbing himself until he was red. Another bucket of fresh water dumped over his body rinsed off the soap and grime from his hard ride. Another bucket of rinse water, this time a little cooler to gradually lower his temperature. A third bucket of ice cold water took his breath and brought him out of his lethargy.

"I wish this sauna was out in the country some place. I could go out and roll in some clean snow to cool off."

Knowing he had no particular place to go, he dressed slowly. He picked up his dirty clothes and towel to give to the old woman out front. He hoped she would know someone who would wash his dirty uniform.

He was surprised to find a young woman in charge. She was blond, blue eyed like most Finns and strikingly attractive. He wondered momentarily if she was there by accident or design. In some areas, a Russian officer was a fine catch for a husband. He wondered if the old woman had sent for her.

Lazily, he looked her up and down. She didn't mind at all. She acted as if she enjoyed his scrutiny.

To his surprise she spoke to him in Russian. They began conversing immediately. Her Russian was not good, so they switched to Finnish. He and all other officers posted to Finland had had to learn the language.

Barloff decided this would be a desirable dinner companion if he could get her to go with him. "Where can a stranger in town get a good meal and a good bottle of wine to go with it?" he asked.

"The Boar's Head down the street has excellent food and wine. I know the owner."

"Do you go there often?"

"Occasionally, whenever I can afford it. I don't make all that much money. I work as a bookkeeper for a shipping company. I help out in the sauna to help pay for my room."

"Then, that older woman's not related to you?"

"No, she's a good friend of the family. She put me up when I came here from the country to find work."

"I just got into town," said Barloff. "I don't know anyone or where to go. If you have nothing better to do, I would love to have you join me for dinner. We could go to the Boar's Head where you know the owner. If I get out of line, you could have him throw me out."

"If you can wait for thirty minutes or so until Gerta gets back, I would love to go with you."

Barloff couldn't have been be more pleased, but he decided to play it down a little so as not to appear too eager. He introduced himself to her, and she gave her name as Elsa Maki.

"Can I pick you up here in about half an hour, then?" he asked.

"No, pick me up at my room across the street. You can see it from the window here. It's the white house with the steps on the outside to the upstairs. I live upstairs by myself so come up and knock. I'll be ready."

Barloff went back to his room to wait. Thoughts about his previous love trysts ran through his mind. He compared the overall good looks and apparent intelligence of this woman to others he had known. She was above anything in his past.

"There I go," he said to himself, "I've already made love to her in my mind. I'll probably get the brush off. Some high-ranking officer is probably dating her. She's probably just looking for a free meal and a night out."

Barloff watched until he saw her leave the sauna for her room.

"I ought to give her a few minutes to get ready," he said.

Another twenty minutes elapsed before he sauntered over to her room. She answered his knock immediately and put on her coat, indicating that she was ready to go.

Barloff was a little disappointed. He hoped she might invite him in. For reasons he could not fathom, he was curious about her room and the way she lived. He wanted to know a lot more about this woman.

Taking his arm for support going down the stairs, she did not relinquish it until they reached the Boar's Head.

He opened the door for her. Wonderful smells of good food cooking and soft voice sounds floated quietly throughout the huge dining room to set him at ease.

Mika, the owner, a huge bear of a man in a white apron stained with most of the day's menu, met them at the door. Mika had an excellent reputation for good food. Finns and Russians alike patronized his place. He was not fond of the Russians, but he didn't voice his opinions aloud as Russians formed a large part of his business.

Mika gave Elsa a big hug, engulfing her in his huge body. He kissed her on the cheek as he let her go, saying in his booming, bull voice, "Elsa, how I have missed your smiling face. You haven't graced my establishment for quite some time."

"I know," she said. "I've been busy at my job and helping Gerta at the sauna. She hasn't been feeling well lately."

"I'm sorry to hear that. I'll have to send her something special from the restaurant."

"I'm sure she would like that. Oh, and this is John, Mika. I just met him at the sauna today."

"Glad to meet you, John. Did you get her to scrub your back in the sauna?" Mika asked jokingly.

John blushed. Elsa added to it by saying, "No, I didn't meet him until he was all through. If I had known how good looking he was, I might have sneaked in there with him."

John knew they were teasing, but he couldn't keep from blushing under the dual onslaught.

"Enough of this," said Mika. "How about a cozy table by the fireplace? You two can watch the fire and still pay attention to each other."

Mika brought a bottle of wine saying, "This is Elsa's favorite. I know you'll like it."

"I'm sure if it suits Elsa, I'll like it," said John.

Mika uncorked the bottle, pouring a little into John's glass for him to taste. John nodded, and Mika poured both of their glasses saying, "This is local wine, rather pleasant. France does not have the monopoly on growing good grapes nor the making of good wine. Unfortunately, the supply is limited. Sometimes I have to hoard a little for special people like Elsa."

Barloff sipped his wine, taking in the huge dining room. Built entirely of logs. Fitted together so perfectly that no chinking was needed, the logs were oiled, giving them a sheen and patina that only came with age and care.

Massive overhead beams supported the upper floor, likely Mika's living quarters. The great maw of a fireplace could take logs as long as a man was tall. Built entirely of stone, it had been fitted together as meticulously as the logs. Some of the stones were immense.

Only brute force would get some of those stones in place, Barloff thought.

Elsa asked, "Just where in Russia do you call home?"

"Well, really," he replied, "the army is home to me now. Both my parents are dead, and I'm an only child. I have a few cousins living in St. Petersburg where I was born and raised."

"You're rather young to have lost both parents."

"Yes," he said sadly. "They both died in one of the many epidemics that swept St. Petersburg years ago. I survived because my parents sent me to my grandparents' farm outside of the city. My grandparents are still living, and I visit them every time I go back."

Mika came bustling out of the kitchen to their table. He acted as if they were the only people in the world that mattered to him at the moment.

"Tonight we have excellent roast duckling or a saddle of venison. We had some baked salmon, but, alas, it's gone to the very last flake."

Elsa ordered the duckling, but John ordered venison saying, "I haven't had good venison for a long time."

Elsa leaned over the table. "You'll like it the way Mika fixes it."

The dinner came about a half an hour later. They ordered another bottle of wine as they had sipped the first one away awaiting dinner.

The dinner was a success. They gave each other tastes, both meals were superb. John immediately appraised Mika as being an absolute perfectionist in the culinary arts.

"Next time I'll order the duckling, if it's available."

"Anything Mika fixes will be good. He's just that way with his food."

They finished their meal slowly, reluctant for the evening to end. John asked for the bill. Mika totalled it up in his head, bringing two small glasses of aquavit, the fiery liquor from Sweden.

"This drink's on me," the congenial host said. "You can't go out on a night this cold without a little internal fire to keep you warm."

John thanked Mika for the wonderful evening and the aquavit.

Walking arm in arm back to Elsa's room, the crisp snow made creaking noises under their feet. It was a beautiful starry night.

"It looks like you could reach out and touch the stars," said Elsa.

John wondered if he would get invited in. Elsa took the initiative, saying, "You can come in for a moment to get warm. You can't stay long, though. I have to get up early for work."

He stepped inside, pleasantly surprised by the neatness and tasteful way she had furnished the room. It was very much like her, orderly, yet not formal. Just homelike—comfortable with everything in place. They both slipped out of their coats. He hung his over the back of a chair, while she carefully put hers away in the closet.

He enfolded her in his arms as she came away from the closet. She readily melted into him. Hard, pointed breasts pressured him as they embraced. He was painfully aware of this beautiful woman in his arms. His loins ached for her. He picked her up, carried her to the large, feather bed and laid down beside her atop the goose down comforter. They sank nearly out of sight in the billowy softness. He kissed her hard on the mouth, and she moaned softly. He nuzzled her ears gently.

"You can take advantage of me very easily because I like you very much," she whispered. "I didn't tell you earlier that I was married for a short time to a sailor lost at sea. I can get very passionate if I let myself, especially with you."

He backed off a moment, not wanting to ruin this friendship that he felt could blossom into something special for both of them. He started to raise up to go when she reached up, put her hand around the back of his head and pulled him down into a kiss. She took his free hand, slipping it under her blouse and onto her naked breast.

It was a race undressing each other. Clothes flew everywhere. She pulled back the comforter to crawl between freshly laundered sheets that still smelled of outdoors. He pulled her close to him, she snuggled up, both of them feeling the deliciousness of their bodies as one on the cold sheets.

He woke up the next morning to see Elsa fully dressed.

She said, "Get up, lazy one. I have breakfast ready. I went downstairs, cooked breakfast for Gerta and us, but I brought ours up here. I'll have to eat and run, or I'll be late for work. Don't you have to report back this morning?"

"No, not until after lunch. I don't know when I'll have to leave for Kiivijarvi, but I seriously doubt that it will be today or tomorrow."

"I would like to have you here forever. We were great together, or didn't you think so?"

"Yes, we were. I thought it was perfect."

They ate breakfast, talking idly about nothing, still a little shy in each other's presence. She got up and cleared the dishes to take downstairs. He finished dressing, retrieving his coat from the back of the chair while waiting for her to come back upstairs. Then he helped her with her coat, and they left together, she for work, he for his quarters.

All morning Barloff thought over the evening's events, feeling pleased with himself and how everything had worked out. He was anxious to continue the tryst.

Promptly at 1:00 P.M., he reported to Colonel Golovin. Golovin was at his desk, as preoccupied as the day before. He looked up when John said, "Lieutenant Barloff reporting back as ordered, sir."

"Yes, lieutenant," Golovin said. "I have thought this matter over thoroughly. I've met with my staff and sent a message to St. Petersburg. We all agree that Jonas should be executed. Due to the gravity of the situation, plus possible repercussions from the locals, I'm sending a full company of our troops with you to strengthen the post. They might be needed to keep order. Karloff was a fool to whip the man, but it's too late to do anything about that now. We don't need this incident escalating into anything bigger. It will take about a week to get the company ready to move. I would like you to stay here until then to advise me on the situation up there. We will be in touch with you at your quarters when I need to talk to you again. Stay fairly close to the base. I know you're young and want to see the sights but don't get over a half day away."

John saluted, and the colonel returned it perfunctorily. He turned on his heel, striding out the door, thinking, "What luck! I have at least another week with nothing to do but be with Elsa."

Chapter 4

Escape

JONAS PACED HIS CELL. They were planning to execute him, of that he was sure. The Russians would not consider anything less than an eye for an eye.

He thought about his beloved Emma, how she must be suffering. He wondered if they might allow her to visit him.

Jonas plotted how he could get some messages out to see if his friends were trying to figure a way for him to escape. He knew that if he could get away, the advantage would be his. He was born and raised in the area and knew it well from his hunting and fishing trips.

The blessing of sleep was a long time coming, lying on his stomach with his back still on fire and thoughts of escape racing through his head.

The next morning he woke to find unwelcome bed partners. He was crawling with lice. Sanitary conditions were not the best in this prison, and Jonas was meticulous about his personal hygiene. The unwelcome guests upset him almost as much as the events that brought him there.

One of the guards was a little sympathetic about the conditions in his cell. The main guard opened up the cell so Jonas could get rid of the vermin filled straw. With a little cajoling he got the guard to bring him a bucket of water and some strong lye soap.

First, he stripped off his clothes to scrub himself with the strong lye soap. Next, he washed out his clothes, wrung them out and hung them to dry. He walked around the cell, naked, scrubbing the entire cell down with the lye soap and water. A bit more hard persuasion got the guard to bring another bucket of water to rinse himself and the cell down. The water was ice cold, but he didn't care. The guard brought him fresh straw which he spread and crawled into to keep warm while his clothes dried. He felt sure he hadn't gotten rid of all the lice, but he would have a respite before they could return in any great numbers. Sleep was impossible because he was so cold, and yet his back still burned.

Thoughts of escape ran through his mind. He could overpower a guard, but then another guard stood at the end of the corridor. This in turn led to the locked guard room where usually three or four guards were on duty or changing shifts. He abandoned that idea as impractical.

He thought about tunneling out, but the cell was entirely of stone. If he could get some stones loose, he would have to tunnel through frozen ground to the outside without the benefit of tools. Then what to do with the excavated dirt? That idea was out. Besides, he guessed he didn't have much time left before his execution.

The single barred window drew his attention next.

A picture of a wooded lake, left hanging on the window bars by some previous prisoner, irritated Jonas. It reminded him of the outside and freedom. Dozing momentarily, he dreamed he was once again free and out skiing and hunting with his friends. He saw himself coming home from a hunting trip, cleaning the game for a feast and joyful get-together. Jonas roused when the guard pushed the dish of breakfast gruel under the cell door. He dressed back into his damp, cold clothes, shivering all the while.

Picking up his gruel and inspecting it carefully, he decided there were no worms in it. He made up his mind to eat, so he could keep up his strength. If an opportunity came for him to escape, he knew he would need all his strength and faculties.

Finishing his breakfast, he pushed his bowl back under the door and turned his attention to the window. It was an odd set up as the window was outside the bars and swung open from one side like a door. The latch slipped up and the window swung open easily. He closed it carefully waiting for the guard to pick up his breakfast bowl before doing any more. The guard came and saw Jonas sitting on the edge of his bunk.

When he was alone, Jonas studied the window again. The bars were imbedded in the stone and leaded in. They would not budge to his tugs.

He looked at the picture of the lake hanging on one of the bars. He was about to tear it down when he noticed the string had worn a shiny place on the bar. The wind, blowing through the ill-fitting window, rocked the picture back and forth on its string, making the worn spot. The thought occurred to him, maybe with some extra help and abrasive sand, he might be able to cut through the bars.

He wondered how long it had taken the string to wear the shiny place in the bar. Knowing it was a near-hopeless plan, Jonas thought about trying to cut through the bars with the string. He considered using yarn from his socks when the picture string wore through. But, hopeless as it was, it was better than waiting for the Russians to execute him.

He awaited darkness to start his project. Prison routine was unfamiliar to him, so he dared not try anything in the daytime. He observed guard movements for future reference. It was going to take a long time to cut through the bars, if indeed, he could cut through them at all. The sands of time were running out for him if he did not do something quickly.

The only other meal they served in the prison was a supper of sorts, which was a vegetable stew. Jonas searched in vain for meat but found none. It did have a slight meat flavor with plenty of vegetables, which he knew he needed. He finished that off with the one slice of hard, dry, black bread. He slid his bowl and utensils back under the door. The guard made sure he returned the utensils so he wouldn't have a weapon.

The guard left and Jonas went to work. The picture gave up its string but would be used later to hide the progress made in cutting the bar. The string was about a foot and a half long. Wetting it with saliva, he dragged it through a small mound of sand and mortar he scraped together. Working the string back and forth he had to stop often to wet it and apply more sand. From time to time he changed the work area on the string so it would last longer. After an hour of back and forth sawing, he could feel a small notch in the bar by rubbing a finger nail over the area. He attacked the bar with new vigor.

There were two more bars in the window. All three would have to be loose to get his body out.

"If they bend easily I might get by cutting only one end loose," he said to himself.

Toward morning the string broke in the middle. By this time he had sawed about one quarter of the way through the first bar. He tied the string back together and rehung the picture. He didn't want anything to look suspicious. He couldn't think of any way to cover up the cut bar as he progressed. The string covered up most of the cut for now. As he progressed, he knew the cut would become obvious.

Jonas laid down to get some rest and make the guard think he had been asleep all night when they came with breakfast. Progress thus far told him he would have to find time to work on the bars during the day. Based on his night's work, he would not cut through the last bar for twelve more nights. There was serious doubt in his mind that he had twelve more days or nights left. He worried that he might need more time to cut through the top bars or at least cut them part way so they would bend out of the way. He needed more string, lots of it.

His socks revealed a loose end he could unravel easily. He unraveled about six feet of yarn.

Jonas thought about the previous day's activity. He remembered the one guard that came on after breakfast. The hobnailed boots made his walking noisy. The guard ran his night stick along the bars as he went, like a child running a stick on a picket fence.

Breakfast over, Jonas went to work on the bar in earnest with one ear cocked for the guard. The wool yarn from his sock worked even better than the picture string. It held the abrasive sand better. The guard was very obliging, coming down the corridor with his loud boots and the clickety clackety of his stick on the bars. Each time Jonas laid down on his bunk as though napping.

By supper time he was half way through his first bar. He was anxious to get through to see if he could bend the bar. This would speed up his escape. He wanted desperately to get word to Emma or his friend Vilho. They could put supplies together he would need for wilderness survival.

Supper time forced Jonas to quit. The delay made him anxious. The new guard who came on after supper made rounds until midnight. This guard carried a lantern whose flickering light preceded him down the corridor. This gave Jonas ample time to get into bed, but it irritated him to have to stop working. But the guard went to sleep about midnight, giving Jonas a long run at cutting.

Sometime in the wee morning hours, Jonas cut through his first bar. For a moment he thought the yarn broke again, but, when he found it intact, he knew he had cut through. Everything he did was by feel. The feeble light reflecting from the snow outside made the cell appear eerie.

He pulled the bar toward him, bending it easily. This meant he wouldn't have to cut through the top bars.

It took several tries bending the bar back and forth to get it to align perfectly. The next problem was how to cover the cut. The cut wasn't visible from outside the cell door even though a bit of light showed underneath. But, if they came inside, they might discover the cut. The picture covered the first bar while he went to work on the second. The stirring of the breakfast crew down the corridor made him give up for the moment.

Breakfast over, Jonas was about to resume his work. He realized that he didn't hear the guard from yesterday. Another guard came down the corridor quietly to look into his cell. Jonas was glad he had waited.

The guard spoke fluent Finnish. He tormented Jonas unmercifully about his short time to live. All of the officers spoke Finnish, but only a few of the enlisted men bothered to learn the language.

Jonas spoke with him at length even though his attitude rankled him. He was trying to find out news of his fate. From the meager information gleaned from the guard, Jonas couldn't make up his mind if a decision had been made or if the clod knew nothing. A messenger would barely have had time to make it to Helsinki, and the directive was sure to come from command headquarters in Helsinki.

Jonas was anxious to get back to his work. When he began answering the guard in curt, one word answers, the man got discouraged and left.

The normal prison routine ordered tours every hour. The new guard had Jonas worried whether he followed procedure. Jonas wasn't sure if it

31

was safe to proceed.

He had no way to judge when guards would make their next rounds.

The new guard came on quiet cat's feet, hoping to catch some prisoner doing something wrong.

Jonas had a sudden flash as to how to keep track of time. He counted the strokes of his string against the bar figuring that each stroke took about a second. Three thousand six hundred strokes would make an hour. He quit at three thousand. He was right. A few minutes after he lay down in his bunk the guard came silently down the corridor.

The guard peered into Jonas' cell. Jonas faked sleep so the guard would go away. The guard went on rather than try to strike up another conversation, much to Jonas' relief.

Jonas went back to work on the bars when the guard returned to the guard room. But he remained nervous about this guard. Jonas stopped for a moment to rest his arms because he had to hold them up fairly high to work the yarn back and forth. Hearing a slight noise behind him, he turned slowly, making sure his body hid the yarn still hanging on the bar.

The guard asked, "What are you doing, Jonas? Trying to figure a way to cut through those bars?"

Jonas' heart skipped a beat, but he forced an outwardly calm and said, "No, I was just thinking what a beautiful winter day it is. What a great day to be out skiing."

"Ha! Your skiing days are over!" said the guard as he walked off.

Jonas decided to quit for the day. It was too risky with the silent-footed guard liable to pop up at any time. He sat on his bunk stewing and fretting all day about his progress. He forced his mind to think of all the items he would need to survive in the wilderness. He had gone into the wilderness for long stretches but never in the dead of winter.

"In the past, if I forgot something, I could go back for it or cut my trip short. This time I can't afford any mistakes. I could die."

The second bar cut through easily that night. The yarn broke more often, though, because he hurried to make up for the lost daytime cutting. Surely, he could cut through the third and last bar in the next day or two. The time table would depend on which guards were on duty.

For supper that night they gave him greasy pork with half rotten potatoes and rutabagas. He toyed with his meat, trying to get up enough courage to eat it. He noticed the burned fat was almost the same color as the bars on the window. Why not use the black fat to cover up his cut marks on the bars? It was cold enough so the fat would remain solid to look like part of the bar. He hid the piece of fat meat in the straw of his bunk before pushing his dish out into the corridor.

When he picked up the dish, the guard remarked, "Man, you must have been hungry. You ate all that slop we gave you."

Jonas replied, "One must eat to survive."

The guard sneered, "You're not going to survive much longer."

"One can only hope," retorted Jonas.

As soon as the guard was out of sight, Jonas used some of the black fat to cover the cut bars. It worked perfectly. Even with close scrutiny they couldn't tell where he cut the bar. The greasy meat covered both cuts.

He had the third bar cut half way through when he decided to get some sleep. In the past three days he had slept for about two hours.

"If the opportunity for escape comes, I'll need to be well rested," he told himself. Dozing, he heard some rustling near his feet where he had hidden the greasy meat. It was dark in the cell, but he was sure it was a mouse. Swatting in the general area with his boot, he heard a squeak and scurrying. He quickly reached for the meat, relieved to find it still there. He put it under the straw near his head, but sleep no longer came.

He lay on the straw and thought about freedom for himself and his country. He had thought earlier about becoming a passive resistor. It came to him now that he must do his bit to make freedom possible in the land.

"If all of us choose to do nothing," he told himself, "then we do not deserve to be free. I have to convince other people to help me and the cause for freedom. There are lots of little things we can do to make the Russian occupation of our land hard enough that they will give up and go home. First I have to free myself from this prison."

Shortly after breakfast, the bar-rattling guard came by to tell him he had a visitor. He cleaned up as best he could under the circumstances. It pleased and surprised him to see Emma. She sat on a chair near the door. The guard stood about ten feet away, watching to make sure nothing passed from Emma to him. They weren't sure if the guard understood Finnish so they talked in low tones.

"Oh, my love," she said, "I have missed you. I have worried myself sick about you."

"Emma dear, you have been on my mind constantly, but we don't have time for idle talk. I know I can safely escape from here. Never mind how. Look for me tomorrow morning or the next morning before daylight. I can't give you a note or anything, so you're going to have to remember everything I'm going to need. Find Vilho and enlist his aid. I'm going into the wilderness if I get out of here. Vilho and I have been there before, so he'll remember some items I haven't remembered."

Jonas went through his mental list once, then a second time with Emma repeating after him so she would remember it all. The guard said the time was up. She blew him a kiss through the bars as the guard marched her out.

Jonas sat for a moment, his heart pounding in his throat. He was putting Emma in jeopardy, but he felt he had no choice if he wanted to live. He thought of taking her with him but rejected the idea as being too dangerous for her.

Now that he had the bar-rattling guard back on duty, he went to work on the last bar in earnest. He quit when the guard came down the corridor and went back to work immediately after he left. The guard must have been extra lazy because he made only two rounds plus supper. This gave Jonas some extra time to work on the bar, for which he was grateful.

Old silent foot returned for the night shift. This worried him, but he had to use a lantern which gave Jonas a little warning.

Some time toward morning, he cut through the last bar. With his greatcoat, blanket, and straw, he made a sleeping man bundle showing only its back to the door. He wished he could leave his boots but didn't dare try to go the several miles to Emma's house barefoot in the winter cold. His socks were gone, used up for yarn to cut the bars. As he made his decoy, his hand found the fat, which gave him another idea. He slipped the fat into his shirt pocket.

He braced his feet against the wall to get more leverage on the bars to bend them inward out of the way. They bent easily.

He opened the window and crawled out, sliding to the ground carefully to make as few marks in the snow as possible. Turning back to the window he reached back in to bend the bars back in place. Two came back to their original place, but the first one he had bent before didn't align itself. He bent it back again, this time it lined up fairly close. He was getting worried that some one would come along the path even though it was dark and early morning. One last tug on the bar brought it back almost perfectly. He took the greasy meat out of his pocket to cover up the cut bars and closed the window. He stepped onto the path alongside the building. He tossed clods of snow into his tracks by the window. It looked like the walk shoveler had thrown the clods there. Then he took off at a brisk trot for freedom.

Jonas ran all the way to Emma's house. Several times, with his breath coming in great gasps, he wanted to slow down to a walk. The sure, sweet, smell of freedom spurred him on. Adding incentive to his speed was not knowing how long it would be before the guards discovered he was missing. The first place they would look would be Emma's house.

One of the many things he had asked Emma to do was keep the sauna hot. He slipped into the back door of the Lehtinen house calling softly to Emma, who came to him immediately.

She started for his arms when he said, "Stay away from me. I'm covered with lice from the prison. That's why I wanted the sauna. Send me some of Matt's fresh clothes, as I'm going to burn these."

.

Without another word he slipped out to the sauna.

He stripped to the skin, throwing his old clothes into the sauna stove. Using hot water he sluiced the sauna down in case any of the vermin got out of his clothes. He washed and scrubbed his body until it glowed red. His whipping scars had healed a little, but the heat and scrubbing made him wince in pain. Climbing to the top bench he threw water on the heated rocks to take on plenty of steam.

He wish he could stay to soak for hours, but he knew he couldn't.

He sluiced his body once more, and gave the sauna a thorough going over. He felt cleaner than he had for days. He felt like a man again.

Emma had been in the changing room with a towel and clean clothes. Her faint odor still lingered. Although she didn't wear perfume she had a sweet, pleasant odor that hung in the air moments after she passed.

He dried and dressed quickly, thinking about Aimo living next door and the chance that he might see him.

He said to himself, "Ah, that lazy one wouldn't be up at this hour."

Jonas slipped into the house. Matt had been dispatched to get Vilho. They were all there, greeting him warmly. Emma gave him a big hug and kiss. Everyone had questions. How did he get out? Did anyone see him? Did he have to hurt anyone? What was he going to do now?

Jonas told them briefly how he had cut the bars and then put them back in place, covering the cuts with the grease.

Everybody laughed.

Vilho said, "I hope they never find out. If they don't figure it out, they'll think the guards were in on it, and there will be the devil to pay."

"It won't hurt my feelings a bit if they start bickering among themselves," Jonas said.

Matt said, "They'll probably call you a ghost that can go through stone walls."

Jonas related his plans as best he knew them. He asked them if they had all the items he wanted. They had, plus some extra items they thought he might need.

"I remember," said Jonas, "an old trapper's cabin back in the hills. I saw it last summer when I was on that wilderness trip on my furlough. I know I can find it again. It was in fair shape. I spent a night there. I thought at the time it could be a cozy retreat with a little fixing. There's a small spring right by the door running down to a stream and on into a series of lakes. In the cabin is a big stone fireplace with cooking swivels built in. The door was out of kilter but the one and only window was still intact. Some trapper spent a lot of time getting it in that kind of shape. He hasn't been there for several years. I wonder what happened to him?

"I'll hole up there for now. I'll be in touch. I know I'll need additional supplies from time to time. I have a little money on deposit with the store-keeper in town. You can use that to repay yourselves for purchases."

They all spoke up indignantly, saying that payment wasn't needed and they were glad to do it.

"I hope the Russians get out of here soon so we can get back to normal living," said Jonas wistfully, though he doubted it would be soon.

Vilho reached behind the couch pulling out a long box saying, "My dear and good friend, I have a present for you. I bought it for myself but, under the circumstances, you have a greater need. Besides I can get another one. Your old rifle won't be adequate for your needs in the future."

Jonas opened the box to reveal the latest Winchester repeating rifle from America along with extra ammunition, reloading tools, powder, primers, and bullets for reloading spent cartridges.

Tears welled up in his eyes. He choked out his thanks, giving Vilho a big hug.

Jonas said, "I better get going. I don't know how much time I have. I'm sure this is going to be the first place they look. While I'm gone, think about how we can get the Russians out of our country. I used to think we could live with them but I have changed my mind."

Taking Emma in his arms, giving her a long, lingering kiss and wiping tears gently from her eyes, he said, "No matter what happens remember that I love you and I will be back." He shook hands with Anna, Toi, and Matt, then gave Vilho a bear hug saying, "Take care of them for me."

"You can count on that my friend!"

Jonas shouldered his heavy pack and slipped outside to get into his skis. He melted into the still, black morning darkness and the forest. Unseen, only the faint *shush, shush* of his skis came back for a moment before all settled into silence.

Chapter 5

Russian Reaction

THE FUROR IN THE GUARD HOUSE reached Gerchenoff by an out-of-breath messenger.

"Captain, I mean, Lieutenant, sir, Jonas has escaped. We can't find out how he did it!"

Gerchenoff bounded up from his desk and said, "Lets's go find out what you idiots have done now! Lieutenant Brezinski," he bellowed, "Follow me to the prison!"

Both men reached the guard room, gasping for air. Gerchenoff sat down and spurted questions between breaths. "What the hell do you mean you don't know how he escaped? He didn't just get up and fly away!"

"Well, sir, it appears so," said one of the guards. "We can't find any way he could have escaped."

"Let's have a look at his cell," said Gerchenoff, jumping up. "When was he seen last?"

"The night guard said he had supper but doesn't know after that," said the sergeant of the guard. "He flashed his lantern in the cell and saw the bundle on the bed and assumed he was sleeping. We didn't realize he was gone until we saw he hadn't eaten breakfast."

Gerchenoff looked around the cell with distaste. It nauseated him.

He looked closely at the bars, shook them but not with any great force. Jonas' grease camouflage held. He looked the cell over carefully for loose stones or signs of excavation but could find none.

Outside, with Brezinski and the rest of the crew following, Gerchenoff searched for clues of Jonas' escape. "He didn't come out that window unless he's part bird. There are no tracks outside the window and it's too far for him to jump to the walk. Somebody had to help him escape, and I'm going to find out who that somebody is!"

Damn, thought Gerchenoff on his way back to his office. *What's headquarters going to say about this latest fiasco? This, coupled with that indiscretion in St. Petersburg will probably end what's left of my army career.*

Back at his office, he slumped down to compose a message to Helsinki. Then he called for a rider to deliver it to Helsinki and await a reply.

In Helsinki Colonel Golovin received the news calmly under the circumstances. He sent his orderly for Barloff who happened to be in his quarters resting from the nightly tryst with Elsa. Barloff reported to Golovin, who filled him in on the escape of Jonas.

"I was seriously considering promoting Gerchenoff to captain and giving him command of that post, but now I don't know."

"Sir, I think Gerchenoff is a good soldier," Barloff said. "I don't know what happened on that escape. It sounds like we might have a traitor in our midst. Gerchenoff has been in charge of that post for only a few days and might not have full control of all his people."

"Yes," said Golovin, "but he should have had some inkling of the quality of his men. Being second in command does not excuse ignorance."

"I suppose not, sir."

"Would you take the post?" asked Golovin.

"Not unless ordered to, sir. Gerchenoff will make a good commander. He is also my best friend."

"Do you think he can handle the post?" asked Golovin pointedly.

"Yes, sir, I think he can."

Barloff thought to himself, *Hell, I wouldn't want that job. No matter who gets it, they're really going to be under the gun with two companies of soldiers trying to catch one man. Well, maybe Golovin won't send the other company up there now that Jonas has escaped.*

As if reading Barloff's mind Golovin said, "I'm still going to send that company from here to help hunt the murderer down. It's even more important that I send them now and catch him quick. When they find him, and I know they will, I want a speedy trial, followed by a speedier execution. We can't have one Finn making us the laughing stock of the area. I'll send a rider, post haste, to Gerchenoff, informing him that we will push up the departure time. The other messenger should get there today. This will inform him of the change in plans. You should be able to leave here in two days with a full complement of men and equipment."

Barloff felt a twinge of disappointment run through him. He knew he would be leaving Elsa sooner than he thought.

When dismissed, Barloff saluted, turned smartly on his heels and left. He made a hasty plan to break the news to Elsa over lunch. A horse and cutter was at his command, but he decided to walk. It was a bright, clear, cold day. By walking, his timing would be about right for her lunch break. He needed the air to think about his role in the upcoming events.

He strolled into the shipping office where Elsa worked. She looked up, surprised and pleased to see him. It was a slow time in the winter. There were no ships in the harbor loading or unloading cargo.

"Come, I'll show you around," she said.

Elsa held John's hand through the office and warehouse as she introduced him to some of her friends.

"What a variety of goods you people ship in and out of here!"

"We ship out and receive goods from all over the world," said Elsa with pride.

The two of them walked arm in arm around the corner to a small cafe where most of the dock workers ate. It wasn't fancy, but the food was good, with generous portions for the hard-working stevedores.

They sat at a small table overlooking the harbor. John wiped the steam from the window so he and Elsa could see the water. A few ships had dropped anchor for the winter. Ice formed around the edges of the bay, soon it would be frozen completely, except for some channels that the ice breakers kept open. The main part would remain frozen until spring.

John toyed with his utensils, trying to find the right way to tell Elsa he was going to have to leave earlier than expected.

He blurted out, "Elsa, dear, I'm afraid I have some bad news. The prisoner I told you about, the one that killed our captain, has escaped so the colonel is pushing up my departure time."

"Oh, I'm sorry. When do you have to leave?" she replied, "I thought we would have more time."

"In two days, maybe sooner if we can get it all together."

"I honestly didn't want to think of your leaving. I have become fond of you. In fact, I think I'm in love with you."

"I feel the same way. I can't believe it could happen so quickly."

They held hands across the table, looking forlornly into each other's eyes. Small tears welled up in Elsa's eyes. The waiter brought their food, forcing them to separate their hands so he could put the food on the table.

Neither of them could finish the bowls of pea soup with thick slices of dark bread that they had ordered.

The waiter came over and asked, "What's the matter? Our food not good enough for you?"

"No," they replied in unison. "It was very good."

Barloff said, "As a soldier, I eat a lot. I guess these dock workers could put me to shame if they eat that much all the time."

Elsa said, "Maybe we should have had small bowls."

The waiter said, "Those are the smallest bowls we have."

They walked back to the office with their arms locked together. She reluctantly let him go, knowing she had to get back to work.

"I'll come for you right after work, and we'll go to the Boar's Head for dinner," Barloff said.

"I'm not sure of the time," she said. "I may have to tend the sauna for a while. I'll try to get out of it if I can. I'll promise to work extra after you're gone. Gerta is a romantic herself, so I think she'll go along with it. I may have to stay for a little while when she goes to dinner. We'll have the rest of the evening to ourselves."

"I hope so," he said as he turned to leave, "I hate being away from you even for a moment."

"Come by early anyway. You can sit with me at the sauna."

"I will," he tossed back over his shoulder as he went out the door.

Barloff went back to his quarters to find a message waiting for him to report to Colonel Golovin immediately.

Barloff reported to Golovin's office to find several other officers there ahead of him. Golovin introduced him to Major Rykov and captains Kotlik and Chekok.

Golovin was busy looking over some papers on his desk. Everyone silently waited for him to speak. The lull gave Barloff a chance to assess the other officers in the room.

Rykov was a major with crisp military bearing, his uniform fitted like a glove, and his boots reflected a high polish. He had an arrogant look on his face made even more pronounced by a faint sneer. His hair—sandy and streaked with a little grey—had started to thin. His nose, while not large, was prominent and blade-like, giving him the look of a hawk or an eagle. His whole bearing reminded one of a bird of prey, ready to pounce on its victim. "A man to be wary of," thought John.

Kotlik, swarthy looking, was probably from strong peasant stock. He was slightly heavy but well muscled with a small waist and large arms and shoulders. His eyes were dark brown under jutting brows, constantly darting here and there, taking in everything. Outwardly calm, his rapid eye movements showed pent-up energy.

Chekok, the opposite of Kotlik, was thin and wiry, with brown hair and penetrating blue eyes. He sported a moustache in a vain attempt to look older. He looked too young to be an officer, especially a captain. He sat in his chair, legs stretched out and crossed, completely relaxed, waiting patiently for the meeting to begin. John assessed him as one not easily ruffled.

Golovin looked up from his papers to note that everyone was present. He wasted no time in getting started. This was the way he did everything. While his body and uniform looked a little sloppy, his work habits and way of doing things were not.

"I want this man caught and soon. This could make others think they can defy our rule. The extra men I'm sending should make the job of hunting him down easy."

"Captain Chekok will command the company here," Golovin

began. "Once in Kiivijarvi, he will be under the direct command of Captain Gerchenoff. I have, this day, promoted Gerchenoff to the rank of captain despite his mistakes. Chekok does have a little seniority but I feel Gerchenoff should command in Kiivijarvi because he is familiar with the situation.

"Barloff, I'm promoting you to first lieutenant to be Gerchenoff's second in command. You will be under Chekok at times because this will be a joint command of Gerchenoff and Chekok in the search for the murdering rebel, Jonas. All other operations are the responsibility of Gerchenoff. Chekok will command the company going north. You and Gerchenoff will command the post once you arrive. Gerchenoff will be the overall commander but I want you, Chekok, to be able to take over if Gerchenoff proves incapable of good leadership. I want this renegade caught and put away before our next training sessions start."

The promotion pleased Barloff. For some reason he thought of Liza, Aimo's sister, back in Kiivijarvi. He thought this strange and felt guilty because he was in love with Elsa. Liza was just a passing fancy.

Golovin interrupted his thinking saying, "Barloff, I want you to brief these men on the situation back in Kiivijarvi. Rykov will be in charge of the operation in its entirety from here in Helsinki while Kotlik will serve as overall liaison officer. I'm sure this operation will not take long, one Finn is going to have a tough time eluding two Russian companies."

"May I remind the colonel," said Barloff, "that most of the men under Gerchenoff are Finnish enlisted men? As such, I doubt they will be enthusiastic about hunting down one of their own countrymen."

"True," said the colonel, "but as soldiers, they will have to follow orders. We'll have enough Russians with them to take care of any slackers in the ranks."

Barloff shrugged, as if to say, "Don't say I didn't warn you."

"Use Rykov's office for the briefing. I have work to do," said Golovin, dismissing the group with a wave of his hand.

The briefing went well enough with Rykov doing most of the talking. Barloff took an instant dislike to Rykov with his domineering arrogance. He thought no one else had anything of value to contribute.

Barloff had heard of Rykov before, none of it good. Rumor had it Rykov was the hatchet man for the area. He wondered if Golovin was under scrutiny by Rykov for some reason.

Rykov gave out orders on the hunt for Jonas, even though he had never been in the area.

"I really can't see what the big problem is running this renegade to ground," said Rykov sarcastically. "He has to make some kind of track in the snow. First off, we restrict all civilian movement in the area. Then we use a checkerboard pattern of patrols to cut his tracks. From there it's a matter of keeping on his trail in relays until we run him to ground like hounds on a fox. If he resists, we kill him, saving us the trial."

"Major, you have put your finger on the problem when you said fox," interrupted Barloff. "I know this soldier. He's an excellent woodsman who has spent most of his life in the woods. He was our best man on wilderness jaunts. He knew where we could find good water, shelter, and wild foods to supplement our diet. It was a joy to have him along on a field trip. He made life a little more pleasant for everyone."

"Lieutenant," said Rykov, "It sounds like you really like this man. I'm not sure you should be one of the people looking for him."

Barloff retorted, "I don't like nor dislike the man. I respect him and have to evaluate the kind of man we're going to hunt. I know the task is going to be a lot tougher than we realize."

"Nonsense," snorted Rykov, "I'll give you two weeks following my plan. By that time you should have him captured or killed. If not, I'll come up to direct the search myself and show you how it should be done. I'll come up there for the trial and execution. I want to be there in case we have trouble with the local people when we kill him."

"Again, sir," said Barloff, "that man has everything going for him. He grew up in the area, he's an excellent survivalist, expert rifle shot; he's a wizard with a knife if it ever comes to infighting. He will have the support of the local people. Quite a few of the Finnish enlisted men will support him even if they don't come right out and say it. If he knows we are tracking him, he can lead us into some horrible traps, summer or winter."

"Barloff, how many times do I have to tell you that this is no big problem. We'll have the man in irons within the month. He's another man, another annoying field problem we have to solve. The tsar has heard of this incident and it has become blown all out of proportion."

Barloff decided then and there that he would be careful about crossing swords with Rykov in the future. Very respectfully, he said, "I still think this is going to be a bigger job than any of us can imagine."

"Well, maybe," conceded Rykov, "you know the man and the country better than anyone. I still look upon it as a simple field problem. Thank you, lieutenant. I have enough information for now. Chekok and Toklat, if you want to pick Barloff's brain some more, feel free, but do it elsewhere as I have work to do. Dismissed."

The three of them walked out into the hallway.

Kotlik said, "Make sure you keep me posted on all events in Kiivijarvi. Pay special attention to the attitude of the people and their relationship with the search."

Chekok said, "Let's go to the Boar's Head for a couple of drinks and talk. I want to know more about the area and this Jonas. He sounds like some kind of man, the kind of man we need on our side."

"That's right," said Barloff, "If this whipping and killing hadn't happened, he would be on our side now. He probably would have stayed in the army after his time was up."

They put on their coats and walked to the Boar's Head where Mika greeted Barloff warmly.

Chekok looked surprised at Barloff and said, "You do get around don't you? You haven't been here long but you found our favorite cafe. Did Golovin direct you to this place?"

"No," said Barloff, grinning, "A special young lady introduced me to the place."

"Hoo-ey, you do get around don't you?" cracked Chekok.

Barloff just smiled at him.

Mika showed them to a table. Chekok ordered vodka, but Barloff, thinking about the coming evening, wanted to stay sober. His mouth was dry, so he asked Mika, "Do you have any beer?"

"You bet," boomed Mika, "The very best. We make it ourselves."

"Beer it'll be," said Barloff.

"Tell me more about this Jonas fellow," said Chekok. "I like to know about the enemy I have to hunt down."

"What do you want to know?"

"Everything and anything that you can think of about the man."

Barloff started in, "Let's see, he came in about eighteen months ago. He had a couple of delays granted so he's a little older than most, twenty-two I think. His mother died and his father was quite ill for some time. He had a lot of expenses with his father. After he died, he had to mortgage the farm. His older brother still lives on the farm. Between his brother and his army income I think they have paid off the mortgage."

"Does he have any other relatives?"

"I believe he has two other brothers and a sister. They were here for the father's funeral, but I don't know where they live."

"We ought to put some kind of watch on them in case he goes to them for help."

"I'll make it a point to find out where they live," said Barloff, "We have a Judas among the enlisted men. His name is Aimo Hakala, and he might know or could find out. He's the one that told Karloff about the fine sand imbedded in the ice rink."

"Damn, I would like to have been there to see that. I bet it was funny. I always thought that Karloff was kind of a stuffy bastard anyway. I really didn't think that the prank merited a public whipping, but then Karloff's feelings got hurt."

"That wasn't all that got hurt," laughed Barloff, "He made several beautiful pratfalls. On the last one, I thought he busted his ass."

"That was a good piece of thinking, putting sand in the rink. I would never have thought of anything like that."

"Nor I," said Barloff. "That shows you the kind of man we will be dealing with when we get there. No joking, this is going to be for real. We're going to get the brunt of it, you just wait and see."

"I hope not," said Chekok. "I hate being away from Helsinki for long. This is easy duty—lots of pretty women, as you have already discovered. There's sailing in the harbor and swimming when the weather is warm enough. I like to lay on the beach and do a little girl watching. A short way out of town you can find good salmon and trout fishing. This is going to be where they hand out promotions. You have to be under the noses of the top brass so they remember you at promotion time. Unless you do something spectacular out in the sticks, you never get the recognition."

Mika came, bearing their drinks. Barloff's beer was in a heavy pewter tankard with a lid. Mika had put it outside in the cold. John's damp hand stuck to the ice-cold pewter momentarily. He pushed the lid back to take a long drink. It was, as Mika said, very good. Wiping the foam from his upper lip, he said, "Now that's what I call good beer."

"It is. I have had it before. This is the place to eat, drink or just loaf."

They had several more drinks, toasting everyone and everything. Time flew by quickly. Suddenly, Barloff remembered his date with Elsa. He knew she would be home by now.

"Captain, if you don't have anything more you want to talk about, I would like to leave. I have a date with that beautiful girl. I'd like to spend as much time with her as possible before we head north."

"I didn't realize it was so late. I have a date this evening myself. How about making it a double date?"

Barloff really didn't want to make it a double date, but this was a captain and his commanding officer, so he thought it best to comply.

"That would be fine, Captain. Where would you like to go?"

"Right here if that suits you, Lieutenant. How about 7:30?"

"That's agreeable, Captain."

Barloff went over to Mika to pay for his share of the drinks but Chekok had already paid for both of them. Barloff thanked him for the drinks, and they walked out together, Barloff heading for Elsa's and Chekok going back to his quarters.

Elsa met him at the door and was positively radiant. He marvelled at her beauty and how lucky he was to have found such a prize.

They embraced as she closed the door. He nuzzled her with his cold nose. She wiggled away from him and said, "Let's not go anywhere tonight. Let's stay here and make love."

Thrills ran through him just thinking about it, but then he remembered the double date.

"Oh, Elsa," he lamented, "I agreed to a double date with Captain Chekok and his girl friend. I wanted to get out of it but couldn't without a big scene. We're going to Kiivijarvi, and I'll have to work with him up there."

"Darn," she said. "I got off working at the sauna, too."

"He's easy going. I think you'll like him. We'll try to make some excuse to get away early. Maybe he'll want to break up early as he doesn't have any more time than I do."

"I hope so," she pouted.

"We have over an hour before we have to meet Chekok at the Boar's Head. We can make a lot of love between now and then."

"I'm for that," said Elsa.

"I just wish I hadn't stayed so long with Chekok. I'll hardly have time to take a sauna and change clothes."

"Let's take a sauna together," said Elsa happily.

"What will Gerta say?" asked Barloff.

"She won't say a word. In fact she'll encourage us. She's been urging me to get a boyfriend ever since I lost my husband."

"I'll get some clean clothes and be right back."

Gerta met them with a mischievous smile as she surmised their purpose for coming. She handed them towels and said, "No one here now. If anyone does come, I'll knock on the wall so you don't take too long."

Both stripped to the skin. Barloff took her hand to enter the heated part of the sauna. The heat hit their bodies like a welcome invisible force after being out in the cold winter air.

He filled a wooden bucket with water to cool down the hot benches. Both climbed to the top bench, and John threw a dipper of water on the hot rocks. He looked over at her, seeing the perspiration beginning to glisten on her body. He still couldn't believe this beautiful woman was his, at least for the time being.

He pulled her close to him, kissing her full on the mouth. It tasted slightly salty. They made love in the heat of the sauna and it was good.

Barloff filled two wooden buckets with water adding hot water to get the temperature right. He started soaping himself.

"Let me," said Elsa.

She began soaping his body gently, all over. He picked up another bar of soap to do the same to her. It was a sensuous experience. The slick soap allowed their hands to slide over each other's body effortlessly. He gently massaged her breasts, watching her bright pink nipples become erect. The second time they made love standing up. He had to hold her up. He was almost a foot taller. It was a matter of reach.

45

After they were through, they both sat on the lower bench to catch their breath. They got up to finish washing, and then sluiced their bodies off with clean, cool water. They went into the changing room to cool off before getting dressed. Neither of them was a bit shy about seeing their naked bodies, it was the most natural feeling in the world.

They dressed, deciding to go to the Boar's Head even though they would be a bit early.

They walked silently arm in arm to the Boar's Head, enjoying the cold, crisp night air. Neither of them felt the need for words, content in each other's company.

Mika greeted them with his usual booming voice and a big bear hug for Elsa. "What will it be tonight? We have fresh sausage I just made, roast loin of pork, an excellent baked salmon or fried trout."

Barloff said, "Let's wait and see. We're meeting Captain Chekok and his girl friend for dinner. You can bring us a drink while we wait."

"What's your pleasure?"

Elsa said, "I'll have a small glass of wine. I'll leave the choice up to you, Mika."

"I'll have beer like I had this afternoon. You do brew some excellent beer, Mika."

"One beer and one wine," said Mika heading for the kitchen.

Elsa and John stood by the fireplace toasting their back sides for a moment. The fire felt good after the cold walk. They stood talking quietly by the fire.

"Yipes!" yelled John jumping away and patting the back of his trousers.

Elsa laughed, "You didn't burn your trousers did you?"

"No, but it feels like I scorched my legs," retorted John.

Mika came over with the drinks asking, "Should I pour the beer on your legs or would you rather put the fire out from the inside?"

They all laughed. Mika led them to a table for four directly across the room, saying to John, "I thought you might want to get a little farther away from the fireplace this time."

Chekok and his girl friend came in shortly. Introductions were exchanged all around as they sat down.

Mika came over and took their food and drink orders. The food was good, but the conversation was dull. Katri, Chekok's girl friend, was good-looking but rather dumb. It was hard to carry on an intelligent conversation.

Chekok seemed fascinated with the story of Jonas. He turned the conversation in that direction, asking Barloff, "Have you told Elsa about the tough renegade we're going to have to hunt down?"

"Well, a little bit," replied Barloff. "You keep calling him tough as if you know that his nick name is *sisu* in Finnish. That's the right translation isn't it, Elsa?"

"Literally, yes, but it means a lot more in Finnish," said Elsa. "It's one of those words that takes pages to translate, and still you wouldn't have it right. It is tough, unyielding—in a man it would be muscular, a sinewy type of muscle structure. It means the ability to endure and survive under the most adverse circumstances. It's akin to a bush that only splits into individual fibers but doesn't break no matter how you bend and twist it. You can go on and on trying to describe *sisu* and still not quite have it."

"I know what you mean," said Chekok, "Knowing both Russian and Finnish, I find words in both languages that carry a meaning that's difficult to translate. Some words lose something in translation."

"I tried to tell Rykov what a hard job it's going to be to track this man down," said Barloff, "but he didn't want to listen. He's in his own element with everything in his favor. The only positive item we have going for us is sheer numbers."

"I agree," said Chekok, "but most men make mistakes of some kind or have some kind of weakness. In this case it might be the woman. What's her name? Emma, I think, isn't it?"

"It's Emma," said Barloff. "But if you harm one hair on her head, he will hunt you down and kill you like a dog. We could create a raging maniac. Right now I think all he's going to do is stay out of our way. I don't think he will kill anyone unless it's necessary for his own survival."

Chekok fell silent. Barloff was afraid he had put a dangerous thought in his head about Emma. Barloff felt he knew Jonas well enough to predict what he would do if any harm came to Emma.

They left early. Both couples wanting to spend some time together before they had to part.

John and Elsa were glad the evening didn't last any longer. It was boring beyond belief. They went directly to Elsa's house.

Morning came, and this time Barloff was up and stirring. He was anxious to get back to headquarters to get a progress report on their move. He hoped for a few more days, but he knew it was not to be; a soldier's life was like that. He was also itching for a little action.

He knelt on the bed, kissed Elsa lightly and said, "I'll try to get away so we can have lunch together."

"All right, my love," said Elsa sitting up revealing her naked body in all its glory. "I'll look forward to it all morning. It'll make the work go faster."

"You'd better cover up, or I'll never leave," said John looking wistfully at her and the inviting bed.

"That wouldn't be bad, would it?" Elsa teased.

"I'd like that too but the colonel will have my hide if I don't show up on time." He kissed her again and spun for the door, not trusting his emotions anymore.

John was barely back in his quarters when an orderly came to his door. "Colonel Golovin wants you to join him and some other officers for a breakfast meeting as soon as possible."

"Yes, I'll be there shortly. Thank you."

John went directly to the officers' mess. He was the first to arrive. This was his first trip to the officers' mess. He had been eating at the Boar's Head, Elsa's, or the little cafe down by the docks. The place was quite impressive. Part of the dining room was more sumptuous, reserved for officers with the rank of major or higher. He looked through the door at the other portion of the officers' mess. It was quite plain in comparison.

An orderly brought coffee. It was good, fresh, strong and piping hot. He had not drunk coffee much until he came to Finland. The Russians were more inclined to drink tea. But here, many had acquired the coffee habit from the Finnish people. The orderly didn't bother to ask if he preferred coffee or tea.

Golovin and Rykov came in, still discussing details of the move north. Tall, lean, well-dressed and immaculate Rykov towered over the short, pudgy, unkempt Golovin. The entire picture was a study in contrasts. Golovin looked as if he had slept in his uniform; Rykov's was perfect.

Golovin sat down at the head of the table. The orderly had a cup of coffee at his elbow immediately. Barloff had guessed right, the colonel had succumbed to the coffee habit.

Chekok and Kotlik came in shortly. Barloff watched Chekok secretly, wondering how he fared the night. He looked well enough. He must have been in his quarters to receive the message about the meeting.

"We'll order breakfast shortly," Golovin said, "but we have a lot to cover, so we might as well get to it. We have the unit ready to march, or rather will have by this forenoon, so make preparations accordingly."

Barloff's heart sank. He would not be able to see Elsa again.

He said to himself, *I wonder if I can get away long enough to say good-bye?*

Golovin and Rykov took turns outlining the order of march.

Over all it would be a seven-day forced march. Three of the nights would be in the open. The other three nights, they would stay at other outposts along the way. Barloff and Chekok would be with the advance units. They would proceed to their first campground.

The men ate breakfast while Golovin went on and on with the endless details of the move. Barloff was fidgeting in his chair, anxious to get out and see Elsa once more.

"Your units are in the staging area. I suggest you check on them yourselves to make sure everything is right with your own unit," said Golovin when they had finally finished.

Barloff and Chekok left together. Kotlik said he would join them later at the staging area. He had a few last minute details to cover, some additional items he would give them later.

At the staging area, Barloff met Nikolai Toklat, Chekok's second in command. He was doing a remarkable job of keeping horses, sleighs, troops and equipment in some semblance of order for the march.

Chekok said, "Here are a few more details I got from Golovin and Rykov." Handing him a sheaf of papers he added, "I'm going to sneak away for a bit to say good-bye to Katri."

"How about I sneak off with you, sir?" asked Barloff, "I would like to say good-bye to Elsa."

"I can see why you would want to do that. She's some kind of woman, that Elsa. Katri is pretty, but she's dumb. If I ever get back here without you, I'm sure going to try to take over for you. Just joking, of course. Come along."

They commandeered a one-horse cutter. They piled in with Chekok grabbing the reins, giving the horse a slap on the rump. They started with a lurch.

"Where do you want to go?" asked Chekok.

"Down to the docks. The Helsinki Shipping Company."

"I know it. It's right on the way to Katri's. I'll pick you up on the way back. We can't stay long. Toklat has almost everything ready to move out."

Chekok dumped Barloff off at the shipping company.

Barloff said, "I'll be here or at that little cafe around the corner."

"Good enough," Chekok shouted, slapping reins to the horse and taking off with flying snow clods from the horse's hooves.

Barloff went inside to meet Elsa at the door.

"You're early," she said looking up in surprise from the accounts ledger in front of her.

"I know, "He replied, "I'm not here for lunch. We're leaving this morning. I just came to say good-bye."

"Oh, my," she said, crestfallen, "I'll see if I can get off for a little while. At least we can go around the corner to the cafe."

She asked her boss if she could leave for a short while, explaining the situation. He grudgingly said yes, asking her not to stay too long.

The two of them ran to the cafe, sat down by a window where they could watch for Chekok to return.

The waiter came by and said, "Well, here are our bird eaters back. What will it be this morning?"

"Just coffee for me, I've eaten breakfast."

Elsa ordered a hot roll with her coffee.

Barloff blurted out, "Elsa, I love you. I know we have known each other for such a short time, but it feels like I have known you forever. I have never been as one with another person as I have been with you. I have never felt like this before in my life. I'm sure it's love."

Elsa started to interrupt, but Barloff said, "Wait, let me finish. Then you can laugh, if you want. I love you and want to marry you. I can't do anything right now, but when I get back to Kiivijarvi, I'll look for a house. I'll send for you, if you're of the same mind."

Elsa said, "I feel the same way. But, I'm afraid you might change your mind when you get away from here and back to your old friends."

"No, I won't," he said adamantly, "I love you. I want you for my wife. Major Rykov or Colonel Golovin will be coming up soon. If you're of the same mind and I've found a house, I could make arrangements for you to come with them."

They talked excitedly about what they would do in the future.

He said, "I'll send letters with our regular courier and have them delivered to the Boar's Head."

"I'll be looking for them every day," said Elsa.

Just then Chekok came down the road in a swirl of snow dust. Barloff walked to the door to flag him down. Chekok saw him and turned the cutter in a giant slide. The cutter slued sideways as he came around the corner. He brought the cutter to a sliding stop yelling, "Get in. We're going to be late for the march."

Elsa ran out to kiss him good-bye.

"I'll pay the bill," she said. "You go on. I love you."

Barloff turned to give her a fierce, hard kiss. Turning quickly, he made three long jumps into the cutter. Chekok slapped the horse with the reins, taking off in a sliding turn for the staging area.

Barloff waved a farewell to Elsa as they rounded the next corner.

They arrived back at the staging area to find all in readiness, thanks to the efforts of Lieutenant Toklat. Toklat had both their horses saddled and tied to the lead sleigh. Kotlik tucked a packet of papers into that sleigh as everyone mounted horses.

Chekok raised his arm waving it forward shouting, "Forward Ho!"

Chapter 6

Hideout

JONAS' SKIS SHUSHED THROUGH THE SNOW after he left the warmth and comfort of Emma's house heading for the wilderness. Looking back at the yellow rectangle of light coming from her window, he wondered when or if he would see her again. He knew the Russians would search the town house by house and then look for his ski tracks going into the woods.

He said to himself, "I have to leave with no trace if possible. The ski trail down to the fishing lake will hide my tracks. I can take that trail and maybe get off without being obvious."

Jonas found the ski trail in the darkness. Skiers had packed the trail hard going to and from the lake, making it a dark ribbon in the snow. He needed to go down the trail far enough so no one could see him from the road while he waited for daylight.

The long winter nights were upon them; it wouldn't get light for quite some time. Even then, daylight would last only a few short hours. But, it would brighten enough soon so he could see where he was going.

Squatting on the trail, he contemplated his next move. As the sky lightened, he could discern features of the main trail in the snow. He remembered where he was and how the ground lay.

"Let's see," he said aloud, his breath thick on the cold air, "there's a gentle slope ahead ending in a ravine. It flattens out some distance before it pitches downward to the lake. Over there is the long ravine with timber in the bottom. The trees go up both sides, almost to the ridge top itself."

An idea came to him for hiding his tracks. He skied off the main trail toward the ravine for a few hundred feet where his tracks disappeared from the main trail. A long arc down the hill brought him back onto the trail. Getting off his skis, he turned them uphill and remounted, carefully patting the snow to hide his foot prints. Skiing a short distance up the slope, he started a herringbone pattern climbing like anyone coming from the lake.

When he reached the point of his first departure, he stepped out of his skis again, turning them down his original detour. He followed this arc, but, this time, when his tracks disappeared from the sight of the trail, he

51

turned up the ravine into the timber.

To the casual observer it would look like someone had taken a short detour to get fresh snow. Unless the Russians actually followed his trail, they wouldn't be aware that he left.

"It'll snow in a few days. Then there'll be no trace of my leaving."

Out of sight of the trail, he started his herringbone ascent to the ridge top. Once on top, he looked towards town, picking up the pin-point light of Emma's window. He sighed and moved on.

"By tonight," he said to himself, "the wind on this ridge will have scoured my tracks clean. If they see my track below, they won't be able to follow me beyond this ridge."

Jonas continued on, staying with the high ground, going from one ridge to another, heading southwest. After twenty miles, he turned off the ridge. More instinct than anything else made him pause. The snow had changed the landscape considerably since his summer visit.

Half way down the slope he stopped, turning his skis sideways to the slope to study the winter-altered terrain. For a moment, he thought he had missed the trapper cabin. Then he saw it. The open door showed a black hole in the snow. The rest of the cabin lay under a blanket of snow.

"Home at last, such as it is," sighed Jonas.

He skied up to the door, which was half full of snow with more inside. Slipping out of his back pack, he hung it on a nearby broken tree limb and then slipped his rifle between the straps.

Using a ski as a shovel he cleared the doorway of snow. Gently, he brushed snow away from the only window to let in a little light.

The cabin looked the same as he remembered it from summer. Examining the door closely, he remembered closing it when he left. Some rodents, probably mice, had gnawed through the top hinge of rawhide, allowing the door to sag open.

Pulling the door closed he remarked, "I'll have to make new hinges of raw hide from the first deer I kill."

He had left a stack of kindling and wood from his summer visit. Good manners had him leave the dry wood, in case someone came in out of a storm or other emergency. He had not expected that person to be him.

Retrieving his pack and rifle, he immediately laid a fire in the fireplace. Flint and steel struck sparks into a bed of tinder. It caught on the second strike. He breathed more life into the smoldering tinder by blowing on it gently. It flamed up, as he pushed it in with larger chips. The larger chips caught quickly, and he added larger pieces to the fire. Soon the fire was crackling merrily, throwing dancing shadows on the walls of the semi-dark cabin. Soon the cabin took on a warm, home-like feeling.

He looked around the cabin remembering details faintly from his last visit. "If I had known then what I know now," he said, warming his hands, "I would have made a little more effort to make this place liveable."

Picking up his rifle, he looked at it closely for the first time. There simply hadn't been the time nor opportunity before. He hadn't bothered to load it. Not knowing where it was going to shoot would be a waste of ammunition.

"Sighting in comes tomorrow," he said, hanging the rifle on some wooden pegs above the fireplace put there for that purpose by the former occupant.

He turned his attention to the back pack. He put away staples such as flour, sugar and the coffee he so dearly loved.

"Ah, what's this?" he asked, pulling out a small sausage skin. Twisting one end of it open, he smelled, "Sourdough starter. That had to be Anna's idea. I was wondering how I was going to get some started. Sometimes you can't get it started at all, especially in winter."

He was like a child on Christmas morning opening presents. He had to trust the people he loved to provide for his survival. From what he saw, they had done a thorough job of it. He found a small ax without a handle. Vilho had to have been sure Jonas could whittle a handle and saved the space in the pack. A buck saw blade rolled in a protective leather cover came out after. The leather he could use for something else after he built his saw. He hadn't even thought of a saw. Vilho must have. After he made a frame for the sawblade, he could save himself hours of back-breaking, ax work. Jonas unpacked everything, putting each treasure away as he went. Emma and Vilho had added a few items that they thought he would need.

He couldn't see much of a problem in surviving. But, while the wilderness would provide many of his needs, he knew he would eventually have to go back to town for more supplies. That was the greatest danger.

While the cabin warmed, Jonas busied himself sweeping out dust and leaves that had blown in through the open door. The melting snow made wet spots on the floor.

Jonas went outside to cut spruce boughs for his bed. Selecting carefully so the fresh cuts wouldn't show, he gathered a big bundle. He laid them on the bunk against the wall, curved side up. He threw his sheepskin sleeping bag on top of this heap and crawled in, falling asleep immediately.

When he woke some hours later, he ate. Then, he took his rifle from the pegs to sight it in. It was nearly on. Within three shots, he was hitting right on target at one hundred yards. He picked several more targets at further distances, firing nine more rounds. By this time he was confident he could hit anything man-sized out to five hundred yards.

Back inside, he reloaded the fired cartridges with the tools provided by Vilho. Later he would vary the loading to try for even better accuracy.

He often commented that an inaccurate rifle was useless unless you intended to frighten your quarry to death.

After he finished with the rifle, he set about making a handle for his ax and buck saw. He had made both before, so it was not a big task. Now he had the tools he needed for several months of survival.

The next few weeks passed uneventfully. If the Russians scoured the countryide for him, he saw none of it. He busied himself with getting his cabin ready for the big snows yet to come.

He put in a good stock of wood, killed game, including a fat buck. He skinned the deer, hanging the carcass high in some fir trees behind the cabin. No one could see it unless they were right under the tree.

It took several days to get the cabin in good order. He repaired the door hinges with raw hide from the deer and chinked up a few open spaces between the logs.

Jonas worried about the tracks he made, going to, and coming from his meat cache. The snow had deepened, making it difficult to negotiate without skis. But the skis left trails visible from the ridge. He solved the problem by cutting some small fir trees, sticking them into the snow in a curved lane. Now his tracks were not visible from any angle. The cabin itself he camouflaged with a few spruce trees set in the snow.

He didn't build a fire during the day. The days were quite short anyway, so, with a good fire going during the night, the cabin would stay warm until dark when he replenished the fire. He didn't want anyone to spot the plume of smoke from afar and decide it was his hideout.

He tried to stay on the high ridges in his forays for meat. In just a few hours, the wind scoured his tracks clean.

On one of his trips, as he topped a ridge, his trained eye caught the glint of something shiny. He stopped immediately behind a small fir tree. He carefully scanned the next ridge just in time to see a ski patrol disappear from sight. The only reason they could be there, was to look for him.

"I wish I had my telescope so I could see if the composition of the patrol was Russian, Finnish or mixed."

The patrol hadn't seen him, or they would have headed his way immediately. They were probably running a checkerboard search pattern, trying to cut his trail. He didn't know how big a grid they were using, so he was at a loss to know when their next trip would be closer. He was grateful for the warning. Now he knew they were coming, but he didn't know when.

"If a big storm moves in, I can follow their tracks to check the size of the search pattern. This will give me a better idea of their time table. They won't go out during a big storm and afterwards, they won't be able to find my tracks. I'll have the knowledge I need to figure out their pattern."

It was as if God answered his prayers. The next day, ominous, black clouds rolled up on the horizon. Scattered at first, they bunched closer and closer as the day wore on, trying to nudge each other out of the way, crowding into one big black, rolling mass.

Jonas knew by experience that this would be a major storm. He quickly donned his coat. He decided on the basis of what he had seen that he could make his scouting trip before the storm hit. If he guessed wrong on the storm, he would lead his enemies to his lair. It would mean he would have to give up his snug retreat. He felt the storm would come and thought the risk worth taking.

A sense of urgency came upon him as he climbed to the top of the ridge directly behind the cabin. From there he skied directly to the point where he last had seen the patrol. The wind had all but wiped out their tracks on the ridge top. Only a seasoned tracker such as Jonas could pick up the small telltale ridges of snow that the wind had not wiped out. Their tracks led him to where their trail turned south. Finding the second south running line two miles east told him their grid was a two-mile square.

Satisfied that he had discerned their grid pattern, he started back to the cabin. As he turned from the ridge to his cabin, it started spitting snow.

He muttered to himself, "I guessed right on you again old man winter. I hope you snow enough to cover my tracks. I like this place too well to give it up to those damn Russkies. I would hate to have to go to ground like a rabbit."

It felt great to return to his cabin and look out at the snow coming down in earnest. There was not much wind with the snow, which made it especially good for covering his tracks. Some wind might keep his tracks open, giving the hunters a clue on which area to concentrate their efforts.

Jonas, knowing the country and their grid pattern, calculated that their next traverse would come close to his cabin.

"I estimate they will be on the grid close to me in the next three to four days, weather permitting. I don't know how far south they were running their grid pattern before they turned west again. They would most likely stop at Lake Lahti. The lake is large enough to form a natural boundary. Dependent on this storm, I can plan on a visit within the next few days. I have to know when they pass my cabin. I can't have any activity or make any tracks until after they pass."

He was sure they wouldn't come close to the cabin unless some freak occurrence made them suspicious. The cabin was on a short finger ridge, jutting out from the main ridge. If they changed their search grid to a smaller one, they still wouldn't come down the short ridge. He was sure they would cross on the ridge directly behind the cabin.

"It will be at least three days after the storm before they come this way. I'll start my ridge top surveillance in two days. After the Russians pass,

I can get back to normal."

He sat in the cabin, trying to think of any small item he overlooked that would give away his location. He couldn't think of anything but still couldn't keep his mind worry free. In his mind he formulated several plans of action if by some chance they did discover his hiding place.

"If I have enough warning I could slip down into the valley on my skis and be gone. They would track me of course, but I know the terrain better and am a much better skier. They would go slow in fear of an ambush. They could only travel at the speed of their slowest man or risk thinning their ranks."

He thought, "If they do catch up to me, I could hold off a considerable force with my new Winchester. It's faster shooting and has a longer range, than the old, single-shot breech loaders they're using. The Russians would send for more help, but they couldn't get here for at least another day. This would give me a chance to slip away under cover of darkness."

All his ideas were good except where he could go for shelter.

"If they don't burn my cabin, I could go into town. There, I could lose my tracks among a welter of other tracks. Then I could take another route back to the cabin. The Russians would concentrate their search in town. If they burned my cabin and all the supplies, I would have to go into town to get more. I know a rundown shack at a small lake that might suffice for temporary shelter. I better make an emergency pack I can grab quickly if something does go wrong."

The snow stopped after three days with a six-inch accumulation. Now there was no way the Russians could find any sign of his movements. The snow helped hide the cabin better. From ten feet away no one would know it existed. If one stepped around the small spruce trees he might see the dark shadow of the door and window, but even those were not obvious.

"Boys," he said, "I give you three days to come my way and then leave me in peace for a while."

On the morning of the second day following the storm Jonas packed a lunch of sour dough biscuits and cold venison. He planned an all-day vigil afield. He guessed they would make their next grid run on the long ridge behind the cabin.

Between the ridge and the cabin lay a blown down spruce tree with its roots turned up in the air like some fallen giant, which indeed it was. The bole of the tree was about four feet off the ground, and the heavy snow nearly covered it. The tree lay parallel to the ridge but on the edge of it closest to the cabin. Jonas skied to it carefully via a small clump of other trees so as not to leave any telltale tracks. If the patrol came down the ridge, they would stick to the relatively open center rather than follow the edge where the spruce lay.

His approach was to the back side of the tree. Using his skis as a shovel, he dug to the ground directly under the bole. Crawling into his snow cave, he pulled his skiis in after him to provide something dry on which he could sit. To survey the ridge, he cut a small peephole under the bole.

"I wonder where their base camp is? I know they aren't going the twenty miles back to town after skiing the grid all day. I'm sure they're working in shifts with men coming and going all the time. If they chase me hard, maybe I could mingle my tracks with those of the relief crew."

His vigil proved fruitless, which he thought would be the case. He didn't want to chance missing them if they were earlier than he calculated.

The next day at dawn, he was back in his cozy snow cave. The interior had iced over from the heat of his body making the walls hard and slick.

Four deer alerted him to the patrol by bounding down the ridge through the heavy snow, taking quick looks back up the slope. The old buck brought up the rear pushing the other deer ahead of him. Jonas knew the patrol must have scared the deer. He was looking out the peep hole when a brace of grouse burst from cover on the hillside and flew close to his lair. His pulse raced with the sure knowledge his enemies were coming. He forced himself to remain calm despite the nearness of danger.

In a few minutes, he counted eight skiers as they came down the ridge and passed within thirty feet of his hideout. The soft shushing of their skiis was all he could hear as they sped by his snow cave. No one looked his way. Even if they had, they wouldn't have noticed the small oblong slit in the snow beneath the bole of the fallen spruce. He recognized some of them. They were using both Finnish and Russian men in the search.

He waited an hour before crawling out of his hole. He didn't realize until then how tense he had been. All his muscles ached from holding in readiness for flight or fight.

He carefully surveyed the area to make sure another patrol wasn't following on the heels of the first. The Russian search pattern was now clear in his mind as he made his way back to the cabin.

Chapter 7

Chekok

THE FIRST NIGHT ON THE TRAIL, they faired better than expected. It turned out to be a warm night. They camped out, pitching their tents in the snow. Rigging shelters for horses and getting the cook tent set up made for a long day. It wasn't a comfortable camp, but everyone survived.

The second night they spent in the town of Torka in a small Russian outpost. Crowded conditions prevailed, but everyone slept inside, including the horses.

The end of the third day meant another night of camping in the open. About noon of that day, the wind picked up, with a few flakes of snow coming out of the northwest. The wind strengthened, blowing up little swirls of snow. The older men said the blow was going to be bad because they could taste salt in the air carried in from the Gulf of Bothnia. When the wind blew fierce enough to carry salt that far, one better hunt for cover soon.

Chekok ignored the storm warnings and the men's grumblings. It was a long way to their planned bivouac area.

At first the snow blew in light, hard particles stinging men and horses alike. The driving force of the wind increased in velocity rapidly. The pellets, driven by the wind, blew almost horizontal to the ground. Their line of march forced them into the teeth of the gale. The men had to lean into the wind at a forty-five degree angle to keep their balance. At times spruce groves sheltered them by breaking the full force of the wind.

Each time they passed a shelter belt of trees Barloff tried to get Chekok to stop. He refused. They had not traveled their allotted miles for the day.

Chekok said stubbornly, "We still have more miles to go. Those are our orders, and I'm in command!"

Barloff retorted, "You keep this up, and there won't be anyone left to command."

"So be it," snapped Chekok spurring his horse ahead to see what lay in front of the column.

John pressed his horse to catch up. He didn't want to give up on stopping the column early.

Barloff faced Chekok again saying, "I know you're in command and we haven't made our distance for the day. But we could lose supplies, equipment, horses, and possibly men. Under those circumstances, Rykov would hardly reprimand you for an early stop. He would really be on you for losing men or supplies due to stubbornness. The weather may clear soon, and we can make up the lost time."

"What if the weather doesn't clear?" snapped Chekok.

"We would be late, but we would arrive without losses," said Barloff.

"You don't know Rykov and what a stickler he can be for staying with the plan, especially if it's his plan," retorted Chekok.

They rode on in silence, their collars turned up against the storm. They turned their heads away from the wind with its stinging particles of snow and ice. The cold weather paled in comparison to the cold that developed between them.

The storm increased in tempo. The snow particles were hard, ice balls, making traction difficult. A soft snow would have been easier. Men and horses slipped back one step for every two forward, making walking more and more difficult and tiring. The troop plodded along in a trance.

The snow and wind increased, cutting the visibility to near zero. Horses pulling sleighs ran into the ones in front, tangling horses and harness. Drivers cursed their teams, the weather, and everything in general. Chaos reined up and down the line of march.

Several times the roadway became hidden by blowing snow. Sleighs ran off into ditches, spilling their contents in the snow. The men had to get off the road to set sleighs upright by sheer brute force and then reload the contents. Several times men unhitched horses from other sleighs to help pull out the ditched ones.

The snow turned wetter, clinging to everything it touched. Drivers had to stop and wipe snow from their horses eyes so they could see. Invariably, when this happened, the team behind ran into the stopped one, causing a chain reaction of collisions. Up and down the line came cursing, yelling, and the cracking of whips. The drivers lashed out at their horses to vent some of their anger and frustration.

Chekok and Toklat rode up and down the line of march pleading, cajoling and cursing the men to move faster. A numbness spread through the group. The men put their heads down, plodding along like dumb beasts.

Chekok rode ahead to scout the roadway and saw the vast, treeless plain Barloff had told him about earlier. He decided they could not survive if they tried to cross in a howling blizzard. The increased force of the wind across the plain convinced him to stop.

He remembered a small grove of spruce trees some distance back.

He pushed his horse into a full gallop to stop the column before they passed the area. His horse knew they were going to quit this nonsense. Horse and rider were glad to turn their back on the raging storm.

He got back in time to stop them at the spruce grove. He told Barloff and Toklat what lay ahead.

"We'll stop here in this grove. At least we'll have a little protection and easy access to firewood. Rykov and his march orders can go to hell," he shouted above the howling wind.

Toklat directed the sleigh drivers into the spruce grove as they came to it. The men put up their tents first. Normally four men could put up one tent but the unrolled tents billowed out like tiny parasols in the wind. It took twelve men to set up one tent. The men were grateful for the early stop and pitched in with a will, helping each other with the tents.

The cook tent, being larger, took most of the company to get set up. Finally, all tents were pitched, horses sheltered and fed. Now they could tend to their personal needs. The men gathered wood for the tent stoves, knowing a cold, miserable night lay ahead. In no time, all the trees yielded their dry wood and branches as high as a man could reach. Several enterprising men got their horses out of shelter. The mounted men could reach higher to throw down more wood.

Most of the tents ran out of wood by morning, resulting in the men getting up early and donning clothes to get warm. The snow abated during the night, but the wind continued blowing.

Breaking up camp took extra time with the snow covering tents and equipment. Chekok ordered all snow removed from the tents before packing. The men started to grumble early in the day about the hardships of the trip.

Chekok galloped up and down the line, trying to get the men to make up for lost time. Despite threats of whippings and court martials he got no results. The men still moved at their plodding pace.

Barloff was sorry for the rift still evident between Chekok and himself. He understood why Chekok wanted to go on. This was his first command, and he wanted it to go well. He watched Chekok pushing the tired men but held his tongue. Finally, he could stand it no longer. He rode up to Chekok and said, "Take it easy. The men are tired and out of sorts due to the storm. If you drive them much harder, you'll have a full-fledged mutiny on your hands. How will that look on your record?"

Chekok started to make a short retort, then realized Barloff was right and said, "I know you're right. I want to apologize for yesterday. I got carried away with the responsibility of my first command. I really need someone like you to steer me straight in situations like this. I know you have to make judgments based on current conditions, previous plans not withstanding."

Barloff breathed a sigh of relief. "Let's give the men a free hand," he said, "Most of them know what to do. I know we'll get more out of them if we trust them."

Chekok's change of attitude made the march run smoother. Men and horses pushed on with a determination not seen before, and they gained lost time.

Chekok commented. "Your soft hand touch is working miracles with this group. I would never have believed it."

"It goes to show you what one can accomplish with a little faith in your fellow man," laughed Barloff.

"Well, I have learned a valuable lesson on this trip," said Chekok.

"We can all learn from situations like this. I've learned a lot from this episode, myself," said Barloff.

"I don't know what you learned. Hell, you were right all along."

"I know, but I pushed the wrong way to get it done. I could have been a little more diplomatic trying to get you to stop. I might have gotten it done sooner. At any rate we both made the right decision by stopping early. I hate to think what would have happened if we tried to cross that open plain in the teeth of the storm."

The journey to the next outpost went fairly well. This was a small fort built in earlier years by the Finns and now occupied by the Russians as a way station. Limited facilities dictated tent pitching again, but, because it was a remount station, the horses had ample space.

All the tents pitched, the horses and people fed, the evening became relaxed. Chekok invited Barloff and Toklat to his tent. He felt mellow with his great crisis past and the probability they would make Kiivijarvi on time.

Chekok had had several drinks before anyone got there and was in a talkative mood. Toklat came in first. Chekok said with a slightly thick tongue, "I never did thank you for the good job you did in the staging area. You got it all so well organized, I had nothing to do."

"It was my job," said Toklat, "I enjoy duty like that. I have to be working all the time, or I get bored."

Barloff came in a little later. Chekok greeted him warmly, saying, "This is my best friend here. He tried to get me out of trouble earlier, but I wouldn't listen. I finally saw the light, thanks to Barloff, here."

Chekok poured Toklat and Barloff each a half glass of vodka saying, "Drink up! It's a good night to get drunk and be somebody."

Barloff wasn't a heavy drinker and didn't want to get drunk with them. He felt someone in a command position should stay sober.

Chekok and Toklat got into a drinking contest. The more they drank, the more belligerent they became.

Chekok chided, "Barloff you're not a good Russian. You can't drink vodka like me and Toklat.

"Oh, I can drink my share when I want, but I've been there before and don't want to suffer tomorrow." Barloff thought to himself, *I'm probably going to have to get this company going in the morning. I know neither of these men is going to be able do anything.*

At one point he thought he was going to have to fight both of them, and then he thought the two of them were going to fight each other. The alcohol finally overcame them both, and they passed out in their chairs. Barloff got some help to put them in bed and went to bed himself. He knew for sure he would have to take over. Neither would be fit to command anything in the morning.

Morning came, bitter cold. Barloff could hear men outside his tent getting ready for the march. The cold made the snow creak under the men's boots. He was reluctant to leave his warm covers but knew someone had to get the troops moving. He was second in command and knew that Chekok would not be able to do anything, even if he could get him up.

Barloff went to the cook tent for breakfast. Several men made snide remarks about the whereabouts of their illustrious leader. Barloff ignored the remarks.

Breakfast over, he ordered the cook tent and the rest of the camp struck and ready for march. He waited until the last minute to strike the tent with Toklat and Chekok. He couldn't get either man to stir. He couldn't delay any longer, so he had pallets made in one of the sleighs. He transferred them from tent to sleigh. Toklat stirred, moaning several times with hangover pain. Chekok never woke up to acknowledge they were moving him. Barloff covered them well and ordered the group to proceed.

Around noon Toklat came to, yelling, "Where the hell am I? What's going on? Where are my clothes?"

Barloff rode over saying, "Your clothes are under your pallet. Your boots are at the foot of your bed. We're a half day out on the march. We'll be stopping for lunch soon."

At the mention of food, Toklat turned green and threw up over the side of the sleigh. He flopped back down under the covers. Finally, he mustered up enough strength to get himself dressed. He did most of it under the covers to keep from freezing. He stayed under the covers for several minutes to get some warmth into his cold clothes.

Chekok slept on. On his rounds, Barloff would ride by to see if he was still among the living. There wasn't much doubt, he lay with mouth agape, snoring loudly.

Barloff said to himself, "The longer he sleeps the better off he will be. No matter when he wakes up, he's going to have one big headache."

By mid afternoon, Chekok came out of it. He stood up in the sleigh, yelling for Barloff, who came at a gallop.

"Where the hell are my clothes?"

"Under your pallet. Your boots are at the foot of your bed. You've been asleep most of the day."

"I'm glad someone had enough sense to get this outfit on the road," said Chekok struggling to get dressed, standing up in the lurching sleigh.

"Do you want the driver to stop the sleigh so you can get dressed without falling on your ass?"

"Yes . . . no! Hell, I don't want you to lose time because of my foolishness. I'll manage." He said, falling down in the sleigh.

Barloff rode off to get Chekok's horse. "I'm glad that's not me riding horseback with a big hangover. Every little jounce and bounce is going to hurt."

"Barloff, you're a good man," said Chekok stepping from the sleigh into the saddle.

"Thanks. Are you going to be all right?"

"I will be in a day or two. Right now I could cheerfully die."

Barloff rode off to check the column, leaving Chekok to follow at a slow walk. Near the head of the column he saw Toklat, off the road, dismounted, throwing up again. Barloff shook his head, thankful that he had had more sense.

Chekok made it to the head of the column, walking his horse carefully, trying not to make any jarring steps.

Chekok said to Barloff, "If you ever let me do that again, make the last drink of the evening hemlock. I don't want to wake up like this again."

They rode for a time at the head of the column with Chekok groaning with each step his horse made. Barloff didn't chide him any more, he felt bad enough.

"At least you had a little something to celebrate last night."

"Oh, what was that?" asked Chekok sarcastically.

"Well, it looks like we'll make Kiivijarvi on schedule despite the storm delay."

Make it they did. By the time they reached Kiivijarvi, Chekok was back to his old self, barking orders like the good soldier.

Chekok and Barloff reported to headquarters. Both listened to the same rumors of sightings of Jonas here and there and the "almost caught him" stories. As soon as they could, they went to their own quarters for some rest in a real bed.

Chapter 8

Ghost

JONAS COULDN'T UNDERSTAND his melancholy feeling when he returned to the cabin.

"What's the matter with me? I should be happy the patrol passed by and won't be back for quite some time."

He slept fitfully, waking during the night with vague feelings of apprehension about his future and Emma's.

"Emma," he said into the darkness, "I miss you so much. I didn't know how much until I saw that patrol today. They made me think how far apart we are right now, maybe apart forever. Just seeing those people looking for me made me realize the plight we're in."

After breakfast, Jonas still felt moody. He paced the cabin and suddenly shouted, "I'll do it. I'll go into town to see my lovely Emma."

The ski patrol had made it possible. He could follow their tracks to camp and wait for the next relief patrol to leave for town. Guessing that the Russians hadn't changed old habits, they should make the relief change on Monday as usual. He hated to wait that long before the relief patrol started into town. It was a bit dangerous, but, having just come through the area, they wouldn't expect him to break cover so soon.

Having made up his mind to go, he looked forward to the trip with joy, thinking of seeing Emma. A warm, tender feeling welled up in him as it always did when he was going to see her. At times he would not admit to himself how much this woman meant to him, his life, the very existence of his being. Now he was going to see her and time moved too slowly.

* * * * *

He climbed the ridge and put his skis in the patrols' track. He made a small loop off and back onto the track, making it look like one of the patrol had made a short deviation. A careful observer might wonder at this, but to the casual onlooker it would hide his entrance.

"I doubt that another patrol will come this way soon, but there's no point in making glaring mistakes this close to my cabin."

It was nearly dark when he reached the camp. Long before it came into sight he smelled wood smoke drifting down the slight breeze. The twinkle of camp fires and the sound of muffled talk told him he was there. Stopping behind a clump of trees, he watched the camp for a long time, trying to determine if this was the new patrol or the old one or both.

After an eternity, two men came out of one of the tents. One complained, in Finnish, about spending another week chasing a ghost when be could be back in town, enjoying life. This confirmed that it was a joint Finnish-Russian patrol and that the other patrol had already left for town.

All I have to do is wait until they fall asleep, he told himself, *sneak through camp and get on the returning patrol's trail. The other tracks around camp will disguise my own.*

Soft laughter welled into his throat thinking of their chagrin if they knew he was this close to them.

The patrol settled down for the night, and Jonas slipped through the camp to find the return ski trail. Good moonlight, coupled with the bright snow, showed him their tracks. The going was easy with the trail well packed.

It was still dark when he reached the hill above town. A few bright lights marked early morning risers. A chance meeting with one such person made him hurry. He stayed on the patrol tracks all the way, not leaving them until he neared Emma's house.

The prospect of danger and seeing Emma pumped adrenalin into his system. He eased into the yard, pulling off his skiis at the rear entry. A light in the kitchen meant Anna was getting breakfast. Thinking of breakfast made him remember he hadn't eaten anything since the day before.

He knocked softly.

Anna asked, "Who is it?"

Jonas returned softly, "It's Jonas."

She opened the door with a *whoosh*, closing it quickly behind him.

"Sit. I'll pull the shades and call Emma. Help your self to the coffee on the stove. It's fresh."

Emma came down the stairs in her robe and slippers, hair tousled and eyes still puffy from sleep. She rushed into his arms to give him a long, lingering kiss.

"I know I should have stopped to fix my hair, but I couldn't wait to see you."

"You look absolutely lovely to me!"

"Oh, Jonas, I'm so glad to see you. How you are, what are you doing, are you surviving all right?"

"I'm here. That's what's important. It feels good to be here to see all of you. It's great to hear another human voice other than my own," said Jonas huskily.

"I bet you could use a bath," said Matt. "I'll heat the sauna. Besides, I know you two would like to be alone for a while."

Matt headed for the sauna. Toivo and Anna retired to the kitchen.

"Oh, Emma, I missed you so. I can stand most anything. All the deprivation and loneliness is possible as long as I know I'll see you again."

She replied, "All I live for is the sight of you. I keep thinking this is all a bad dream and I'm going to wake up and find everything is fine."

"It can't last forever. Something will break to let us be together."

"Jonas, what would you think of us escaping to Sweden or America or someplace like that? We could start all over."

Jonas was a long time making a reply, groping for the right words, he said, "Emma, I would go to the gates of hell for you. I would do it gladly if that's what it would take to keep us together. But, think about our country. What's going to become of our heritage if we keep running away or turning the other cheek to all the Russian indignities. Someone has to fight them. Maybe I'm the start. I don't want us to live as slaves or fugitives. I feel I have to stay, at least for a while."

Emma was silent for some time. "It was a thought," she finally said softly. "I keep thinking what will happen if the Russians catch you. We've heard they have sentenced you to death. Vilho heard Chekok say that, if they caught you alive, the trial would be a mere formality, followed by a swift execution."

"I know," he sighed, "I've thought of all that. I still don't know what to do. There are rumors of unrest in Russia. If they have internal problems, that would be the time for us to break away. Writers like Runeberg and Snellman have told us to be ready in case Russia goes to war with someone. I think we have to try to wrest our freedom from Russian hands somehow."

"Oh, Jonas, that would be such a monumental task."

"No, it just takes a few dedicated people who value freedom more than anything else."

"Even me?" she queried.

"Without freedom what would we have? I couldn't live the life I would like or keep you and our children in bondage."

"I know you're right, but it doesn't appear so to me."

"It's not just us we must think about. What of our children and their children? Will they grow up as slaves with no say over their destiny? As much as I love you, I love freedom for both of us more. I know that's hard for you to see, but it has to be that way, or we are forever slaves."

"I don't know, Jonas. Will it ever come to pass?"

"I know that somehow God will help us achieve our goals and make our lives really amount to something. There are many people who think like me and are willing to fight the Russians. It just takes someone to get it started. Most men are followers, not leaders. We need leaders to free this country. I'm not sure I can be a leader, but I have to try. I think that, once we get started, some real leaders will come into the fray."

Matt came in to announce, "The sauna's getting warm. I loaded it with wood because I know you like it hot."

Matt's walking in put an end to their conversation. Jonas felt there was a small rift in their relationship for the first time. He felt sad. Maybe she would come around to his way of thinking in time.

A hot sauna after breakfast made Jonas feel much better. The rest of the day Jonas and Emma talked idly about events in Kiivijarvi.

Jonas listed the supplies he needed. The list was split between Matt and Vilho. A big amount of supplies might set too many tongues wagging about their destination. Chances were that none of the local people would say anything, but some Russian might see the extra supplies and put two and two together.

With the chores done and Jonas' supplies packed in his rucksack, Anna fixed coffee to go with some of her fresh-baked cinnamon rolls. Then Jonas rested. He slept fitfully, worrying about the Russians being so close. He made up his mind to stay the day and leave in the morning.

At breakfast, Jonas broke the news to Emma and the rest of the family that he was going back into the wilderness. Emma was crestfallen but softened a little when he explained. "I'm putting you and your family in great danger by staying, but I'll come back to see you soon."

"Don't worry about what the Russians would do to us. Most likely nothing, or they would have the whole area down on them," said Matt.

"They don't care what you or the other town people think!" replied Jonas. "They would execute all of you for harboring a criminal to make an example for the rest of the town."

That evening Aimo, the next door neighbor, came home from duty. He said to his sister, "I think there's something going on next door. I think Jonas is there or has been there. They pulled the shades early last night. Vilho was nervous on duty all day, and then I saw him with a big load of groceries. He wouldn't buy that much at once unless he was going to give them to Jonas. I'm going to wander over there to see what I can find out."

"Oh, Aimo," his sister said, "You're always imagining one thing or another. What would you do if you did find out Jonas was over there?"

"It would be my duty to turn him in. After all, he's a murderer."

"You know that was an accident. Besides, Emma's a good friend of mine, and I wouldn't want you to hurt her. It would really hurt her if something happened to Jonas."

"Well, she shouldn't have taken up with the likes of him, anyway!"

"Oh, sour grapes! She never gave you a second look even though we've been neighbors all these years."

"Well, I'm going over there anyway," said Aimo with finality.

Aimo walked to the back door and knocked. Jonas slipped quietly up the stairs as Matt went to answer the door.

"Well, hello Aimo," said Matt loudly so Jonas would know who was there. "Come on in and visit. Mother was just talking about putting on a pot of coffee."

They planned earlier that, no matter who came to the door, Jonas was to go upstairs. His heavy clothes were up there in case he had to jump out the window.

Jonas cursed himself for leaving his skiis in the back entry. They were standing up in the corner where it was quite dark, but Aimo might recognize them as they were distinctive with his special bindings. He sat on the floor, listening to the conversation drifting up to him. He knew Aimo was a big windbag and would not leave until he had talked himself out and eaten all of Anna's baked goods.

Jonas worried that Vilho might come in any time with the rest of the supplies, which would be a dead give away. He need not have worried. Emma had slipped into the living room and raised the shades. She knew Vilho had to walk by the windows and would know something was wrong with the shades up.

Emma barely sat down when Vilho came knocking. Jonas held his breath, trying to think what they would do if Vilho did come in with the supplies. He need not have worried.

Vilho came in, saying, "I smelled fresh coffee brewing a half mile away, so here I am."

"Well, sit down at the table. I was about to pour. Emma would you get another cup for Vilho?"

Coffee dragged on with everyone impatient for Aimo to leave.

Vilho said to Toivo, "I want to talk to you privately about a little business proposition you and I might work out when I get out of the army."

Aimo finally took the hint and left.

At home Aimo said to Liza, "I still think there's something going on over there."

"It's just your imagination. Go to bed."

"No, I'm going to watch for a little while. If they pull those shades with Vilho still there, then I'll know something is going on."

"Suit yourself. I'm going to bed."

"It's not just my imagination. I swear I saw Jonas' skiis in the entry way. You know they have that high ridge up the middle that you don't see on many other skiis. It was quite dark in the entry, so I can't be sure. It looked like they had those special bindings he made."

"Sometimes, brother, I wonder about you," Lisa said flatly. "You could make a good spy or a bad one. Those could be skiis and bindings Jonas made for Matt or Toi. I don't like snooping into other peoples business. I get angry at you, catering to the Russians when they're our enemy!"

"You don't understand what's going on in our country at all!" retorted Aimo, walking off to watch the Lehtinen house.

Vilho was the one that thought they ought not to pull the shades. Emma started to pull them, but Vilho said, "Aimo will know something is going on if you pull the shades while I'm still here."

Emma said, "I know you want to visit with Jonas some more. With him upstairs, that'll be hard to do. If we go into the other room or upstairs it'll look suspicious. We need to let Aimo see us and not Jonas.

"I know," said Vilho, "Have Jonas come part way down the stairs. We can talk from here. No one can see the stairwell. Toivo and I will act like we're talking to each other where Aimo can see us through the window."

Jonas and Vilho carried on a conversation with Vilho sitting on the couch and Jonas sitting on the stairs half way down. They could see each other but Aimo couldn't see Jonas.

"I got all the supplies you needed plus a couple of surprises for you when you get back to your wilderness camp. I left them in the sauna. We ought to leave the supplies there until you get ready to leave. Aimo may be watching."

"All right," said Jonas, "I think you people are all wrong about Aimo. I know he's weak, but I doubt he's an informer."

"No, we're not wrong!" said Vilho vehemently, "We're sure he's the one that told Karloff about the sand in the rink."

They talked on about freedom for Finland, how they could accomplish it in their lifetime. Could they get help from the outside? What could they expect from the unrest in Russia? Would that be a help or a hinderance? Many questions. Most of them had to be left unanswered but became food for thought, a step in the direction of freedom.

Vilho got up, came around the stair well to look his friend in the eye and bade him Godspeed. He left via the back door, creating some clatter that might tell Aimo he was leaving. It was pretty far for any sound to carry, but he tried.

At six o'clock in the morning, Jonas woke to a black winter day. He had to leave; that was all there was to it. He arose quietly and dressed. Emma must have been awake or heard him because she tiptoed down the stairs. When he hugged her, he could feel the soft suppleness of her body through the practical flannel night gown she wore in the winter. He wanted to hold her forever, but he gently pushed her away.

He whispered, "You better get dressed, you little vixen, or your father will be after me with a shotgun."

She laughed softly as she turned to go upstairs. Her soft laughter stayed with him the whole while she was gone. It made him feel worse about having to leave.

"I wish I could save that soft laughter for all the lonely nights I'm going to have to face in the wilderness."

Emma came down the stairs, and Jonas said, "You look so beautiful coming down those stairs. I'll keep that picture in my mind on those lonely nights out there."

She flew into his arms, and they embraced for a long time, not saying anything, content to be holding each other.

Jonas said, "Don't wake up your parents or Matt. I hate good-byes. Saying good-bye to you is bad enough. I'll get my supplies packed into my rucksack."

"Don't forget what Vilho left in the sauna."

"I'll get them as I leave."

"Let me fix some breakfast for you before you leave. You need the strength for your long trip back."

"No, you better not. Your folks will get up and delay my leaving. I better be gone before some early riser sees me. You might fix a little snack for my pocket."

Jonas packed the supplies into his rucksack while Emma made him a sandwich. He shrugged into his big sheepskin coat, kissed Emma quickly before he could change his mind and stay. She slipped the sandwich into his coat pocket. He stepped into the entry way to retrieve his skiis and went to the sauna to get what was left by Vilho. It was difficult to close the pack with the additional supplies. He wondered at the parcels he stuffed into the pack. It took a lot of effort to swing the pack to his back. He stepped out the door into his skiis, slung the rifle over his shoulder and headed for the woods.

As soon as he was in the protection of the timber, he paused to look back at Emma's house. He could still see the light on in her window and knew she would be crying even though she hadn't shed one tear when he was leaving. He noticed a light go on in Aimo's house.

He said, "Well, at least I got away without Aimo seeing me leave."

He was wrong. Aimo had watched for a while before going to bed, but his sleep had been restless. He rose to look out the window at the Lehtinen house. Early lights made him suspicious, wondering why they were up so early. Then he saw the light from the back entry make a yellow rectangle in the snow. It was quickly blotted out by a shadowy figure. The door closed, and the figure went into the sauna, soon to emerge, don skiis and head for the forest. He knew immediately who it was. He sat there, stunned.

"I was right," he hissed between his teeth, "Jonas was there last night while I was visiting. Vilho did get supplies for him. I'm sure the Lehtinen's did the same. What to do? What to do?"

He made up his mind quickly, "I'll report it! This ought to put me in good with Gerchenoff."

When the shadow of Jonas disappeared into the forest, he lit his lamp to get dressed. That's what Jonas saw. If Jonas had known, he would have been in more of a hurry to be gone. He took one last, long look before he started his leisurely trip away from his beloved.

Aimo literally threw his clothes on, shouldered into his coat as he ran out the door. It was a long run to the Russian compound. His breath came in great gasps as he ran. The cold air seared his lungs and throat, but he ran on. He thought Gerchenoff would still be in his quarters and ran directly there. A light was on. He didn't relish waking Gerchenoff, but he practically burst the door down getting in. Gerchenoff showed his irritation when he saw it was Aimo, saying, "What the hell do you want at this hour of the morning?"

"Jonas, Jonas," he gasped.

"Out with it man! What about Jonas?"

"He was here. He just left the Lehtinen house headed for the woods. I saw him. I know it was Jonas."

Gerchenoff finished getting dressed, his mind racing.

He said, "Go wake Chekok and Barloff and tell them about Jonas. Then go to the first platoon and tell Sergeant Markov to get his best skier-shooter combination of ten men. Have them ready to go in five minutes."

Aimo rushed out to tell the people, his sense of importance and pulse rising rapidly. "This ought to show people around here a thing or two," he muttered to himself as he ran.

Gerchenoff was under extreme pressure from Rykov in Helsinki to bring the culprit to justice. With this new information, he was already receiving the plaudits, mentally, from headquarters for a job well done. He did not see any way Jonas could escape.

Aimo roused both Barloff and Chekok with much grumbling from both until they heard the story. They both bounced up with the news, anxious to get this ordeal over once and for all.

Markov cursed Aimo when awakened but cheered up when he heard the news. Markov had been on the checkerboard search continuously and wanted to get back to Helsinki. He roused his men, sent two of them to the mess hall for two days' rations for twelve men. The kitchen people were already up and working. They grumbled about the extra work, fixing that many rations in a hurry.

It was a remarkable piece of efficiency. The ten-man troop plus Chekok and Gerchenoff were ready to go in less than twenty minutes. Altogether only about fifty minutes had elapsed since Jonas entered the forest. It would be another hour before daylight allowed them to follow his tracks, but Gerchenoff wanted his men on Jonas' trail as soon as possible.

The squad shouldered their skiis and rifles to double time down the road with the two captains leading. Aimo chugged at the rear. Opposite the Lehtinen house, they stopped to wait for Aimo to catch up so he could show them where Jonas had entered the woods. There were other ski tracks around, and they didn't want to get on the wrong one. Aimo remembered right where Jonas entered.

"I noticed two birch trees growing close together that Jonas blotted out as he passed," said Aimo.

The squad got on his track but could only go a few feet at a time because of the darkness. Gerchenoff called a halt to await better light. He was afraid Jonas' tracks would mingle with others and get lost.

Gerchenoff dispatched Aimo back to the company area to give a message to Barloff and Toklat to take charge of the company. Gerchenoff ordered another two ski patrols on the alert and ready to relieve the first one if the chase became extended.

* * * * *

In the meantime, Jonas made his circuitous route off the lake ski trail and was heading for the ridge top, heavy hearted. Even though it was dark, he knew the area well enough to go forward. He was fortunate that he was getting this much of a head start on his pursuers. It would be lighter in an hour, and he could make better time. He was not in any hurry.

The wind picked up, heralding the dawn. It began by softly sighing through the spruce trees. He liked the sound of solitude, it quieted his being.

Jonas' out-of-balance pack irritated him. He skied down the ravine bottom and then up the hill in his usual herringbone-pattern climb. It took almost an hour. When he got to the top, the sky was starting to turn to gray daylight. Moving along the ridge where he could look back on the town and his back trail, he paused to repack the supplies in his pack.

Swinging the pack to the ground, he opened it to move several items around for better balance. When he swung around to catch the pack for shouldering, he looked down his back trail. He thought he saw movement in the ravine. He strained his eyes through the semi-darkness of dawn.

"There they are!" he said through his teeth. "Following my tracks. No doubt about it. Someone had to have seen me leave. There are too many other tracks for them to be following mine by chance."

It was not random. They followed Jonas' tracks until they mingled with the other tracks to and from the lake. Gerchenoff ordered flankers out on both sides of the main trail to see if he left the trail before the lake. They found where he made his little circle route to leave and surmised immediately it was their quarry.

Jonas estimated at least an hour for them to get to his present position. An idea formulated quickly, but he needed time to make the plan work.

First, he had to lead them away from his true destination. He didn't want them to concentrate their search near his cabin. The area he had in mind would do just fine. He hurried down the ridge where he turned down through some dangerous trees, rocks, and blown-down trees to try to gain the needed time. He skied a bit recklessly, pellmell down the slope. He had to be careful not to go down too steep a slope if his plan was going to work.

He skied down a long gradual slope going in and out of groves of trees, knowing this would delay the soldiers. Fearing an ambush, they would approach the groves cautiously.

He came to the area he wanted. It was much as he remembered. He noted the tall pine tree, landmark for the big clearing just ahead. The clearing was not visible from the pine tree, but Jonas knew it was there. He skied under the pine to give him a direct line to the clearing.

He skied down the gentle slope feeling sure his plan would work. When he got out in the middle of the clearing, he stopped.

* * * * *

The patrol hit the clearing with Gerchenoff leading. The tracks simply ended, they went no where. Gerchenoff put up his hand for a silent stop as he surveyed the tracks in front of him. He called up Chekok and Sergeant Markov.

"What do you make of it?" asked Gerchenoff.

"I don't know. Maybe he back tracked and turned off somewhere," said Chekok.

"No," mused Gerchenoff, "we would have seen his tracks branching off somewhere. There's no sign of him turning his skiis around to back track. Look how his tracks disappear in a taper as though he flew out of here. There's no hill or anything to give him speed to make a jump. Let's hold here for a while. I'll send two men back tracking to see if we missed where he might have gotten off. Anything over a mile, and he would have run right into us. This is the second time he disappeared without a trace. I'm beginning to believe he's a ghost. These Finns are rumored to have supernatural powers. Maybe it's true."

No one in the group disagreed with him.

Search as they would, no place was found where Jonas could have left the trail. He had disappeared. Finally, they were forced to go back to town. Gerchenoff dreaded having to report this one to Rykov, but he thought of no way to avoid reporting the incident with Chekok present.

The town heard the news and had a big laugh at the Russians' expense. Even they did not know how Jonas had given the soldiers the slip, but he had humiliated the Russians again.

Rykov intercepted the dispatch before it came to the attention of Colonel Golovin. Both men were incredulous that the commanders in the area even implied that Jonas might have some kind of supernatural powers and could disappear at will. There was considerable talk of sending Rykov to Kiivijarvi immediately to solve the problem once and for all. Golovin turned the matter over to Rykov with a shrug of his shoulders.

Rykov's manner was not nearly so nonchalant. The missive he sent back to Gerchenoff as to their incompetence would have blistered the ears of the devil himself. Rykov questioned their sanity or the possibility they were imbibing too much vodka. The implication was clear: get the job done right or get out.

Chapter 9

Ski Jump

Six weeks passed before Jonas needed to go back to town for supplies. He waited impatiently for a snow storm to cover his ski tracks. Several mornings later dark clouds gathered, heralding a big storm.

Grabbing his rifle off the pegs and swinging his pack to his back, he headed for town. He hadn't skied far when the sky started spitting hard particles of snow. He smiled to himself for guessing the weather right.

Jonas timed his thoughts to the *shush-shush* of his skis. "I can evade any patrol out here because I know these woods better than any one," he told himself. "I don't want them to find my cabin. I would have to find a new place. I know nothing to compare with the safety of my cabin."

The snow and wind increased in intensity, slowing his progress. He kept a sharp watch for familiar landmarks. He was thankful for the snow, knowing no Russian patrols would be out.

The ridge top where he could normally see the town below was shrouded by the snow storm. The town lay below somewhere, along with his beloved Emma, but he couldn't see it. Still, his pace quickened in anticipation of seeing her.

Down the ravine he zoomed, hitting the hard-packed ski trail that went from town to lake. Snow would soon cover his tracks so he didn't bother to hide them. His skiis fairly flew over the snow for the short distance to Emma's.

Slipping into the back entry, he put his skiis in the corner and knocked softly. Emma answered. Seeing him, she blushed, fell into his arms to give him a long, lingering kiss.

Emma's mother called, "Who is it, dear?"

Emma was still kissing Jonas when Anna came to see who it was. She said, "Step inside before someone sees you. I'll pull the shades."

Emma and Jonas stepped into the warmth of the kitchen. Jonas took Emma by the shoulders, holding her at arms length, and gave her a long, loving look. As he leaned over to kiss her gently on the cheek, a small tear trickled down her face. Oh, how he ached for her love.

Anna pulled the shades and they went into the living room. Jonas took off his greatcoat to better toast his back side against the blazing warmth of the fireplace.

Toivo came downstairs to greet Jonas warmly. They exchanged small talk about events in the area. Jonas sensed a feeling of tenseness but didn't know what it was about.

Toivo became serious, saying, "Jonas, you know they have a price on your head? The Russians are really mad. They've spent all this time and energy to capture you with no results. They're offering a reward to the townspeople for information leading to your capture. A point in your favor is that the local people just laugh at the offer of reward."

"Well," said Jonas, "they've been close to me several times but haven't caught me yet, as you can see. About the townspeople—I doubt anyone would give me away even if they could. As a safety measure, I haven't told anyone, including you good people, where I'm hiding. It's not that I don't trust you, but the Russians might resort to torture to get the information. You can't tell them what you don't know."

"What about Aimo next door?" asked Emma. "We're pretty sure he turned you in on that ice rink episode. We're also fairly sure he's the one that put the Russians on your trail last time. You really did make a fool of them. We still don't know how you managed to fly away."

"It wasn't easy, I first realized they were on my trail and I got this idea but had to have a good lead. I remembered this big pine tree with an overhanging limb. I skied under it out into this open field where I made an upward taper with my skiis as if I left the trail flying. It was a little hard, standing on one ski at a time to make the right tracks, but I got it done. I turned around on the skiis without turning them around. It was a little awkward skiing that way, but I made it back to the big pine tree. I grabbed that low limb hoisted myself, skiis and all, up into the tree. I had a few bad moments up there when I saw some big flakes of bark on the snow that I knocked down in my climbing, but I managed to sprinkle snow from the boughs to cover most of them. The Russians came along the trail and went right under me and never looked up. I climbed down when they were out of sight and got on their trail to come back into town. I reentered the forest about a mile down the road."

They all had a big laugh.

"Back to Aimo," said Jonas, "I agree he's weak and possibly dangerous to us because of where he lives. I know he likes to feel important, but I don't believe he would go that far. I believe he's a loyal Finn."

Matt said, "Aimo's been friendly with several Russian officers who had him promoted to corporal. A leader he's not, and the men resent it. I believe the promotion was a reward for services rendered!"

"Maybe it's true, then," said Jonas reluctantly.

"Off that subject for a while," said Matt. "Vilho wanted to know as soon as you came in. Should I get him?"

"Yes, please do. I would like to talk to him about the latest Russian activity."

Matt donned his greatcoat to get Vilho. Anna went into the kitchen to prepare some food. Toivo followed her, ostensibly to help, more to leave Jonas and Emma alone.

The two of them were on the couch. Emma pulled her feet under her and nestled against Jonas' shoulder. Neither spoke for quite some time, being close was enough.

Matt returned with Vilho in tow. Vilho slapped Jonas on the back when he stood up from the couch.

Vilho almost shouted, "Man, am I glad to see you! Looks like life in the big thicket agrees with you."

They made small talk for a while, but Vilho had to hear how he outwitted the Russians this last time. Jonas told the story again, giving Vilho a big laugh.

"If it had been me," said Vilho, "I would have picked them off one by one with my rifle when they came down the trail.

"That's not my way," said Jonas.

"That's all the Russians understand, killing!"

"Oh, Vilho, most of those men are just taking orders. It's the higher ups that are to blame. I can't bring myself to kill in cold blood just because they're taking orders."

"Let's kill the higher ups then."

"We would have to start in Helsinki and go all the way to St. Petersburg and kill the tsar. We might be able to get the ones in Helsinki, but I doubt we could get close to the tsar."

"You're probably right." said Vilho reluctantly.

"I don't know if I'm right or not, but I don't condone wanton killing."

Vilho changed the subject, "You look good, Jonas. I thought you'd lose weight eating your own cooking."

"I eat well, thanks to your supplies and good hunting. I really miss being back here with you, Emma, and the rest. It really gets lonely out there in that little cabin."

"You can change all that loneliness right now," piped Emma. "I'm ready to marry you and go back with you right now."

Jonas threw her a fond look and said quietly, "I would love that, too, but it's much too dangerous."

Emma looked disappointed. "I don't care if it's dangerous. I want to be with you."

"Out of the question. I love you too much to put you in such peril."

Vilho interrupted with, "Did you know they have a price on your head? They're offering a reward for information on you."

"Toivo told me the bad news."

"They intend to make an example of you with a well-publicized execution. Now tell me you don't believe in killing."

Emma blanched, "Oh, Jonas, what are we going to do?"

"Don't worry your pretty little head about it. First they have to catch me, and then they have to hold me."

"If they catch you, they'll watch you closer this time," said Emma with fear in her voice.

"Let's not cross bridges before we get to them," said Jonas, trying to allay the fear rising in Emma.

Vilho said, "They're going to double their efforts while we still have snow because it's so much easier to track you. Your freedom is causing other people to resist in many small ways."

"That's all right," said Jonas. "I've scouted the wilderness thoroughly. I have several different escape routes if they do happen to get on my track. I know the area better than anyone. Plus I can out ski those Russians any day of the week and twice on Sundays."

"They plan to have several crack ski units in reserve all the time in case they do get on your track. They'll have fast skiers relaying information back to control so they can intercept you or put a fresh unit on your trail. I think it would hurt our growing movement if they managed to catch you."

"Like I said," Jonas said quietly, "they have to get on my trail first."

The talk went on about what to do. Jonas' mind drifted to all the alternatives he had planned. He modified them based on this latest information from Vilho.

Vilho said, "There's some talk that if they don't get you by spring, they'll bring in a unit of Cossack cavalry. They'll hunt you down with horses and dogs."

"The horses I don't worry about. They can't go where a man can go, especially in this country. Dogs I do worry about. If they get dogs on my trail I might have to kill them, and I don't like killing the dogs. They're only doing their masters' bidding. I would have to be close to the dogs to kill them, and that would make it easier for the Russians to chase me with the horses. I'll have to give that some thought before summer; they can't take me this winter. In fact, I don't intend for them to take me at all."

"Just thought you ought to know," Vilho said. "Headquarters is really putting on the pressure to get you. To have two full companies trying to catch one man is embarrassing. Even the kids have taken up the chant. 'Can't catch Sisu, Can't catch Sisu, and no Russian ever will.' Even Nicholas in St. Petersburg is fuming at the ineptitude of the troops."

"I hope the kids are right," said Emma. "They still refer to you as the ghost from that back-tracking ski incident. They still don't know how you did it. Some say that you've left the area because they haven't been able to find your tracks. I guess the reason they aren't going along with that theory is because I'm still here. I think if I went to Sweden or Helsinki, you could meet me there and they would give up the search."

"No," said Jonas. "At least not yet. We've created a lot of nationalism, and it might grow big enough to oust the Russians for good. I'm showing the people what one man can do to make them look like fools. Think what a few hundred could do over the whole country. I spent a lot of winter nights thinking how we could get this nationalistic feeling going strong."

Vilho said, "Really, they're playing into our hands with their high-handed tactics and outright abuse of the people. The resentment is building. All we have to do is fan the flames of liberty a little."

"True, but we do need some good reliable men to fan those flames here and in other places."

"You're right!" Vilho shouted. "I know several good men, including myself, that are ready to join you right now!"

"Not so fast," said Jonas. "We need lots more men and materials before we can take on the Russian army. I've given this a lot of thought. Right now we need to go slow and plan well. A few mistakes could cost us. We better be ready when we move with the program, but we will move."

"I know, I know," said Vilho, "but I get so mad when I see all the abuse heaped on our people."

"Slowly but right is my motto," said Jonas, "We can do it. We need to plan well, train some people so they can move into other areas and set up resistance. Even subtle, passive resistance is better than nothing."

Vilho replied, "This town is resisting, but it's right under the Russian thumb. Other towns not so closely connected need organizing. We must get them involved in the fray."

"That's why this is a good place to start," said Jonas. "We can start some harassment, theft of weapons and supplies right here. Right now they have a lot of extra weapons and supplies not closely guarded. A few quick raids while their vigilance is down might pay off handsomely."

"Sounds good," said Vilho.

"I'll start formulating plans for a raid," said Jonas. "In the meantime keep a sharp look out for some good help. Check sentry schedules for the different warehouses and what's in them."

"Will do," replied Vilho.

Emma had most of the supplies Jonas needed. The next morning, she and Vilho split the remaining list of supplies, going separate ways to

avoid suspicion. Vilho bought powder and primers for reloading empty car-
tridge cases. Emma bought most of the staple grocery items.

Jonas and Emma lolled around the house the rest of the day. Emma
talked about getting married, and Jonas kept putting her off because of the
uncertainty of his future. He did want to take her for his wife but felt it unfair
to her and a great risk for her family.

That night a knock on the door sent Jonas scurrying up the stairs.
It was Aimo from next door, supposedly to borrow a cup of sugar, but more
to check to see if Jonas was there. On the way out he saw the skiis and was
sure they belonged to Jonas.

Aimo turned out the light in his house to make it look like he was
going to bed. He slipped out the side door to make his way to Russian headquarters.

"Captain Gerchenoff," he said breathlessly, "I think Jonas is in the
Lehtinen house!"

"What makes you think so?" asked the captain.

"I'm sure I saw his skiis standing in the corner of their back entry."

"That's not much to go on, everyone around here has skiis."

"Jonas made his own skiis, and they are different from most. The
ones I saw sure looked like his to me."

Gerchenoff called a hurried meeting of officers. Some were for an
immediate search of the Lehtinen house, dragging Jonas out by the heels
and executing him on the spot.

Gerchenoff vetoed the idea saying, "There might be shooting with
some innocent people getting hurt. We have the townpeople mad enough
at us already."

Chekok retorted, "Innocent . . . hell! They're harboring a known
criminal!"

"Nevertheless, I think we should try to take him out in the open, if
at all possible."

They decided that Aimo would go home and keep an all-night vigil
on the house to make sure that Jonas really was there. If Aimo saw him
leaving, he was to report back immediately. A ski unit would be ready for
immediate pursuit. If they killed Jonas, it would be away from prying eyes.

Aimo returned home to take up his vigil. He could see nothing in
the Lehtinen house because of the pulled shades. He fumed and fidgeted,
wondering what was really going on over there. The lights went out, but
Aimo kept his vigil.

Toward morning, Jonas woke to peer out the window. To his dismay, it had stopped snowing. He felt he had to leave despite leaving tracks
they could follow. Aimo made him feel uneasy, along with the knowledge
that he was putting the Lehtinen family in jeopardy.

He dressed quietly and tiptoed into Emma's room to wake her. She woke sleepily, smiled and kissed him good morning. He felt her warm, firm, body touching his through covers. His primal urge surged anew. He tore himself away. He went downstairs to light a lamp while he waited for her.

Jonas started breakfast, but Emma came down to take over the task. He busied himself with his pack to keep from touching her. He knew that would only make matters worse. It was going to be hard enough to leave.

Aimo became alert seeing a light so early in the morning. This further heightened his suspicions that Jonas was in the house.

Jonas and Emma ate breakfast without waking the rest of the family. Emma had that sad look in her eye, thinking of Jonas leaving again for God only knows how long.

She said, "I wish we could be together like this from now on."

"I would like that, too, but you know the situation. We'll find a way for us to be together. I can't go on this way much longer. I would take you with me right now, but I think too much of you to have you live in that shack I'm living in now."

"I wouldn't care just as long as we were together."

"After a while it would make a difference."

"No, not as long as we're in love."

"It's not something we can do now, anyway. I have to be on my way. Daylight will be here soon, and some of the early risers might see me."

Aimo saw light as the back door opened up into the entry. His senses picked up immediately. Shortly, a figure, unmistakably Jonas, emerged with a pack on his back, carrying his skiis, and heading for the woods. Aimo waited a few minutes to make sure Jonas couldn't see him, then hurried to Russian headquarters.

"He just left! He just left!" cried Aimo out of breath to Gerchenoff.

"Are you sure it was Jonas?" asked the captain.

"I'm positive," said Aimo still gasping for breath. "There is no mistaking that man. He had a pack on his back and carried his skiis to the lake trail."

"Get the patrol out fast," snapped Gerchenoff, "We'll get him this time!"

Jonas donned his skiis when he reached the edge of the woods. Some sixth sense gave him an uneasy feeling as he looked back over his shoulder. Seeing nothing, he shrugged and moved out.

He lamented to himself, "Damn, this snow will make it easy for trackers if they do get on my trail."

His precarious position heightened his mental activity. He would have to try to leave a path that would be difficult to follow. He also knew the Russians had some good trackers that he couldn't easily fool.

Instinct for survival, as with any long-hunted animal, made him extra cautious. He decided on a more circuitous route to the cabin in case they followed him. The new trail was one where he could check his back trail often from vantage points.

He went directly to the lake, acting like he might be an early morning fisherman. He went part way out on the ice, and then back tracked to a small clump of trees with a knoll, where he jumped off the trail. He knew if anyone looked closely they would figure out what he did, but the move would buy him some time.

He mused, "It will also be a dead give away that I am trying to hide my trail. At least I can look back from the far ridge. I can tell if there's anyone on my back trail."

The alerted patrol mounted swiftly, with Lieutenant Barloff in the lead. Aimo took them to where Jonas had put on his skiis. They were in hot pursuit. Momentary confusion at the lake, but the trackers soon found where Jonas had jumped off the trail. They lost an hour unravelling the tracks, but soon they were back on the trail, smelling blood, Jonas' blood.

Jonas made good time on the new powdered snow. The trees hung heavy with snow, giving the woods a fairytale appearance. He felt good. The air was crisp and clean. He sucked his lungs full several times, feeling good to be alive, then he pushed rapidly onward.

Habitual to most long-hunted animals was the checking of their back trail. Jonas was no exception. He stopped on the ridge top above the lake to survey his back trail. Far down in the valley he thought he saw figures moving around where he had left the lake. This time he had his telescope, which he retrieved from his back pack. Looking through the telescope, with its better light-gathering abilities and magnification, he confirmed his suspicions. He paused for a minute to let them get strung out on the trail so he could see how many were in pursuit. He counted nine. He sucked air into his lungs quickly as the adrenalin began pumping through his system. He swung his pack up, taking off at a fast pace, his mind working furiously.

A plan formulated in his mind, but he needed time and distance. He hoped they were not familiar with the area, or his plan wouldn't work.

Two hours of hard skiing widened the gap between him and his pursuers. He neared the place he had in mind and noted it would be ideal with the fast, powdery snow.

He dug his poles in to get extra speed for the long down hill run to a cliff with a two-hundred-foot drop straight down. If he missed, he would be just so much meat on the rocks below. If he could soar far enough, he would land on the down hill side of the far slope. He estimated the jump to be a hundred feet down and one hundred fifty feet out to clear the lower hill top.

It looked like any other hill, except this one had a one-hundred-foot gap, like a pie wedge, cut out of the middle. Any other jump he could land anywhere with not much more than injured pride if he fell. On this one, he would have to clear one hundred fifty feet to pick up the far down slope or get smashed on the face rock.

He crouched low, building up momentum for his spring from the brink. He soared like a bird from the precipice. His clothes popped like pistol shots as he soared toward his goal.

He felt exhilarated as he flew through the air. He caught himself saying, "Even if I don't make it this is a good way to go, soaring like a bird to instant death."

From above it looked like Jonas' trail ran straight down hill. They couldn't see that the trail ended at the cliff.

The patrol came down the hill at breakneck speed, intent only on their quarry and ignoring possible danger ahead. One had to admire their skiing ability, they were really good. If any of them knew in advance what lay ahead, they could probably clear the hill. They didn't see the danger until it was too late.

The first skiier left the lip, saw the problem, tried to soar to clear the gap. The second and third skiers were in the air before the first man hit with a sickening thud, his skiis clattering among the rocks. The man was dead. The next two hit in almost the same place. The rest of the troop followed like they were playing some crazy kind of follow-the-leader game. The second to last in line saw the problem with the rest of the men. He tried to execute a mid-air turn and land on the back slope, but his forward momentum was still too great. Losing his balance in mid air, he tumbled to the rocks below like a giant rag doll.

It was eerie that no one uttered a sound as they flew to their death.

Lieutenant Barloff, the last in line, saw what was happening on his way down the slope but knew he couldn't stop in time. He was probably the best skiier in the group. Immediately determining the problem, he made a snap judgement to go for it. He gave a tremendous spring at the edge of the cliff, soared like an eagle, stretching with every fiber of his being toward his goal. He nearly made it, but one ski brushed a tree top sending him cartwheeling down the slope.

Chapter 10

Turmoil

INCREASING TURMOIL FACED RUSSIAN headquarters when the ski patrol failed to return. The first night after the ski patrol left, concern was minimal, Gerchenoff thought the patrol likely in hot pursuit. He expected a messenger in the morning. When none came, concern for the patrol escalated.

A second patrol was mounted to find the first. Their search proved futile as a snow storm hit and wiped out the tracks. They had established a general direction, however, a place to begin when the storm let up.

Gerchenoff fumed, saying, "We should have mounted a second patrol earlier. Maybe we would have caught up with them before the storm hit. We never do anything right when it comes to this Jonas. And they should have sent a messenger back by now. I'm beginning to believe Jonas leads a charmed life or is a ghost."

No one disagreed with him.

After the storm, Gerchenoff mounted more patrols.

Gerchenoff knew that the patrol's food supply would have been reduced to nothing by the time the rescuers were sent out. He hoped that, when the the patrol saw a storm threatening, they had holed up to wait it out. It was also possible that they sent a messenger back and something had happened to him. He believed there was also a chance that Jonas had killed the entire patrol. The longer the patrol stayed missing without any word, the more certain of this he became.

The search parties fanned out in different directions from where the patrol's tracks had last been seen. On the seventh day of the search, one of the patrols discovered the first body. This was the one that tried to make the mid air turn. He had landed on wind-swept rocks. They discovered the rest of the bodies, except Barloff, lightly covered with snow. The cold had preserved the bodies except that some animal had gnawed the flesh off one man's index finger, leaving it bone white, bare and pointing to the sky as if in accusation. The men sickened at the sight of the carnage and cursed Jonas for leading their comrades into such a trap. The search for Barloff continued without success.

Gerchenoff said, "He's probably under the snow somewhere. For all we know, Jonas might have died as well and been covered with snow. We can't know for certain until spring. I don't know who's going to tell Barloff's girl friend. Me, I suppose. He had said they were planning to get married. Too bad."

Moods were grim at Russian headquarters when they brought in the bodies. Sentiment ran high. Some talked of wrecking vengeance on the townspeople, who believed that Jonas was not dead, that he had, in fact, successfully completed the jump. The Russians had to concede that, if that were true, it was a fantastic jump on the part of Jonas. It had to have been a desperate, calculated risk. He must have known about the spot before hand; even then it took a lot of courage to try it. Only a man in fear of his life would have taken the chance.

Russian headquarters in Helsinki issued an ultimatum, "Find that man and bring him in, dead or alive. If alive, we'll make an example of him, but bring him in!"

Meetings were held, and plans were formulated, discussed and discarded. No one knew how to catch Jonas. Everything had been tried before. None of the solutions worked.

Gerchenoff said, "We'll bring the Lehtinen family in for questioning. At least they'll know we're aware that they have been helping Jonas."

There was a long silence before Brezinski said, "Sir, that may create a lot of animosity among the locals."

"To hell with the locals! Their careers are not on the line; ours are, yours and mine! This could be our career high point or its end, take your pick," screamed Gerchenoff.

Brezinski said timidly, "There must be some other way. Even if the Lehtinen family did help Jonas, I doubt they know where he is now. He probably doesn't stay in one place. If we bring them in for interrogation, we lose the advantage of Aimo as a spy next door. They'll know that's how we know and will be on the alert. Short of brute force or torture I doubt they'll tell us anything. These Finns aren't easy to break down."

"Brezinski, I've had enough of your insubordinate remarks. Go pick up the Lehtinen family for interrogation," snapped Gerchenoff.

Brezinski sulked glumly out of the room to follow orders. He didn't like the task at all. He was dating a young Finnish girl. For this and other reasons, he was in sympathy with the Finnish people.

Brezinski picked up a squad of enlisted men to go with him on this unpleasant task. He didn't use Finnish enlisted men, fearing it might aggravate the problem even more. There was a lot of grumbling among the men having to do this disagreeable task. This was not soldiering. Most of the men knew the details of how this problem came about. Few were in sympathy with the high command. They felt their commanding officers weren't acting right, which resulted in strained relations with the Finns. With a little effort they could have cordial relations with the Finnish people.

Brezinski knocked on the front door. Anna answered.

Brezinski apologized politely saying, "I'm sorry, but I have orders to take all of you in to headquarters for questioning."

Anna turned ashen and asked, "On orders from whom?"

"Captain Gerchenoff."

"I might have known," said Anna recovering her composure. "Matt isn't here right now, and I don't know where he went. The three of us will be ready in a few minutes."

She quietly closed the door in his face.

Brezinski didn't know what else to do but stand there and wait for them to come out.

Anna called Emma and Toivo into the kitchen explaining the situation. "I don't know how much they know. We better tell them part truths based on what Aimo would know to tell them. Tell them, yes, Jonas was here, but we don't know where he is now, which is the truth. We admit nothing of his past visits or that we have been helping him. I'll leave Matt a note to let him know what's happening. I wish there were some way to warn Jonas before his next visit. I don't know how long they plan to keep us. Even if they let us go, I'm sure they're going to keep a close watch on the house. Jonas could walk into a trap. I'll put the shades all the way up so he'll see our danger signal."

They stepped out on the porch, ready to leave with Brezinski. Anna and Emma cast backward glances at their home, wondering if they would ever see it again. Toivo walked with downcast eyes, not wanting anyone to see his tears. He was sure none of them would ever come back.

They marched in silence back to headquarters. One half of the squad in front, the other half bringing up the rear, as if they had some criminals that might bolt for freedom. Several of the local people saw the Lehtinens with the escort, and word spread quickly. They talked of dire consequences if anything happened to the Lehtinen family.

Vilho was one of the first to hear about the ordeal. He was livid as he said through clenched teeth, "If they harm one hair on those people's heads, there will be hell to pay. Revenge will come from me and Jonas and a whole lot of other people."

"Easy does it, Vilho," said Arne, "You can't fight them all."

"The hell I can't!" exploded Vilho, "Look at what Jonas is doing to two companies of men by himself!"

"Yes, but this is different, they've done nothing but bring the Lehtinen family in."

"Just that is enough," retorted Vilho, "I would like to know why Gerchenoff wants them."

Arnie replied, "It's probably just routine because Emma and Jonas were so close."

"That may be, but they have known about that relationship for a long time. Why take them now? Are they connecting Jonas to the ski incident for sure? Are they going to take it out on the Lehtinen family? Do they think they're tied to the resistance movement?"

"I doubt they'll get anything from them, even if they do know what happened," said Arne.

"Arne, they know how close Jonas and I were. If I go snooping around the orderly room, they'll kick me out. You could get away with a little eavesdropping to find out what's going on."

"What if I get caught?"

"You won't. Use any old excuse to go in. Ask to see the duty roster. Say you can't remember when you were scheduled to pull guard duty."

Arne went off, half afraid to spy for Vilho, yet more afraid of his wrath if he didn't do his bidding. He wandered into the orderly room. From there he could see the Lehtinen family through the partly opened door. Emma sat on the edge of her chair with her handkerchief in her hand.

Sergeant Markov said gruffly, "What do you want Arne?"

"I just wanted to see next week's duty roster."

"I haven't posted it yet. It's right there on my desk. Look at it and then tack it up on the bulletin board."

Arne picked it up, glancing through it idly. He noted that his name wasn't on it, but he was more interested in the events going on in the next room. He pretended to look for a nail and hammer to put up the roster. He heard a lot in that few minutes.

Gerchenoff's voice, "We know you've been helping Jonas. I am asking you again, where can we find him? We just want him for questioning in that ski incident to see if he knows anything about it or where Barloff went. We dismissed the killing of Captain Karloff as an accident."

For an instant Emma's heart gave a leap of joy thinking that Jonas might come back in peace.

Toivo having gained his composure, retorted, "If that's true, why are you still looking for him? There's an extra company of Russian soldiers still here for the express purpose of finding him."

Emma's hopes faded with the realization that the Russians were lying to get information .

"Nonsense," replied Gerchenoff glibly, "They haven't received orders to move out yet. You know how long it takes to get orders from Helsinki."

Gerchenoff switched quickly from the quiet confidant to the rough, tough, interrogator.

"Jonas was seen leaving your house in the early hours of the morning heading for the forest!"

Simultaneously four people—the three Lehtinens and Arne—came to the same conclusion, that Aimo was a traitor. He had been spying on the Lehtinen family for the Russians.

Arne couldn't wait to relay this information to Vilho. He didn't want to hear any more. He sauntered out the door, heading back to the barracks and Vilho. Excited about what he heard, it was hard for him not to break into a run to deliver the news. He forced himself to walk casually as if he didn't have a care in the world.

Arne barely closed the door when Vilho asked, "Did you find out anything?"

"Did I?" said Arne proudly. "They're questioning them about the ski accident. They said Jonas was seen coming out of the Lehtinen house early in the morning heading for the forest."

"It had to be Aimo," said Vilho. "He's the only one that could have seen Jonas. No one would stay out in the cold to watch the Lehtinen house in the off chance that he was there. Yes, it has to be Aimo. He could watch from the comfort of his house and be close enough to recognize him."

Arne said, "I'm sure you're right; it fits so neatly."

"I'll catch that Aimo out alone one of these days," said Vilho, "and beat the truth out of him. That Aimo can't stand pain. Even the threat of violence makes him sick. He'll talk when I get my hands on him."

In the orderly room, the interrogation of the Lehtinen family went on relentlessly. Gerchenoff alternately ranted and cajoled, shouting one minute, and the next minute he was sweet and soft. Nothing made the Lehtinens talk. Gerchenoff was losing patience. He didn't know where to push. Emma looked like the weakest link, but, when he questioned her, she became resolute in her silence. Perhaps it was her love for Jonas that made her strong enough to resist the bullying. Toivo seemed weak and undetermined at first, but his courage soon made him the strongest of the three.

Gerchenoff sat like a huge, fat toad eyeing three flies before him. Which one should I take? He felt euphoric in his power over these people, yet helpless in his inability to make them talk. He had the power to bring them in for interrogation, but he couldn't bend them to his will. Here again the power of *sisu*, the resolute, quiet defiance that transcended verbal communication stymied him.

"You know," said Gerchenoff in a stage whisper, "I have the authority to have you put to death. I can charge you with harboring a known criminal of my country."

Toivo retorted, "I thought you said a while ago that Jonas was no longer considered a criminal. You realize that, if you did anything to us, you might have thousands just like Jonas to contend with in this area. Right now you can't catch one Jonas. Think of thousands."

Gerchenoff flushed beet red and slashed Toivo across the face with the back of his hand. Toivo sprawled off his chair. He picked himself up with dignity, sat back in the chair with a slight smile, knowing he had beat this Russian. It was worth the slap in the face.

Gerchenoff knew he was beaten. "Turn them loose," he said to Sergeant Markov.

Markov shoved them out of Gerchenoff's office.

"I'm not through with the three of you yet," spat Gerchenoff. "I know where you are and can pick you up any time."

As Markov escorted them out the main door. They heard Gerchenoff mutter, "I don't know how to handle these stubborn Finns."

They walked in silence away from the building. Each of them thinking Gerchenoff would call them back any minute.

Out of earshot, Toivo broke the silence, saying, "I was never so glad to be out of a place in my life. I believe Gerchenoff would have killed us all if he thought he could get away with it without problems from our people."

"All of us thought the same thing," said Anna putting her arm around Emma. She wanted to keep her from breaking up over their predicament and the trouble Jonas still had.

They walked on in silence steeped in their own thoughts and how the situation involved each of them.

Anna thought to herself, *Such a beautiful winter day. The sun is shining, the snow so fresh and clean. No harshness like the ordeal we just faced. Look how the fence posts all wear little white caps of snow. They look like sentinels at attention, watching us go by. Here's my daughter, in love with Jonas and helpless to do anything but love him, mostly at a distance. I pray this will end soon so they can have some semblance of a decent life. I want her to experience some of the joy Toivo and I have had over the years. We're comfortable together, kind of like an old pair of shoes.*

Toivo thought, *I'm so weak! I should have stood up and punched that Gerchenoff in the nose. Well, I should have, but where would that have led? Where is all this going to end? Are we ever going to get out from under the oppressive yoke of the Russians? I feel more sorry for Emma than anyone. She has the rest of her life ahead of her. Anna and I have lived most of our lives. If something did happen to us now, we wouldn't lose much. I don't want to go yet, but I could.*

He chuckled out loud.

"What's so funny?" asked Anna.

"Oh, not much, I was laughing at myself."

"Well, I'm glad to see you can laugh in the face of all this," said Anna.

All three broke into spontaneous laughter, like a dam releasing all the tensions of the day.

"When we get home, I'll fix a special supper," said Anna, "We'll try not to think about this too far ahead."

Chapter 11

Mika

TWO WEEKS PASSED AFTER THE DISCOVERY of the ski patrol smashed against the rocks. Golovin was receiving tremendous pressure from St. Petersburg to catch Jonas.

Golovin and Rykov conferred on the matter and decided that Rykov should go to Kiivijarvi to take charge of the hunt personally.

Rykov said, "I'll get started on it immediately. It'll take me a few days to put it together. I'll show those clods how to hunt a man down!"

"The sooner the better," snapped Golovin "We are getting reports of Finnish defiance all over the country. They're not paying taxes in money or agricultural products. We're getting many reports of draftees not reporting for duty. The tsar and I think it's because this damn renegade is still avoiding capture."

Rykov left, glad to be out from under the thumb of Golovin. He resented him for his sloppy, unmilitary-like bearing but admired his administrative ability.

He said to himself, "I'll run this rascal to ground and get credit for it. The least they'll do is jump me two ranks. It would be great to be on an even footing with that damn Golovin."

Rykov had learned early in his career how to delegate authority. Back in his office, he snapped orders to get his move started. It was late in the day, and he was tired out from the long, tense meeting with Golovin. He decided to go to the Boars Head to relax over drinks before dinner.

Mika sat down with Rykov for a minute to pass the time of day. He mentioned, "Elsa is taking it hard about Barloff still missing. She's been distraught ever since she got word from Gerchenoff that they couldn't find his body. She's absolutely convinced he's still alive."

"Possibly so," said Rykov, "but I wouldn't bet on it. That we didn't recover his body doesn't prove a thing. There could be a hundred reasons why they didn't find him. He could have been hurt and died on the way back. We may find him in the spring, or we may never find him."

"She's been working for me part time to keep her mind occupied.

She's a good waitress, I wish she would come to work full time.

Rykov mentioned his upcoming trip to Kiivijarvi and that he would be taking another company of men with him.

Mika said, "You're going to have an outpost there bigger than this one if you keep sending troops. My good customer list is getting smaller all the time. I might have to move up there and start another restaurant. My head cook wants to buy into this one. I have a notion to sell him the whole works and go with you."

"Why don't you? I'd like to see you up there myself. Leaving your good food is one of my many regrets in leaving here. It would bring a bit of relief from the monotonous duty up there."

"It might not be monotonous chasing Jonas all over the country."

"Oh, it won't take long to run him down," snapped Rykov coldly.

Mika made a snap decision as was his way. He called in his head cook and explained the situation to him.

The cook said, "I don't have enough money to pay you in full."

"I'm not worried. You can pay the balance on a monthly basis."

"What if I can't make it go?" asked the cook.

"Just stick to the same routine we've had for years. It will go; the people won't even know I'm gone."

Elsa came in, looking a little drawn and haggard. She brightened up considerably when Mika's booming voice greeted her. Seeing Rykov, she asked, "Has there been any news about John?"

Rykov replied in the negative. She showed a little disappointment but brightened back up. "If you haven't found his body, then he could still be alive. I just feel it."

"It's good to have faith," rejoined Rykov.

"I've made the decision to go to Kiivijarvi and open a restaurant there," said Mika. "All my good customers are winding up there anyway, so I'll join them. I've been thinking about doing this for a long time. I've wanted a smaller place, preferably near some good fishing. Fishing is my weakness. I know it's good around Kiivijarvi; I've been there before. There are so many lakes and streams that have barely been fished. I would like to drop my hook into a lake where no one has ever been before. The success of my restaurant is secondary. I like everything I saw up there."

"Oh, Mika," said Elsa, "Take me with you. I would work for you up there. I just want to be around when John comes in."

"But it'll be months before I get the restaurant going."

"I have some money saved. I'll get by until you need me."

Mika turning to Rykov asked, "Will it be all right if we accompany you to Kiivijarvi?"

"It's fine with me. Barloff intended to have Elsa come north on one of the freight runs anyway. But, it'll be a rough trip in the middle of winter."

Mika felt a sense of elation after making the decision to leave. Helsinki and the daily routine at the restaurant had been getting him down. He needed a change in his life, and this seemed most opportune. The sudden decision left him little time to do everything before the convoy left. He made arrangements with several of his suppliers, first to start sending material and then food supplies for the new restaurant when it opened. Mika set the timetable in his mind to be open by the first day of spring. That would be pushing it hard, but he wanted to be open before good fishing started. If there were delays, he would have to adjust. One had to start somewhere. He was extremely happy with the decision he made.

Elsa stayed to work the evening shift. Her mind was in a turmoil about leaving, but she felt it would be better being close to where John disappeared. She didn't have much to do to get ready. Saying good-bye to Gerta and telling her boss she was leaving would be hard. Getting her clothes and a few personal belongings together wouldn't take long.

Rykov had a few more drinks, he felt his muscles relax as the drinks took effect. He sat alone, making notes of everything he needed to do. Elsa came by with his dinner order. He hardly looked at what he was eating as he scribbled furiously on his note pad. Dinner over, he went back to the office to leave notes for his subordinates in the morning.

At the Boar's Head, Mika was in a jubilant mood.

Elsa said, "I haven't seen you look this happy in a long time."

"I am happy. I feel just like a school boy out for recess. I've been wanting to do this for a long time. It's like being let out of jail."

Elsa and Mika talked for a long time, with Mika doing most of the talking, all enthusiastic about his new venture.

The next morning, Rykov gave more orders for everything that needed to be done for the trip. The one exception was his personal transportation, which he planned to supervise himself.

Commandeering a big sleigh and several carpenters, he set them to building a small cabin on the sleigh. He planned it complete with table, chairs, cook stove, and full-sized bed. He would have his own cook take care of his meals while on the trail.

Golovin gave Rykov carte blanche for the trip, but, if he had known about this extravagance, he would have blown up. Golovin didn't believe in creature comforts in the field.

The sleigh evolved into an elaborate cabin, nicknamed "castle" by his soldiers. It required a four-horse team to move the rig instead of the usual two. He planned to travel in style and keep warm to the point of using another sleigh to haul dry wood. He had to have dry hardwood for heating and cooking.

Elsa's boss said, "We'll miss you Elsa. You've been a good worker. I hate to see you leave. I hope your man is alive, as you believe. Let us know what goes on up there. I'll pick one of the other girls to take your place. I would appreciate it if you would spend some time with her before you leave."

In two days, everything was ready except the Rykov castle. Rykov kept making excuses to Golovin why they couldn't get under way. At dawn on the fourth day, they were ready. After several false starts, of horses, sleighs, and men getting tangled up in the semi-darkness, they moved out.

Mika's light sleigh was similar to Rykov's fancy one, but long time usage had trimmed it down to bare essentials. Elsa planned to ride with him. A small partition gave her some privacy.

Mika's rig was directly behind Rykov's. He and Elsa had many laughs watching Rykov's orderlies doing his bidding. It looked like a great queen ant with worker ants running around tending to her every need.

The biggest laugh was his toilet, which was a small room in the back of the cabin with a bucket directly underneath. Whenever he used the toilet, he rang a bell for the orderly. The orderly in charge of the bucket brigade would run, pick up the bucket and empty it.

Mika had a small stove for cooking and taking the chill off inside the rig. He and Elsa had some memorable meals on the trip. Elsa marvelled at the efficiency of Mika's cooking while traveling. Elsa took the reins while they traveled, looking back occasionally to see how he was doing. She did her best to keep everything on an even keel. Occasionally a pot did slop over. Mika had clamp down pot holders to keep everything secure while under way. The inexperienced Rykov cook wound up chasing pans all over the stove. After several disastrous spills, Rykov resigned himself to cold meals while under way.

Travel was difficult for the men. The weather turned bitter cold, freezing food and drink. Rykov, snug in his little cabin pushed the men hard. The short days and long, cold nights took their toll. They didn't have time enough to make a good camp at night, resulting in many cases of frost bite. The men, not in good shape, fell exhausted into their beds at night. That same night two men froze to death.

Rykov dismissed the whole episode saying, "You men better learn to soldier in the field. This is a good example for the rest to learn survival."

From the back ranks some soldier said so Rykov could hear, "If you would give us a little more time at night we could make a good camp!"

Rykov, livid with rage, roared, "Who said that?"

Silence in the ranks.

"I'll teach you men the meaning of time. We'll make the rest of the trip a forced march so you will learn discipline!"

"Yes," another soldier said under his breath, "Your damn road castle can catch fire during the night. Then we'll see how you survive the cold."

The next two days were pure misery for the men. Rykov drove them unmercifully. He ducked in and out of his snug cabin to harangue them to move faster. Many more cases of frost bite occurred. The men pulled closer together in their mutual hatred for Rykov.

Late on the third night out, Rykov's castle mysteriously caught fire. Rykov and the cook came bounding out in their underwear and boots. Rykov managed to grab a jacket and the cook grabbed a pair of pants. The fire completely destroyed the rig. No water was available to put it out because it was all frozen. A few men tried, halfhearted, to throw snow on the fire but it did no good.

Several teams hooked onto the burned rig and towed it off the road. It looked forlorn, a few blackened pieces of timber that had been Rykov's pride and joy. The men in his command chuckled, wondering who had had the courage to set it afire. The fire definitely started on the outside.

Mika, parked right behind Rykov, made sure no sparks had landed on his rig. He sat wrapped in a blanket, watching the clean-up operation.

Rykov came over and said to Mika, "I'm going to commandeer your rig for the rest of the trip. Elsa can stay if she wants."

Mika grew red in the face and said in a small, growling voice, "You better not. This is my rig, and the army doesn't have any authority over it."

Rykov said, "I have authority over everything here, including you. I can easily have you shot and left beside the road, if that's what you desire."

The veins on Mika's forehead popped out, and Elsa could see he was about to do something drastic. She clutched his arm trying to get him to look at her.

Elsa said calmly, "Mika it's just a few more days. You and I can make out just fine in one of the supply sleighs. We can spend the rest of the night in the cook tent. Don't let this spoil all your dreams for Kiivijarvi."

Mika calmed some, gritting his teeth. He picked up his and Elsa's bedrolls and personal gear and headed for the cook tent. Rykov made a formidable and unforgiving enemy.

Mika and Elsa literally took over the kitchen. The men loved it as he really knew how to put out good meals. Morale improved considerably with the good food.

Rykov eased off on the forced march, realizing that other mishaps could occur on the trail if he pushed too hard. He could have a full-blown mutiny on his hands.

The rest of the journey was relatively peaceful.

Elsa and Mika got to know each other well on the trip. They talked about everything under the sun. Elsa's intelligence delighted Mika. She gave him many good ideas for his new restaurant from a woman's point of view. Not many women patronized restaurants as they were considered men's domain. The few that did patronize them were usually of unsavory character. Mika's was an exception in Helsinki. Mika's place was still not what Elsa thought of as a family restaurant, though. Elsa convinced Mika that he could change the image of the new restaurant to one more genteel and acceptable to women.

"I'll try it," said Mika vehemently, "I'll probably get a few objectors, mostly those I wouldn't want in my place even without women present."

"You're big enough to ask most anyone to behave. They will do it."

Mika laughed saying, "Yes, that's one advantage of being a big, old clumsy bear."

"You're big, but you aren't old or clumsy. I admired your agility in that small kitchen in your rig."

Mika beamed. He liked having compliments passed his way. It was the main reason he was such a good cook.

Until this trip, Mika thought Rykov an efficient soldier. The trip showed what a tyrant he could be to his men. Rykov didn't know what a formidable enemy he had created in Mika. The confiscation of his rig Mika could overlook, but his abuse of people to show his power rankled him.

Arriving in Kiivijarvi, Rykov gave Mika's rig back to him without even a modest thanks. Mika and Elsa left the company area. They were going to find themselves a place to stay.

As they drove away, Mika said, "I feel as if I should have this rig scrubbed down from top to bottom after his being in here. Physically, he wasn't dirty; it's him or his mind that makes me think of dirt."

Elsa's need for a place to stay came in the form of a room with an older couple. It was airy and clean, and the people were pleasant.

"This is just temporary until John comes home. He wrote that he found a house at a reasonable price. I have no idea where it is or I would go there."

With Elsa settled in, Mika looked for a suitable building for his restaurant. None suited his purpose.

"I know I could use several of the buildings we looked at," he said to Elsa, "but I wouldn't be happy with the inconvenience. I don't have to get back into it right now. I'm enjoying this vacation away from meal planning and preparation. I'll build my own building."

"You'll have to work hard to be open by spring if you have to build it from the ground up."

"I can do it if I can find the materials and the right men."

In his quest for men and materials, Mika kept hearing of Ivar Reyonen.

96

Everyone said, "Ivar is old and independent, but if you can get him, he's the best builder around."

Mika found Ivar at his house and talked to him about building his place. Ivar's house was built of logs so carefully put together that Mika decided no one else would do to build his new place.

"Ivar, I've heard a lot of comments about your building. I can see from the construction of this house that you're one fine craftsman. I'm going to build a restaurant. I want you to supervise the building of it for me."

"I don't do much any more. Just getting too old and tired."

"I don't want you to do any physical work. I just want some one supervising who knows what he's doing, and I believe you do know what you are doing."

"I'm not sure. Good help is so hard to get now."

"I know, but I'll pay top wages with no quibbling for you and who-ever you choose to help you."

"I don't know if I want to take on a task like that. I had some logs cut last summer to season out. I planned to build a couple of houses in the next few years. I like to keep my hand in doing something, but I'm still not sure if I want to do this for you."

"I'll pay you top money for your logs. I sure don't want to build with green timber."

"I would like to see your plans first."

Mika took the plans out of a sheaf of papers. They both looked at them with Ivar nodding approval. Ivar made several small corrections and suggestions. Mika knew he had him, but wouldn't say anything until Ivar confirmed it.

"Yes, I'll build it for you. I like your plan and the way you think. What convinced me to do it was your refusal to build with green timber. Most people wouldn't care, but there's a lot of shrinkage in green timber. No matter how carefully you fit everything, a few months later it looks like a sloppy job. I don't build anything that way."

"I'm glad. I don't like anything that looks sloppy either."

Mika and Elsa went back to town. Mika was pleased with the bargain he had struck. A superior craftsman and some seasoned logs with which to build.

"I like the old man," said Elsa, "I'm sure he'll do a good job for you."

"I know he's going to do a good job. And when we were looking for a place for you to stay, I saw some property that would make a good location for the restaurant, but I don't know who owns it or if it's for sale."

By inquiring around, Mika found the owner. He paid a little bonus for the property but felt that Ivar and the location would pay off in the long run.

"Well, Elsa," sighed Mika, "that job is done. I just have to stake out the way I want the building to sit. Some of this is going to be hard to get started in the snow."

There were indeed some extra problems starting to build in the winter. Frozen ground to break through, building a temporary roof over the basement wine cellar, keeping fires going so the mortar wouldn't freeze before it set properly.

Elsa was with Mika a lot as she had nothing else to do, and they enjoyed each other's company.

Ivar liked the way Mika did everything. Despite the hardships of winter building, everything went smoothly. Mika knew he would be in his restaurant by spring.

Chapter 12

Jonas and Barloff

JONAS WATCHED AS SKIER AFTER SKIER DIED ON THE CLIFF. Then Barloff tumbled down the slope. When he stopped, Jonas covered him with his rifle. Barloff moved slightly, testing for broken bones. A sharp, stabbing pain told him his left leg was broken. Cautiously moving the rest of his body, he found it to be functional. He looked up to see Jonas coming at him with his rifle at the ready. Barloff decided it would have been better if he had smashed himself to bits on the rocks along with his men.

Jonas approached cautiously, sliding his skiis to a stop just above Barloff. He relaxed, seeing Barloff's rifle under him and inaccessible. "Are you hurt?" asked Jonas.

"I think my leg is broken."

Though his better judgement told him this was the enemy and that he should kill Barloff or let him die, Jonas' compassion proved stronger. Barloff wouldn't survive the night if he left him. Jonas couldn't force himself to kill him or leave him to die alone on this slope.

Jonas bent down near Barloff and took out his knife. Barloff's eyes widened in fear. He breathed a sigh of relief when Jonas used the knife to slit his trouser leg to look at the break. It appeared to be a simple break with no bones out of place. What to do? Against his better judgement, he went to the timber for splints. He cut strips from Barloff's pack to tie splints to the broken leg. Jonas went back up the hill like a scavenging bird of prey looking for good skiis or anything else in the patrol's packs that might be useful. He got sick viewing the carnage he had created and sat down for a moment to recover.

"I had to do it. They were out to kill me," he said. Then he reasoned that he could have escaped some other way. But how? The argument raged back and forth in his mind. There was no answer, no solution. It was done.

From the group he found three skiis still intact. With the help of some broken ski pieces, sticks and strips cut from packs Jonas managed a makeshift sled.

Rolling Barloff onto the sled, shrugging into a harness made from more leather strips, he started pulling the sled and the harness broke. Back up the hill he went for more material to strengthen the harness. While he was up there he stripped two of the men of their coats, for additional covering for Barloff. He grew sick anew viewing the bodies lying twisted and contorted in death.

Towing Barloff on the sled was terribly hard. The terrain was rough. The sled kept getting caught in brush, forcing Jonas to go back and free it.

Each time the sled got hung up, Barloff said, "Why don't you just kill me and get it over?"

Jonas wondered why also but said nothing. Night was closing fast. Jonas knew he must find some shelter, or they wouldn't survive the night. Ahead of them loomed a grove of spruce trees. He struggled toward it. He tugged, pulled, pushed and freed the sled a dozen times before he eased it into the shelter of the spruce grove. It was cozy there, with no wind. Jonas felt like lying down, but he knew sleep would be fatal. He forced himself to find dry twigs to get a fire going. Barloff's teeth chattered from the cold and his face was blue. Jonas wasn't cold, just exhausted.

The spruce twigs caught fire quickly. He added larger and larger branches until the fire spread its circle of warmth as it consumed more wood. The flames threw dancing shadows on the surrounding spruce trees. Barloff's teeth stopped chattering when the warmth of the fire reached him. He managed a half smile, the first since they left the hillside.

"Jonas," he asked, "why all this trouble for me?"

"I don't know. I'm just dumb, I guess."

Jonas turned away abruptly to go cut spruce boughs for their bed. He interlaced them with the curved side up for a softer, more insulated bed.

Tired and sore, Jonas forced himself to fix something to eat. Rummaging through his pack he found some roast beef and bread that Emma had lovingly put in there. He heated the roast beef slices over the fire with a green stick. He felt they needed something warm to combat the cold.

Jonas slept fitfully through the night, waking up when the cold hit him to replenish the fire. Barloff slept well through the night. This made Jonas grateful because he knew the next day would be even worse than the one they just came through.

Jonas woke and busied himself with breakfast. Barloff woke to the smell of cured pork cooking on sticks propped over the fire. Jonas melted snow in a small pot he always carried. First he boiled some eggs in the water. When they were done he made some coffee in the same pot. Under the circumstances it turned out to be a good, nourishing breakfast.

Jonas repacked his rucksack, loaded Barloff onto the sled for their continued journey to his cabin. Jonas had misgivings about going back to the cabin with Barloff but didn't know what else to do other than give him up to the elements.

It was an ordeal to say the least. Up hill, down hill, around boulders, through brush and trees, push, pull, tug, move out again and again. Jonas had to take a more circuitous route than normal because the sled wanted to pass him going down hill. He was afraid it might bounce off some trees and hurt Barloff's leg even worse.

Jonas' could barely move his tired body when he came to the cabin. He couldn't see it but he knew it was there. A person would have to pass within thirty feet to see it. The difficult task of pulling the sled plus lack of sleep had drained him. It took him an hour to negotiate the last half mile to the cabin. He stopped to rest often. Barloff's teeth were chattering again, and his skin was blue from the cold. Jonas worried that Barloff might get pneumonia to complicate matters.

Finally, they came to the cabin door. Jonas opened up, shedding his pack and rifle just inside the door with a sigh. He towed Barloff, sled and all, inside. The cabin was cold but still much warmer than the outside.

Jonas soon had a roaring fire going. He pulled Barloff, still on the sled, close to the fire. It took nearly an hour before his color returned to normal and his teeth stopped chattering.

"So this is your hideout," said Barloff. "It certainly is cozy. I can see why we never ran across it. I didn't know we were here until you opened the door."

Jonas replied curtly, "Well it's a good hideout, but I'll have to move. When you get well and get back to your outfit this will no longer be my sanctuary."

"Not on my account," replied Barloff, "I appreciate what you're doing for me. I couldn't tell anyone how to find you anyway; I don't have the faintest notion where we are. I was out of my mind most of the time, and it was cloudy so I have no idea what direction we took from the slope. Most of the time you had me wrapped up like a cocoon, so all I could see was gray sky."

"I'll still move out, but that's a long way off. First we have to get that leg of yours healed."

"I'm sure it's just a simple break. The pain is less now than it was."

"If you're warm enough, we better have a look at it."

Jonas lit a candle to see better. He stripped off the splints. The leg looked bad—all black, blue and swollen. Jonas gently felt the area. As he did so, Barloff winced.

"Damn, that hurts."

"I don't doubt that a bit. It looks ugly, but I'm sure you're going to be all right. I don't think I'm going to have to amputate," he said jokingly.

Jonas replaced the splints. A temporary bed by the fire would keep

Barloff warmer. The two of them managed to get him rolled on to a pallet.

"What about my men?" asked Barloff.

"What about them?" rejoined Jonas.

"Are we just going to leave them there?"

"I don't see any way we can deal with them now. If I had stopped to bury them with rocks, you would be dead from exposure. There was no way I could have dug graves."

"I understand, but I still feel sad about them."

"So do I, but I couldn't help it."

"Sure you could, you could have given up when you knew we were on your trail. You could have gone in some other direction."

Jonas spun angrily toward Barloff saying, "Yes, and get shot on the town square the next day!"

Silence.

After a time, Jonas asked, "How did you know to take out after me?"

"We had some inside information that you might be at the Lehtinen house. Somebody saw you leaving there, heading for the woods."

"Their good neighbor, Aimo, no doubt!"

Barloff blanched but said nothing. His silence told Jonas what he wanted to know. Worry immediately jumped to his mind about the jeopardy in which he had put the Lehtinens for harboring a known criminal.

"What do you intend to do with me?" asked Barloff.

"When that leg gets better, I'll get you back to your company, but I'll have to find another place for me to hide. There's no way I can get you back in your present condition. I thought a lot about it on the way here. I'll get you close, where I know you can make it and still give me some escape time."

Jonas unpacked his supplies, putting everything in its proper place. He went outside to cut strips of venison from a hind quarter he had hanging to use for a stew. Soon he had all the ingredients in the stew pot and swung it into the fireplace. Only then did he squat on his haunches to resume his conversation with Barloff.

The heady aroma of the stew filled the cabin as they talked of the many differences and similarities between them.

"Supper is almost ready. Think you can sit up to eat it?"

"I can if you help me up."

Jonas helped him into a chair, propped his broken leg on another chair. Barloff grumbled a little about the pain but brightened considerably when Jonas handed him a bowl of the hearty stew.

After eating his fill and soaking up the warmth of the fire, Barloff grew quite mellow. They talked on into the night about the Finnish-Russian relationship and its ramifications then and in the future for both countries.

Barloff talked about the woman he met in Helsinki. Jonas knew by the way he talked and said her name that he was in love.

In the wee hours of the morning, Jonas helped Barloff to his bed. Jonas slept on the pallet thinking Barloff needed the rest more than he did.

He lay there for a few minutes contemplating the turn of events over the past few days. Shortly, he was asleep, thoroughly exhausted, and he slept for ten hours. When he woke, Barloff was still snoring. He looked outside to see that they had received three to four inches of new snow during the night. He said a quiet prayer of thanks as this would cover all trace of his leaving the hill where the other skiers had died.

The days passed with Barloff getting better and better. It was pleasant having company in the cabin. Jonas worried as the time came nearer for him to get Barloff back to Kiivijarvi.

Without much else to do but eat, sleep and talk they got into a lot of discussion. Their biggest arguments came when they discussed the Russian occupation of Finland. Barloff came around, grudgingly, that the Finns did have a case for their own government and freedom.

Jonas came to the conclusion that he could really like this man, even though he was Russian and his sworn enemy.

The days wore on, the animosity between the two lessened. They became fast friends. Barloff, without knowing it, was becoming more and more sympathetic to the cause of the Finns.

Jonas perceived the change early, thinking about how this could possibly help their cause. At least he would be less of an enemy.

Jonas made a crude crutch so Barloff could walk around the cabin. From there he progressed to a cane. Jonas knew the time was coming near when he would have to return him to his unit. He thought of ways he could possibly keep him here, but no workable solution came to mind.

Barloff sensed the same problem, broaching the subject shortly after breakfast one morning. "Jonas, I know you're in a dilemma about me. Feel sure that I won't give you away. I have no idea where we are. I can look out the window and see only a small portion of the valley below. There are no distinguishing landmarks that I could identify again. Take me back and leave me. I'll take my time to report in, giving you a head start back."

"That's all well and good, but the officers will not believe you. They would mount another ski patrol like the last one to follow my tracks back here."

"Let's wait until we get a big storm blowing in, so it'll cover your tracks. Headquarters won't mount a patrol in the teeth of a storm, knowing full well that it would be an exercise in futility."

"We'll see," said Jonas dismissing the subject for the moment.

The days went by with no storm in the offing. They became more and more friendly. All the while, the tension to part mounted.

Jonas woke one morning while it was still dark in the cabin. He thought he was up early, but, when he looked outside, he could see huge, black clouds building in the southwest. He could smell the salt sea air from the Bay of Bothnia, a sure sign a big storm was in the offing.

He wakened Barloff, asking, "Feel up to skiing back to Kiivijarvi today?"

Barloff came instantly awake and said, "If you think we can do it safely."

"Today is probably our best chance. I know there's a big storm on the way, as I can taste the ocean salt in the air."

"I can be ready any time you are."

"I'm going to have to blindfold you. I know that's going to take us longer. I can't take the chance they'll make you talk or that you might have a change of heart and turn me in."

Barloff grew indignant saying, "You know me better than to say I'm not a man of my word."

"It's not that. Your fellow officers can devise some ingenious ways to make you talk if they think you're holding back information. This way you won't have anything to give them under any circumstances. On top of that, they wouldn't understand me not protecting myself. They would know you and I have become friends and would really go after you."

"I guess you're right," said Barloff.

"You know I'm right. Get your gear together. We might have to camp out one night if this storm comes in a little later than I think it will."

"How will you find your way back here if the storm proves to be a real howler?"

"I have come this way so many times, that, even with poor visibility, I can find my way back."

Jonas put a makeshift hood over Barloff's head, and then fitted him with a lead rope. Shouldering his pack, they headed back to Kiivijarvi. Jonas tried to go the least hilly route, but, even then, Barloff ran into him several times going down slopes. Nothing serious happened, and they laughed like school boys with each collision. Jonas tried to give ample warning, but, unable to see, Barloff found it difficult to control himself on skiis.

The clouds kept building with intensifying winds. They arrived at the outskirts of Kiivijarvi as the first flakes started falling.

Jonas said, "Now that's what I call good timing. The snow is just starting. I didn't relish being out overnight, waiting for the storm to hit."

Jonas took the hood off Barloff to say good-bye.

"It has been great knowing you, John. I'm going to put the hood back on and tie your hands. Leaving them no doubt as to your not being able to direct a search for me. I'll leave you here by the side of the road. I'm sure someone will be along soon to free you."

Barloff said, "I'm glad I got to know you. I hope we can meet again under better circumstances."

"Me too."

With that, Jonas put the hood back on Barloff's head and tied his hands behind his back. He left him standing in the road. Jonas went into the forest a short way to see if anyone came down the road to rescue him. Shortly, he heard sleigh bells. He watched as two people undid his hood, untied his hands and helped him into the sleigh.

Jonas gave a sigh of relief as he headed into the teeth of the storm back to his lonely cabin. He knew he would be lonelier than ever. He was going to miss John's companionship.

* * * * *

Rykov threw questions at Barloff, "Why do you suppose he didn't kill you like the rest. Did you really break your leg or was that just some excuse for your bungling the chase?"

Barloff grew livid with rage at Rykov's implications. He had to restrain himself to keep from striking the arrogant officer.

"Do you suppose you could lead us back to his hideout cabin. Surely, you have some idea as to your location while you were in captivity, if it really was captivity."

"No sir! As I said, I was out of it when he pulled me in, and it was cloudy so I couldn't see the sun for any kind of direction. I never left the cabin until we got ready to come back here, and then it was cloudy again, and he had the hood over my head. Jonas wouldn't bring me back without some idea that snow was coming to cover his trail."

Rykov was not satisfied, but he said, "You're dismissed for now."

After Barloff left, Rykov turned to Gerchenoff and said, "I don't like the looks of this one. I think he might have been in league with Jonas. He'll bear some watching in the future."

Gerchenoff merely shrugged, thinking that this was another one of Rykov's demented ideas.

Chapter 13

The Cossacks

SPRING MOVED IN WITH ITS FIRST WARM, SUNNY DAYS. The troops were sitting around enjoying the warmth when Vilho walked up.

"They're here," said Vilho to his fellow conspirators.

"Who's here?" asked several in unison.

"The Cossacks, that's who," snapped Vilho.

"What makes you think so?" echoed several of the men.

"Jacob saw them down by the Rock Creek bridge, getting themselves and their horses cleaned up. I'm sure they're going to ride into town and put on a show for us."

Rumors had circulated earlier about a Cossack horse troop coming to run Jonas down. Clearly, the rumors were true.

This elite troop of Cossack cavalry was reputed to be the best in the world. The troop came into town mounted four abreast with banners and pennants flying. Their colorful uniforms added to the illusion that they were something special. Red with gold striping down the sleeves and trouser legs, the white piping around the edges of the jackets and jacket pockets made a strong contrast.

Their leader, Captain Ustinov, dismissed them. Individuals of the group put on a show of their own. They vied with each other in demonstrating their riding prowess. They were good, no doubt about it.

First one and then another would ride through the area, throw his hat to the ground, then swing by to pick it up. All this at full gallop without dismounting the horse. They dismounted at full gallop and remounted on the fly. They would slide to the horse's rump, slide off hanging to the horse's tail to make a flying leap back into the saddle, impressive indeed.

After their show of horsemanship, they tended their horses and then themselves.

The next morning, Rykov briefed the Cossacks on Jonas and his possible whereabouts.

"It will be a two- or three-day romp through the forest to catch the renegade. There's no way a man on foot can elude a cavalry troop as good

106

as this one," said Ustinov.

Ustinov was tall and slim with brown hair slightly streaked with silver. Blue eyes under bushy brows darted rapidly around the room, recording it in the dark recesses of his brain. His skin was tanned and leather looking from many years in the outdoors. He ruled his troop easily with little hard discipline. His men liked and respected him. He had hand picked each man personally.

After briefing, the men saddled up to ride off into the forest with banners flying and tack jingling. The consensus was that, even if Jonas did hear them coming, they still could ride him down. The first day was fruitless. They didn't see Jonas, but they did roust a love-making couple close to town. A lowly wood cutter was scared half to death when they rode up and surrounded him. They rode back into town hot, tired and dusty. The dash and enthusiasm of the morning had waned. This routine went on for days on end. They chased down rumors of sightings with hope but to no avail.

They would catch him in time, they assured all who would listen. Time was making them the laughing stock of the area. "Maybe they could ride, but they couldn't find their butts with both hands," commented Vilho.

Emma voiced concern to her brother Matt, "I don't know if Jonas knows that the Cossacks are here and are looking for him. I worry about him as he's due to come for supplies any day. He could run into them before he knew they are in the area."

"I'm sure Jonas is aware and will take safety measures if he comes into town. Even if he's low on staples, he's capable of living off the land," replied Matt.

In fact, Jonas was well-aware of what was happening. He had watched them from hilltop and ridgetop several times. He couldn't help admiring their riding ability. Horse and rider looked to be one unit, bent on one purpose. Jonas didn't worry; his hideout wasn't readily visible from any horse trail. He watched the troop enough to know they could negotiate almost any kind of terrain except heavy brush and timber. He doubted they would venture through the thick brush and spruce trees around his cabin. His philosophy boiled down to watching them and being careful not to venture out in the open where they could ride him down.

It became a game to wake up and anticipate where they would start their morning search. He positioned himself where he could watch. The enjoyment of guessing exactly where they would be every morning gave him an adrenalin high. Their search pattern was so predictable that soon he never missed being at the start and finish of their day's search.

Jonas tired of their antics after several weeks and went about his business knowing just where his pursuers would be hour by hour. They were as predictable as sunrise and sunset.

107

Jonas' supplies were running low, and he wanted to see his Emma again. He had the Cossack search down to a predictable pattern, so he decided to chance a trip into town.

"If I get up early, I can determine their direction. I can get to town about dark without fear of them surprising me in the few open spaces I have to cross."

The next morning Jonas was on a hilltop overlooking a beautiful valley where the Cossacks had ended their search the night before. As repetitive as sunrise, the troop came jangling down the hill to resume the search. Jonas couldn't help notice that much of the fire was gone from the troop. They rode from daylight to dark without so much as a glimpse of their quarry. The tedium had to be taking its toll.

As soon as they were out of sight, Jonas turned in the other direction for town. He stayed on the high ridges with lots of brush and trees, not easily negotiable by men on horseback. Up high, he could see or hear them if they decided to change tactics. Every few hundred feet, he would visually pick out a dense clump of trees or brush that he could run to before the horsemen could get to him.

His trip into town took a little longer than usual, as he was sticking to dense cover. He went to his favorite hilltop overlooking town and the trail to the lake. The Cossacks went out and returned by this trail in their daily search for him.

He heard the soft jingle-jangle of tack and the creak of leather coupled with the muffled sound of hooves on the forest floor before they came into view. Occasionally a desultory remark from one rider to another floated up to him. They passed within a few hundred yards of his hilltop.

"If you damn Cossacks knew where I was right now, would you be surprised," laughed Jonas.

They rode out to the main road where they turned toward their bivouac area.

Jonas followed, slipping up to Emma's door in the soft shadows of early evening. At a soft tap on the door, Emma answered, saw him and gave a little squeal of delight as she rushed into his arms. Silence reigned for a moment as he gave her a long, lingering kiss.

Anna knew from the sounds who it was and gave them a minute. She went to the door herself saying, "Get in here, both of you, before some one sees you kissing in the light of that open door."

They stepped inside quickly closing the door as Toivo came down the stairs to see what all the commotion was about.

"You're a sight for sore eyes. We've been worried about you ever since the Cossacks got here. Are you aware that they have a whole cavalry troop out looking for you every day?"

"I've been watching them for weeks as they scour the countryside for me. I have their search pattern down, so I know exactly where they will be hour by hour."

"I really wasn't too worried," said Emma, and everyone laughed. "I knew you could take care of yourself," she said. "I knew you would be coming for supplies soon, and I didn't want you to bump into the Cossacks. We have been stocking up on supplies gradually, so the suppliers won't get suspicious. Is there anything special you need this trip?" asked Emma.

"No, not really. Mostly, I wanted to see you."

Toivo said, "Jonas, you better leave by morning. The Russians have been checking often to see if you're here. I doubt they'll come again for a few days. They were here yesterday. Those Russians are very predictable in their ways."

"Yes, I know. I watched that bunch of Cossacks for weeks and never missed predicting where they would be at any given time. That's why I decided it would be safe to come into town."

Anna busied herself in the kitchen cooking up a big meal for all of them. She knew how Jonas liked her food.

Jonas and Emma went into the living room to be alone. Emma cuddled up to Jonas as they sat on the sofa.

"I miss you so," said Jonas, "I don't know how much longer I can stand being away from you for such long stretches."

"I miss you, too. I think of you night and day and try to project myself into your thoughts wherever you are."

"You're succeeding because I think of you every night plus lots of times during the day. When I'm fishing or doing other things you like, I think of you. Off the subject for a minute, do you know when Matt is coming home? I need him to get Vilho so we can talk."

"Matt should be home shortly. He never misses a meal, and it's almost supper time."

Minutes later when Matt came in, Jonas asked him to get Vilho.

Anna heard the conversation and said, "Don't be long. Supper is almost ready. Ask Vilho to join us if he hasn't eaten."

"I will, Mama. You can bet Vilho will come eat with us even if he has already eaten. He's like Jonas about liking your cooking."

Matt and Vilho came back just as Anna announced that supper was ready. They all sat down to a repast fit for a king.

Jonas marvelled at how good the food tasted. He heaped his plate a second time.

"I sure get tired of cooking for myself," he said. "It's great to have someone else cook the meals."

"Oh pshaw," said Anna, blushing. "Anything would taste good to you right now."

"I wouldn't stuff myself a second time on something that wasn't good."

Anna got slightly flustered with all the attention. She went to her stove to hide but was pleased that Jonas liked her cooking.

After eating, they sat around the table talking about the local situation. The Russians had become more and more belligerent toward the townspeople. The underlying cause was their inability to catch Jonas.

"Maybe I should turn myself in," said Jonas, "if I'm causing that much hardship in the area."

"Don't even think about it!" said Matt, "You can't believe how this helps our morale."

Toivo chimed in, "He's right. The townspeople know that you come here for supplies, but no one breathes a word to the Russians even though they suspect. People see me in town and tell me to tell you to keep it up, drive the Russians crazy. You're their knight in shining armor."

"I haven't thought of giving up just yet, but I have thought of moving out of the area. This would take some of the pressure off Kiivijarvi."

"Don't," said Matt, "People around here look to you as a leader. You're capable of getting a revolution started to kick the damn Russians clear out of here."

"Matt, I wish you wouldn't swear," said Anna. "I know you hate the Russians . . . and so do I, but I don't swear about it."

"Oh, Mama, saying damn isn't really swearing."

"It isn't nice talk."

"Let's talk about more pleasant subjects," said Jonas.

"I'd like to talk about getting married," said Emma.

Jonas blushed mightily and replied, "I would like us to get married, but what kind of a life would that be, married to a fugitive?"

"I don't care, at least I would have you for my own once in a while. I could come out in the wilderness with you. I'm almost as good a cook as mama."

"I wouldn't even consider that right now. It's hard to outwit the Russians by myself, but having to worry about you would be too much. I wouldn't put you through the danger I go through evading the Russians. I love you too much for that."

Emma sat quietly and pouted.

Matt said, "Just bide your time, Emma. Soon the Russians will get tired of chasing this ghost and give it up as too costly. Then we'll get back to the way things were."

"Yes, but when?" rejoined Emma, "By then I'll be an old maid."

"Soon, soon," replied Jonas.

"Matt mentioned you wanted to talk to me about something in particular," said Vilho.

"I want you to enlist some of the men you're training into our group. We should start moving out to other areas soon and start more resistance groups. It's not enough that we confine our efforts to this area."

"No problem," said Vilho. "I already have a few in mind who have made remarks that suggest they would fit into our group."

The two men discussed how best to use the new men and how to train and arm the recruits they would pick up in other areas.

After a while, Vilho went home, and Emma and Jonas retired to the living room. They sat side by side on the sofa talking, content to be close to each other. Jonas finally got up, saying, "I better pack if I'm going to leave early in the morning."

"I wish you could stay longer," said Emma, "but I know it's dangerous for you."

They went into the kitchen. Emma watched him pack his usual supply of staples into the rucksack. She felt melancholy at his leaving even though it wouldn't be until morning.

The packing finished, they returned to the sofa with more talk and more loving, until Toivo said, "Leave him be, Emma. He needs a good night's rest in case he has to outrun those Cossack horses tomorrow," and everyone went off to bed.

Jonas woke early with an uneasy feeling. He went into the kitchen to fix himself some breakfast. He didn't intend to wake anyone, but Emma heard him and came tiptoeing down the stairs. She took over the breakfast preparations. They ate in silence, both feeling sad about having to part.

"I have to go sweetheart," he said. "I'll miss you terribly. It gets worse each time I have to leave."

"I feel the same way, but I know you have to leave. Let's pray conditions will get better soon."

"They'll get better, but they might get worse first."

"What do you mean?"

"Well, we have to get the Russians out of this country before we can have any real peace."

"What do you think is going to happen to make that come about?"

"The only way is for the people to get their backs up and push them out. The Russians have some problems at home right now, so I think the time is nearing."

"And you will be in the thick of it?"

"Someone has to get it started and push it toward victory."

Emma lifted her chin bravely. "I know you'll come out of it all right. I foresee us married and having a whole lot of children and living in peace,

111

if you can live in peace with a house full of children."

Jonas kissed her lightly and slipped quietly out into the gray dawn.

As Jonas was slipping into the woods, a Cossack raised up from the ditch, where he spent the night in a drunken stupor. He raised his head enough to peer at Jonas and ask, "Are you that damn Jonas we've been chasing for weeks?"

Jonas didn't answer but hurried on his way.

"What rotten luck," Jonas thought. "Who would have thought some drunken Cossack would be sleeping it off right where I go into the woods. Maybe he'll go back to sleep and forget about it. If I was blood thirsty like Vilho, I'd go back and kill him."

The more he thought about it the more concerned he became.

"Best not take any chances. I better plan my movements so I can go to quick cover where a horse can't follow. I can outrun any of them if they're on foot, but it's extremely difficult to get a cavalry man off his horse."

The drunken Cossack lay thinking whether to go back to sleep or get up to report the incident. "Here I am absent without leave, drunk and a poor example of a cavalry man. No matter what happens I'm really going to be in trouble. If I bring news of Jonas, maybe they'll forget about me being absent without leave."

The thought of becoming a hero gave him enough strength to get up and start for camp at an unsteady run. He careened into camp, more or less sober but exhausted. He stopped to grab a few mouthfuls of air before he pulled the flap on Ustinov's tent.

"I have some good news for you!"

"Who the hell is it at this hour of the morning?"

"It's Corporal Malinkov, sir, I just saw that fugitive, Jonas, slipping in to the woods with a pack on his back."

The Hetman was fully awake now and asked, "How do you know it was Jonas?"

"I'm not absolutely sure, but the description fits, and, what with the curfew, there shouldn't have been anyone out at that hour of morning. He was also near the Lehtinen house."

The Hetman came out of his tent, hair tousled, pulling up his pants.

"Where were you when you saw this man?"

"As I said, down by the village near the Lehtinen house. I was . . . I was sleeping off a drunk, sir."

"So that's why they reported you missing last night, but forget that for now. Go wake the bugler. Get the troops up and we'll chase that rene-gade bastard to the ground!"

Malinkov ran to the bugler's tent, rousing him and said, "Get up and blow assembly. I just saw that outlaw Jonas going into the woods. This is by order of Ustinov."

The bugler stuck his bugle out the tent flap and blew assembly. Moans, groans, and curses erupted throughout the compound.

A voice floated down the line of tents, "They're getting us up in the middle of the night to chase some ghost we haven't had a peek at yet! We'll never see Jonas. We're going to go on hunting him for the rest of our lives."

Dutifully, they assembled in front of the Hetman Ustinov, most of them in all stages of dress and still grumbling about the hour.

"We think Jonas was sighted leaving the area," Ustinov said. "Hop to it, boots and saddles. Let's run him down."

A mighty cheer went up as they ran to finish dressing and get their horses ready.

* * * * *

Jonas heard the assembly call off in the distance and knew immediately what had happened.

"That damn drunk. He did get up."

Jonas paused for a moment considering his alternatives. His brain rapidly calculated how long before the woods would swarm with horsemen. He studied his alternatives. "The high hill with all the brush? No, they'd surround it, and a few would walk through and chase me out. The creek? No, they would split up on each side of the creek and eventually force me out into the open. Run for it? No, I don't have a chance on foot; they'd run me to ground and have great sport doing it. The muskeg bog?" He paused while his mind raced. A plan began to form. He figured it would take him an hour to reach the bog even with a mounted skirmish line on his heels. Still, it was his best chance.

Jonas took off at a dead run for the muskeg bog where he knew horses couldn't go. He thought of abandoning his rucksack to lighten the load and give him more speed but thought better of it, knowing he would need the supplies if he escaped.

After what seemed a long while, the bog came into view. A muskeg looks like a flat field to the uninitiated, but really it's a lake grown over with vegetation. A man could walk on it by sticking to the heavily vegetated areas, but more open areas consisted of black, oozy mud with little more than thin grasses over it. Occasionally the center had open water, looking for all the world like a lake with a grassy shore. But a bog was a trap for a horse with its weight and single hooved feet, allowing it to break through the thin, soddy layer of grass.

* * * * *

113

The Cossacks were ready and mounted in minutes, chafing at the bit to run this renegade down like a fox with hounds.

The Hetman ordered, "At full gallop. Follow me."

Corporal Malinkov rode in front of the column to point where Jonas had entered the woods. Malinkov was in all his glory, blown up with importance, as he directed the group.

"That is exactly where he went into the woods, sir."

"Men, form a skirmish line at twenty-foot intervals. We'll catch him this time and hang his hide out to dry."

Jonas was still moving at a dead run for the muskeg bog. He had been there several times before. Going through the bog saved time going around, and he had learned where to step to do just that. And, because the bog covered a large area, a horse and rider couldn't ride around it to intercept anyone going through it. So, if Jonas could reach it ahead of the troops, he had a chance to escape.

As the skirmish line topped a small ridge, they saw Jonas running all out for the bog. The cry went up like hounds baying at the sight of a fox, "There he goes. Let's get him!"

The commander yelled, "By twos at full gallop!"

The skirmish line closed to form a column of twos behind Ustinov and Malinkov.

Jonas hit the edge of the bog with the Cossacks closing fast. The calvary troop moved as one unit, eager to get Jonas. They were like a pack of dogs hot on the blood of their quarry and closing in for the kill.

Jonas ran hard and talked to himself to concentrate on how to negotiate the way through the muskeg. "Soft here on the edge," he reminded himself. "That log'll carry me across that real soft spot. Jump to that hummock. Good! Skirt that other soft spot. Done! Now straight ahead."

Jonas looked back over his shoulder as the leaders hit the edge of the muskeg. At first the horses stayed on top even though the ground rippled and quivered underfoot. This moving ground spooked the horses, slowing down their forward movement. The rest of the troop, coming at a faster pace and eager to close with their quarry piled up into a boiling mass of men and horses. The rear troops pushed the forward troops right into the soft spot that Jonas avoided by crossing on a log. First one horse and then another broke through the grass to the ooze below. The rear riders piled into the front group pellmell. More and more riders hit the soft spot breaking a bigger and bigger hole into the black ooze to engulf horse and rider. The thousand-year-old black ooze stirred up by men and horses put out an awful stench. This ooze was hundreds of feet deep.

Horses screamed in terror, nostrils flaring, eyes rolling wildly. All tried to get to solid ground, trampling each other and riders in their way.

One rider tried to leap from his horse to solid ground. But the horse lunged, and he landed in front of his horse. The horse tried to use him as leverage to get to solid ground. The trooper disappeared beneath the horse into the ooze. The horse didn't make it either.

Men and horses screamed in terror. Men pleaded or cursed for help, but the black mud was strangling them all. The horses' major problem was they couldn't swim well in the mud, and when they did get to the edge, the grass broke away under their hooves. With no leverage for their back legs, their front legs kept breaking away more and more grass, creating an ever bigger hole. They became exhausted and succumbed to the mire.

Some of the men stayed close to their horses. When they got near the edge they climbed over their horses' heads onto solid ground. Some made it; some did not. Those that didn't make it on their first try were trampled under the ooze by the terror-stricken horses.

Jonas watched as men and horses went under in screaming, unremitting terror. He was horrified at what he had created. He thought they would know enough to turn back and not try to cross the muskeg . He would have had plenty of time to make his escape if they had pulled away from the bog and gone around. It had not been his hope to kill the whole troop. Sickened, he turned and headed into the wilderness.

The horsemen on land tried throwing ropes, reins, or anything to the ones still in the black ooze, but they dared not get too close to the edge. They could become engulfed themselves.

Hetman Ustinov survived, but the man who started the whole disaster, Corporal Malinkov, did not.

Out of the troop of one hundred and ten men, sixteen men and sixty horses perished in the muskeg. Only the last few riders were able to stop on solid ground. All the surviving men and horses came out caked with black, stinking ooze. Ustinov gathered them all on solid ground.

They were a miserable sight, nothing like the troop that rode into the area with shining boots, multi-colored uniforms, banners, and pennants flying. This bedraggled bunch didn't represent the pride of Russia now.

They waited by the mud lake, hoping for survivors to pop to the surface, but all that came up from the ooze was an occasional bubble. Reluctantly Ustinov gave the order to return to camp.

Those that could, mounted double on the surviving horses. The rest had to walk. Walking was terrible for a cavalry man especially bedraggled and caked with mud.

As some of the rag-tag group rode into town, rumors started flying. "What kind of trap did Jonas set this time? What happened out there?"

Ustinov and his survivors knew there would be no merriment in their camp this night and for many more nights to come.

Chapter 14

Fire

A MONTH PASSED SINCE THE BOG EPISODE and Jonas needed meat for the larder and decided deer meat would do nicely.

"Got to get a little farther away from my hideout in case someone hears the shot. There's a lot of wind today, so it will be difficult to tell where the sound is coming from even if someone does happen to hear it."

Several ridges later, he stopped just off a well-used deer trail. He barely sat down when a doe ambled up the trail. It was evident a buck followed her the way she kept looking back over her shoulder. Jonas sat quietly and let her pass to wait for the buck.

It wasn't long before his eye caught some movement down the trail. The buck was much more wary than the doe. He had his nose to the ground, following her scent, but stopped often, raising his head to test the air all around. If he saw Jonas, he didn't pay attention. Jonas sat quietly until the buck stopped with a large tree between him and the buck's head. He quickly raised the rifle and waited until the buck stepped into the clear. He squeezed the trigger, dropping him dead where he stood. The shot echoed through the woods for several seconds. Jonas sat quietly to make sure no one heard the shot and came running.

He congratulated himself when he got to the deer, "That was a good head shot. No use wasting meat."

He quickly skinned the deer. He didn't like being in the open, even though the Cossacks, their numbers replenished, would be far away.

The deer was a fork horn, large and heavily laden with summer fat. It would take two trips to transport the meat and hide back to camp.

His first trip proved uneventful. The meat was hung and peppered well to keep the flies away until he could reduce it to jerky.

He finished packing the second half of the deer into his rucksack when he heard them. A short shiver of fear passed over him before the adrenalin started flowing.

"Those damn Cossacks aren't supposed to be in this area, at least not according to my calculations."

What Jonas didn't know was that this was a special day in the life of Hetman Ustinov, his birthday. The Cossacks liked to party, and Ustinov promised a good one.

The troop was having that Friday afternoon off to get ready for the gala celebration. They would have the rest of the weekend to celebrate and recuperate. The mood of the troop was jubilant. The morale had been poor ever since the muskeg episode. The replacements had begun to fit in, making a cohesive unit once again. This was another reason Ustinov decided a big party was in order.

By Jonas' calculations the calvary should have ended their search miles from where he was, and indeed they would have were it not for the half-day vacation. They were heading back to town by the shortest route, resulting in them catching Jonas in the open.

They headed straight for Jonas, but they hadn't seen him yet. Unable to hide in the open, Jonas set down the venison, picked up his rifle and broke into a dead run for a nearby cedar swamp, the only available cover.

Jonas chided himself as he ran, "That's what I get for not being real attentive. I thought they were far from here. If I'd paid more attention, I would have sensed they were in the area and could have slipped away."

The lead scout spotted Jonas as soon as he started to run. He signaled back to the rest of the troop. The troop yelled a blood-curdling battle cry in unison. Here was their enemy, the ghost, the wraith, the killer of their fellow troopers. Their yells made Jonas' hair stand on end but pumped more adrenalin into his system, helping him pick up speed.

The small clump of cedars stood nearly a half mile away. Little more than a half mile long and a quarter mile in width, the swamp was completely surrounded by open country. Fallen trees coupled with the ones still standing would make an impassable barrier for horse and rider, Jonas hoped.

The lead riders were practically on him when he reached the edge of the cedars and literally dived in. The rest of the troop looked for a way in but could find none.

Jonas crawled on hands and knees to get further into the thicket. It was tough going, fallen trees and brush were practically impossible to negotiate. He hoped that if he had such a tough time of it no horse and rider could make it. He knew they could dismount and search on foot, but they would try everything before they would demean themselves by dismounting.

Ustinov gave the order, "Surround the thicket. It's small enough that we can cover it from all sides. This time he will not escape."

He directed the men all the way around the perimeter of the swamp. Jonas could not slip between any of the men.

Jonas crawled on hands and knees, under, over and through the

117

thickest places he could find. When he was sure he was where no horse or man on foot could penetrate easily, he stopped to catch his breath. His breath came in short, hard gasps that he hoped they couldn't hear.

He looked ruefully at several long scratches made in the rifle stock when he dragged it through the brush. He checked the action to make sure it functioned. They would not get him without it costing them dearly.

"If I can hide until after dark, maybe I can figure some way out of here." He prayed for a good dark night with no moon.

Ustinov had the same thought, which he voiced to one of his men, "That damn Finn ghost will slip away on us as sure as anything when it gets dark. We're spread out fifty yards between men. At night he'll slip through our lines almost anywhere."

"What's the solution?" asked the sergeant.

"We ought to burn him out while there's still daylight. The wind is from the west, and this swamp runs east and west the long way. He can't come back over the burned area. All we have to do is fire it on the west end, and then follow the fire along. He'll either have to come out or burn to a crisp. I don't care much either way. This would be a fine birthday present for me. We could turn his body over and head back to our homes."

The sergeant voiced a concern, "What if it's not Jonas and the body burns beyond recognition?"

Ustinov said, "I don't think it'll burn that bad. If it does, it just does. If that isn't Jonas, it's some other renegade afraid of Russians."

"Well, if it is Jonas, and he comes out alive, that would be a real feather in your cap," said the sergeant.

"I want some men at the head of this cedar grove to make sure he doesn't slip out under cover of heavy smoke. You may have to dismount and go on foot. The horses won't go into the smoke," said Ustinov.

"What if he comes out shooting?"

"Shoot him down like the dog he is. I'll ride the perimeter and inform the troops what we're doing. I want some extra men at the end of the thicket. I think that's where he'll make a dash for freedom.

"Peter, you and John set the fire at this end. Marko, gather your squad and go to the upper end. Sergeant, you take the upper side, and I'll take the lower side when the fire gets going good. Gather men as you go, following the fire as it sweeps through the cedars. Try to stay close together to make sure he doesn't slip through on either side of us."

John and Peter waited until Ustinov had made his circuit around the cedar brake before they lit the fire.

There was a small wisp of gray smoke and crackling as the dry cedar twigs caught fire. It took only a few minutes for the boughs and downed timber to build into a healthy blaze. A few more minutes, and the blaze turned into a roaring inferno. Live trees super heated by the fire and wind exploded ahead of the main body of flames. The fire built in intensity, creating its own draft. It literally tore through the cedars faster than any horse could run alongside.

Jonas smelled the first puffs of smoke as they drifted on the west wind. He immediately surmised the reason. "They're going to burn me out!"

Jonas remembered a small spring coming out of the swamp to the south. "I can't remember if it's a year-round spring or just rain fed. At any rate, I have to find it right now and hope for water or the fire will be on me."

He assumed that most of the troop would follow the fire line. The roaring fire covered the crashing he made hurtling forward, looking for the spring.

"Where's that spring? I have to be close. I hope I didn't pass it by. I think it started in the middle somewhere."

Looking behind him, he could see the fire gaining on him.

Debris from the fire blew around him. Birds flushed ahead of the conflagration, and animals ran by, trying to get ahead of the fire. Unless the animals ran right or left out of the swamp, they would burn. There was no way they could outrun this fire.

Jonas knew the danger of fire was not only burning but suffocation as the fire used all available oxygen.

Providence or good luck, a root tripped Jonas, and he fell within a few feet of the spring. He quickly buried his head in the water and took a long cool drink. The fire was gaining momentum. He rolled his body around in the shallow spring, getting himself wet all over. He buried his face in the wet moss bordering the spring hoping the moss held enough oxygen to sustain him until the fire passed.

* * * * *

"Maybe the fire ran over him before he could get out, said the sergeant. "There is no way in hell anyone could survive that fire."

"Well, he's in there," said Ustinov, "of that we have no doubt. He couldn't possibly have made it to the other end before we got there. We'll just have to wait until it cools to find his body. I can forego my birthday party for another day if I know I'm getting that kind of birthday present."

"It'll take time to find him," said the sergeant.

"Corporal Marko, front and center!" yelled Ustinov. "I want you and your squad to patrol the perimeter by twos until morning to make sure he doesn't duck out, if by some miracle, he managed to survive. The rest of us will bivouac by that little stream coming out of the swamp. It's full of ashes, but the water looks all right. It looks like it has enough flow that it's starting to clear up."

Marko gathered his squad together to give them their orders.

"Well, maybe this will relieve us of having to go into that hot ash pile tomorrow to look for the body."

The fire had swept over Jonas quickly. If it hadn't for the speed of the blaze, he probably wouldn't have survived. As it was, he had to put out spot fires on his shirt. The hot air made him duck under quickly, and the smoke still drifting downwind made him cough. He buried his head in the water to muffle the sound. *I hope they didn't hear that cough,* Jonas thought. *I have to have them think I'm dead. I may be able to sneak out of here tonight by following this stream.*

At full dark, Jonas slithered, snake like down the small stream. The water was cold despite all the hot ash dumped in it.

"I hope I don't start shivering. My teeth chattering would give me away."

As he neared the edge of the swamp, he heard voices. Looking up, he said, "Damn! They *would* have to camp right where I want to sneak out. Maybe I can get by later when they fall asleep."

Jonas lay shivering in the cold water, watching the camp fires dying out and the men bedding down for the night.

"I've got to move or my teeth will chatter." He slithered down the stream further heading through the camp. A trooper walked to the stream, canteen in hand. Jonas inched back to hide as best he could behind a clump of grass. He watched as the man filled his canteen, took a long drink and proceed to relieve himself. It spattered a few feet from Jonas' head. The strong ammonia smell almost made him sneeze. He held his breath to stop it. The trooper returned to the camp fire, letting Jonas continue on out.

Far from the camp, he raised out of the stream to let water drip from his clothes while he emptied his boots. He circled back, retrieved the rest of his venison and headed back to his cabin.

As the sun rose bright and golden in the east, Ustinov called his troop together for the day's orders.

"Men, we have a job ahead of us. We have to comb that burn until we find Jonas' body. A week's furlough to the man who finds him."

A half-hearted cheer went up from the men. No one was looking forward to going into that burned-over area.

"You'll have to go in on foot. Soak your boots in the stream so you won't burn your feet on the hot ash. Make sure you have full canteens so you can slake your thirst and wet down your boots. We'll start the search from the east end. Move out."

The sergeant said, "I might suggest we start at the west end. The wind will be at our back, giving us less smoke problems."

"Once you're in the burn, it'll make no difference. Starting with the sun at our back will give us a little better visibility."

"Yes, sir."

The skirmish line formed on the east end of the burn. It was rough, tough, dirty work. The timbers were still hot, and ash burned their feet, blistering them, despite the cooling water. Blackened timbers, like a jumble of jack straws, forced the men to climb over, around and through.

A shout went up, "I found him!"

They started in the direction of the trooper's call when the man called back, "False alarm. It's just a deer, well cooked."

The search continued through to the west end. No Jonas.

Ustinov said, "I know he's in there. We have to find him."

The skirmish line went through again, this time from west to east. The men were grumbling. One trooper voiced the thoughts of most, "He's not here. He really is a ghost and flew out before we torched the area."

Footsore, blackened and weary they emerged empty handed.

Ustinov wouldn't budge, "We go through once more, this time from the north. I know he's in there."

Much grumbling came from the ranks, but they dutifully formed another skirmish line to go through once more. Again, no Jonas or evidence of his body. The men were soaking their hot, blistered feet in the stream when Ustinov rode up.

"You've covered it well enough. I don't know how he survived that fire, though. He either got out and we didn't see him, or he survived the fire and escaped during the night. I don't believe the rumor that he's a ghost."

The men didn't agree. The legend of the ghost was reinforced in their minds. He was either a ghost or a superior human being with great ability to survive.

Chapter 15

The Trackers

USTINOV REPORTED THEIR FAILURE to find Jonas' body to Rykov. "I don't know how Jonas could have escaped. One possibility was a small stream coming out of the swamp. He might have survived in the stream and slithered down past our noses during the night. That's the only possibility for not finding his body . . . unless he really is a ghost."

"You and I know he's no ghost," said Rykov. "The enlisted men may believe that rubbish, but I do not! He's alive and must be found!"

Rykov and Gerchenoff called a meeting of all officers to discuss the problem of not being able to catch Jonas. Rykov stood up in front of the group, saying, "We all have a serious problem here, one Jonas Kekola. His continued freedom is an embarrassment to the Russian army. Worse, it encourages Finns to defy our rule.

"The search for this one man is costing us time and money. Worst of all, it has flagged the attention of the tsar. He's suggesting strongly that we get on with it and remove this thorn from the side of Mother Russia.

"This discussion will be free and open. Any suggestion will be considered. We want input about the best possible way to solve this problem."

Rykov sat down, indicating the meeting was open for discussion.

The first officer to speak said, "Why not take the whole town hostage or at least part of it until Jonas turns himself in?"

Gerchenoff answered, "We thought of that. We doubt Jonas would give up. Also, we'd have a hard time holding that many people. Further, we would aggravate sentiment to the point where we could have a full-scale revolution on our hands. Jonas has proven to us that we can't fight these people on their home grounds. The population is so scattered that we could only gather a fraction of them. The word would be out and the rest of them would vanish into the forest. Good try, but it wouldn't work. Next."

A young, gangly junior officer stood up to ask, "What ever happened to the blood hound and killer dog idea? I saw the dogs for a while, but now I haven't seen or heard about them."

Rykov answered, "Some of you were in on it, but, for those of you who were not, I will relate the circumstances. Jonas simply outwitted the dogs by leading them on a wild chase or dusting his trail with pepper. One time we thought we had him and sent killer dogs in, he killed both of them with a wooden spear. He didn't bother to waste a bullet.

"Another time he climbed into some slender birch trees, then bent one over into another into another into another and so on. He moved through the trees like an ape for about a quarter mile. He dropped into a creek to emerge from it about a half mile away. The dogs bayed at the first tree as though they had a treed animal. They were thoroughly confused. By the time we unraveled that one, he was long gone. Then it rained, washing out all scent. We could keep using them, but we think he would keep confusing or killing them. Next."

So it went, idea after idea. Some were tried unsuccessfully in the past and others discussed and discarded.

Another officer stood up addressing himself to the Cossacks, "What about you Cossacks? You were supposed to catch him in a few weeks."

The Cossack Hetman stood up, angry, red faced and embarrassed at being pointed out as a failure to catch Jonas. He said, "He goes where horse and rider can't go. By the time ground troops arrive, he's long gone."

A few boos and catcalls from the commanders of the ground troops.

Rykov said, "Hold it! I don't want this to disintegrate into a name-calling contest. I want to solve this problem."

Hetman Ustinov said, "I have a grudge to settle with that man. He killed many of my men and horses in that bog. I didn't want to say anything yet, but you'll know soon anyway. Two trackers are coming from our part of the country that are the best in the world. They're better than dogs because they can think. I have seen them follow a trail on the ground at full trot and not lose it. These men have never failed to track their man. They should be here in the next few days, and then we shall see."

Rykov stood up saying, "We have discussed a lot of ideas here today, but this is the first one that shows some promise. When the trackers get here, I want part of our foot troops mounted. When the trackers get close or Jonas goes into heavy timber or brush, our ground troops will follow."

Ustinov said in typical Russian exaggeration, "Either of these men could track a deer that died of old age back to the place he was born."

That afternoon, Vilho heard about the trackers coming. Vilho was anxious to warn Jonas of the latest danger. His first thought was going into the forest to find him, but he had no idea where to look.

* * * * *

Jonas had an uneasy feeling for several days but couldn't put his finger on it. Pacing the cabin incessantly, he went outside every few minutes to check for anything unusual. Everything was quiet, too quiet.

It came to him, "That's it! There are no unusual noises anywhere. That means the Russians haven't been on patrol at all. No crows have given an alarm or any birds acting frightened. I haven't seen deer or any other animals in flight from forest invaders. Something's up. I better find out what."

Now that he knew the reason for his anxiety, he felt better. He ate breakfast, thinking about ways to discover what was going on.

The trackers came in from the Cossacks part of Russia. Both were young, lithe, bearded and dressed in soft, tanned deerskin right down to their boots. They walked with the lean grace of panthers. They talked little to anyone but each other. The only visible weapon was a knife on each waist.

At first glance, they looked like brothers. Vilho found out later that they were good friends in the same line of work. They were the kind of men who didn't say much but instinctively people gave them a wide berth, the kind of men one would want on his side in a crisis.

Vilho had heard of these men by rumor only. A demonstration of their prowess was staged for the Russian officers earlier.

The Russian officers picked their best men to go out in the forest and try to cover their tracks while making a circle back to the demonstration area. The trackers gave them a two-hour head start. The trackers came back to the demonstration area just behind the men.

The officers didn't believe the trackers followed them step by step. They thought the trackers guessed their route back into the area.

The trackers had themselves blindfolded while two other men made a small circuit through the brush. Everyone could see the men except the trackers. They removed the blindfolds. The trackers ran the same circuit following exactly in their tracks. This feat impressed the Russian officers.

"This is what we need to track down Jonas," Rykov said, "men that can track like a dog and think too. Those men are the best I've ever seen. If I didn't know better, I'd swear they followed our men with their noses."

Rykov called a meeting to plan how best to use the trackers. After much discussion, Rykov decided the trackers would be used like tracking dogs. The cavalry and infantry would follow to make the capture or kill.

The trackers asked Rykov to give the forest a rest to eliminate any possibility of confusing signs. This might make Jonas complacent about leaving sign. All travel was banned in the forest. Rykov ordered guards posted up and down the roads and at all entry points. Any tracks found would, more than likely, be those of Jonas.

That was what Jonas heard, or rather, didn't hear. The forest was too quiet, which set up a danger signal of sorts with Jonas. For a little while, he thought they had given up the search, but he quickly discarded the idea.

It was a pleasant thought, and he let his mind dwell on that for a few minutes, thinking of the peace of not being chased.

"I know they're up to something, but, until I find out, there's nothing I can do about it. I might as well go fishing."

With that he packed a rucksack with a few extra supplies, thinking he might have to stay away a little longer than planned.

Jonas was fishing in a small stream when he became aware that something was happening in the forest. The sounds changed ever so slightly. It alerted his keen sense of one long hunted.

He climbed into a rock fissure, just above the stream bed. It was high enough so he could see above the low willows bordering the stream. This afforded him a good view of the fairly open forest. He saw them as they entered the valley. At first he couldn't understand what they were doing. Two men were running ahead of the main force, casting back and forth like hounds trying to find the scent of the fox. Then it came to him what they were. Trackers! Rumors had circulated about some trackers who were better than dogs. He shrugged it off as Russian bragging.

Jonas pulled his telescope out of his pack to watch them.

"I was right on my first guess. They are trackers!" he muttered.

He had to admire them as they ran back and forth, scanning the ground ahead of them in a low crouch. Their stamina had to be incredible to be able to do that all day.

Then the thought hit him that, if they doubled back, they would cross his tracks. He hadn't been especially careful hiding them because of the lack of activity on the part of the Russians.

Immediately, he began to think of different courses of action if they made a second sweep of the valley. He sat for a long time, watching for their return. Their sounds grew fainter and the forest settled down to its usual quiet, letting Jonas know all was well for the moment. He climbed down, noting how all his muscles ached. Only then, did he realize how tense he had been, sitting up in that rock fissure for so long. It took a few more minutes for him to unwind and think about his plans.

On the next sweep west, the trackers would find his tracks. He worried they would backtrack him to his cabin.

"Better make it easy for them to follow me out of this area and away," said Jonas to himself as he moved out. He hoped for a rain soon, but the clouds didn't look very promising.

As he left the stream, he deliberately made a few foot prints in the soft mud so they would be highly visible. He acted as though he was extremely careless in leaving a trail. He wanted to keep them on his trail until after dark. Rain had to come soon to wash out his back trail.

Jonas had to get back to the cabin to get food, blankets and rain gear to survive the tracking. With that in mind he started covering his tracks while he headed for some high, rocky ridges. It would be next to impossible for them to track him in the rocks.

A small cave in the rocks was his next stop. Until it rained, he dared not go back to the cabin. He didn't have much food and chided himself for not making better preparations. A little bread and the trout he caught along with salt and pepper was it. The pepper was mostly for dusting his trail in case they started tracking him with dogs again. It was very effective in temporarily making the dogs lose their sense of smell. It was not going to be effective on the human trackers.

Thinking of the fish made him realize he hadn't eaten since breakfast. Now it was getting close to dark. He gathered dry wood as he walked, being careful not to break anything that would leave a clue to his passing. There wouldn't be any wood up on the ridge where he headed. By the time he reached his chosen spot, he had gathered enough wood for a small fire.

He looked over the cave site carefully, and then checked his back trail to make sure they were not following him. Pursuit wouldn't be immediate as it was almost dark. The trackers were good but not that good.

Jonas piled a few rocks near the entrance to hide the flames of his fire. He lit the fire just before dark so it would burn to coals by dark. As the fire burned, he looked into the flames, reflecting on the day's events. He relaxed for the first time since sighting the trackers.

The last rays of sun shone directly on the rocks behind him and would hide the few flames of his fire. He couldn't avoid an occasional curl of gray smoke coupled with a spark now and then. The fire spread a circle of warmth in the small cave, engulfing Jonas, making him sleepy. He shook himself out of his lethargy to start supper. The trout were laid directly on the smoldering coals for his supper. He was so hungry he could hardly wait for the fish to finish cooking. After eating, he pulled his jacket close around him, curling up to sleep.

Looking out the cave at the first gray of dawn, he flexed his sore muscles. Checking his back trail for signs of pursuit, he gave a sigh of relief, seeing no one. He picked over the supper remains, thinking about his next move.

The sun came up over the bluff behind the cave, lighting the valley below and making sharp contrast between the dark green of the conifers and the lighter green of the birch and other hardwoods. Before the sun came all the way up, the valley became muted, mottled green, and, as the sun rose higher, it turned the forest into shining splendor.

Jonas thought of all God's glory in the valley below him while, in the next valley, men wanted to kill him. He might even have to kill some of them to save his own life.

"Did God intend for life to be ever thus?"

He shook himself out of his reverie to clean up his camp, leaving no sign of his recent habitation. He knew the trackers were good, but he doubted they could track over the hard rock face he traversed the day before.

Jonas decided to head back to his cabin for the extra supplies he needed. He knew the Russian mentality well enough to know that they would stay with their original search pattern.

He continued down the rocky ridge as far as he could before breaking off for his cabin. By this time he was several miles away from the search area. He calculated that they would stay in the area, especially if they found his sign at the stream side. He surmised they would lose his trail in the rocks and spend countless hours searching there. He hoped rain or a high wind would come up to wipe out his tracks. Jonas doubted they would ever find where he had left the rocks.

Back at the cabin, Jonas had to gather what he needed for a long stay in the wilderness, including some items specifically used to hide his trail.

By mid afternoon, it started to rain. Jonas breathed easier, knowing they could track him no longer.

Jonas thought this a good time to replenish his larder. The rain would muffle the sound of his shot, and the rain made the ground soft, muffling the sound of his walking. He didn't go far before he came upon a fat buck, grazing in the rain. One shot brought him down. Killing of game always saddened Jonas, even though he had to kill to live. He cleaned it and hoisted it to his shoulder for the short trudge back to the cabin, where he finished processing the deer. Then he cut up some liver and onions to cook for supper.

He made up his mind to stay put as the trackers would have to come within a few feet of his cabin to see it. If he didn't make any tracks out in the field, he would be safe. Venturing out in the rain-soft ground now would leave very definite sign. It would be easy for the trackers to follow him.

The rain stopped, and the sun came out to dry everything. Several days passed, and Jonas became fidgety, wanting to know more about the trackers. He knew something had to be done, or he wouldn't have any freedom of movement. Experience with the Russian search pattern told him where they might be found.

Toying with his breakfast, he made up his mind to seek them out. This latest threat to his well-being had him worried.

He packed his rucksack for a long stay away from the cabin. Jonas didn't know what he would face after he left its relative security.

While he was reasonably sure where the trackers were, he still had the uneasy feelings of the long-hunted animal. The hair stood up on the back of his neck just thinking about the danger. He moved cautiously through the woods, stopping every few feet to survey everything. He had an observation spot in mind but didn't want to rush into a trap getting there.

Arriving at his selected hilltop, he hadn't yet seen any patrol activity. He calculated the whereabouts of the patrols.

Jonas used this same hill for an observation point many times in the past. It gave him a good view of the valley below. Watching patrols from a distance, he could usually discern their pattern and go about his business. This was different. The patrols in the past didn't have the help of trackers like these.

Jonas found his usual blown-over tree with roots spreading in all directions. This made a chair, complete with arm rests. He hung his rifle off his right side so it would be within easy reach. His rucksack hung on a root on the other side. He sat down to wait. He was sure they would come, though it could be a few hours or a few days. Not seeing them for a long time, he couldn't pin point their schedule with accuracy.

Time dragged as he sat there, brushing away an occasional fly. The warm sun made him drowsy. He was dozing off when something jolted him to full alert. He didn't know what woke him so he let his instincts take hold.

Jonas swiveled his head slowly, making sure he didn't make any sudden movements. From the north, two crows gave the alarm call before they came flying down the valley at tree top height. Jonas knew something had made the crows move. He swung his pack to him, taking out his telescope to have a better look in that direction.

A buck and doe eased quietly down the slope into heavy timber. His senses were now keenly on the alert.

His scanning telescope picked up the trackers as they came into view. Crouched low and moving at a trot, they scanned the ground in front of them. Just behind them was the cavalry with the infantry bringing up the rear. The cavalry was easy to spot. Not so the infantry; their gray uniforms blended well with the rest of the forest. The one item that really stood out was their black boots. At times it looked like only boots moved through the forest. Jonas watched in fascination as the trackers moved out.

"They're really good or are putting on a good show for the men following them," he said. "I have to think they're that good, or the Russians wouldn't have brought them in. I wonder just how good they really are? How far did they track me last time before the rains came?"

After they disappeared from view, he sat thinking for a long time. The search pattern told him they would cut his sign the next day. They would cross the area where he was presently sitting.

"Well, now I'm in the middle of it. If they're that good, they'll pick up my sign. Will they both follow me, or will they split up and one back track me to my cabin? If they're smart, they'll track me both ways. If they do that, then my hideout is gone forever. They'll surely burn it to the ground."

He was reluctant to move, knowing full well that they would be on his trail.

"I have to make them follow me and not my back track. I see no rain soon, which means I'll have to keep on the run for several days. Watching the trackers in action tells me that this isn't going to be an easy task."

Rapidly, Jonas reviewed his possible choices getting out of his latest dilemma. "I could kill the trackers, but I want to avoid killing if possible. I could run false trails making them take extra time to run each of them down. But if they hit the right trail on the first try, they would be hot on my heels. I could pick out various streams and stay in them for a time. They would have to split up to find out where I came out of the stream. It all depends on how good they are," he said to himself. "I'm going to have to find out. We'll play your game, trackers, and see just how good you are."

This was going to be a game in deadly earnest. Adrenalin pumped through him, turning up his energy level. It was a game he would have to play out to the end. It was the challenge that excited him the most.

Jonas knew he had another day before they crossed his trail and decided to rest in preparation for the hard days ahead. He was going to have to use all his woods skills to outwit these two.

He set up his camp in a small hollow near a fresh spring. "I'm certain they won't be by until tomorrow, so I'll set up a comfortable camp. When they find the camp, I want them to think I didn't know they were in the area."

A rabbit snare garnered his supper. While the rabbit roasted, he pondered all the possible moves he could make to elude his pursuers. He ate and fell into an exhausted sleep still thinking of all the possibilities.

Jonas woke refreshed, luxuriating in his bed for a few minutes before getting up to fix a cold breakfast from the remainder of the rabbit.

His curiosity kept getting the best of him, wondering just how good the trackers really were. It was a game to him even though very dangerous.

After cleaning up his camp, he climbed out of the hollow to a vantage point overlooking his camp. It would be early afternoon before they could track him to his camp. He knew they would cross his trail close to where he watched them the day before.

The sun shone down through the trees. An occasional bird flitted through the area giving him a curious glance. A butterfly came along, testing one flower and then another. He watched the forest scene as though detached from it all. The hunters closing in on him were foremost in his mind. A young deer browsing toward him, caught his attention. He sat perfectly still to see how close it would come before it realized something was wrong. The deer came within ten feet of him when it decided that something was not right about the large lump in front of it. It stood, stared and sniffed the air, trying to get a smell of this strange something. Apparently, it hadn't seen a man before. The deer skirted Jonas, sniffing and staring all the way. Jonas slowly turned his head to follow it. After several swift bounds, the deer stopped and looked back at the strange lump. Jonas laughed to himself. Again curiosity got the best of the deer. Cautiously, it returned, advancing a few steps, sniffing and retreating, its tail up and twitching, ready for flight. Neck stretched out, it came forward trying to get a better smell. It would push backwards a few steps and advance again. Finally, it came within a few feet of Jonas to get a good smell, decided he was harmless and went on browsing.

"I wish Emma could have been here to see this. She would have enjoyed it very much."

Thinking of Emma saddened him. He said to himself, "When will all of this end, so she can enjoy scenes like this with me? Where will it all end?"

All this brought him back to the problem at hand. What to do about the trackers? Jonas estimated the time to be about eleven.

"Probably be a couple more hours before they get here," said Jonas.

The words were hardly out of his mouth when he discerned movement on the other side of the hollow. He looked through his telescope to see what it was. The trackers. He whistled softly to himself, saying, "They are good. They're here two hours earlier than I estimated."

The trackers came into the hollow at a run, following his tracks as though he had laid a white ribbon down for them to follow. They made a quick examination of his camp before they picked up his outgoing trail.

"I'm relieved to see both trackers. That means they're not following my back trail."

Jonas, rifle in hand, swung his pack to his back as he moved rapidly out of the area.

"Well, I found out how good they are! They're really good. It won't do me any good now to cover my tracks. I have to find an area where I'll leave no tracks for them to follow." He quickly ran the inventory of places he knew. His mind made up, he moved out quickly for some rock bluffs.

"I hope I can get there with time to spare. I need to change into my moccasins, they'll leave less sign in the rocks. And I need time to get to the other side of the bluff. There's no cover there."

Jonas reached the bluffs slightly out of breath. Sitting on a large rock, he changed from boots to moccasins. The light moccasins made his feet feel like they had wings. He quickly stuffed his boots into his rucksack.

Picking up his gear, he traversed the hard bluff rock to a point where he could swing to the other side of a large pinnacle.

When he was sure he couldn't be seen, he climbed the far side to watch his pursuers. He didn't have long to wait. The trackers came into view, covering the ground with a long, easy gait. The mounted troops were keeping up to the trackers, but the foot patrol had a hard time keeping pace and had scattered back in a long, scraggly line.

The trackers stopped when they reached the rocks to let everyone catch up. Jonas noticed their easy nonchalance as the surveyed the possible routes he could take into the rocks.

Toklat came up, checking if there was a problem.

Gregor, the tallest of the two trackers and usually the spokesman for them, said, "He knows we're on his trail otherwise he wouldn't have gone into these rocks. I suspect he has known since yesterday that we were tracking him. Josef and I discussed the sign seen thus far and suspect he watched us yesterday. We saw some evidence on that hill where we first picked up his tracks. We weren't sure until now as he was not making any effort to hide his tracks. Now we're sure he had this area in mind all along."

"That takes a lot of courage for him to let you track him here," Toklat said. "Are you sure you can track him through these rocks?"

"Yes," replied Gregor, "but it's going to be extremely difficult. Make sure your people stay back. If he doubles back or something, we want to be able to unravel the sign before your people destroy it."

Toklat asked, "What if he decides to kill you? We won't be close enough to do you any good."

Gregor shrugged, "If it is to be, it is to be. I doubt that he's thinking of that. If he wanted to, he could have ambushed us both before you could have done anything about it."

"Then, you're sure he knows we're on his trail?"

"Reasonably so. We'll know after we try to track him in these rocks. If he's going on through, we should be able to follow him easily. If he takes pains to hide his trail, then we can be sure he knows we're on his trail. I wouldn't be at all surprised if he's sitting up there in the rocks watching us right now."

Toklat swiveled his head uneasily, looking up into the rocks and wondering if he was a target for Jonas' superb marksmanship. He said nothing to the trackers. A knowing, half smile to each other said without words that they both saw the niggling fear creep into Toklat's face.

"I'll hold the men back," said Toklat. "Wave us on when you think it's all right for us to advance."

Turning quickly on his heel, he was glad to be out of Jonas' range. He made sure he had other men between himself and the rocks when he got back.

Jonas watched all this from his vantage point high in the rocks. The trackers scanned the ground, then began the hunt. Jonas didn't anticipate

131

how quickly they would find his track or how fast they moved on it.

"I'm going to be very careful where I put my feet down," he told himself. "Anything I do is going to give them a clue. Even with these moccasins, it's going to be difficult not to stir up a rock or some sand."

It was slow going. He watched where he placed each foot. Looking ahead, he planned his route in advance so he could be on hard rock all the time. The rock ridges forked. He had been there before but couldn't remember how they lay and which would be the best for not leaving tracks. The higher one looked better because of less vegetation and sand.

He picked his way carefully, wincing occasionally as the rocks hurt his feet through the thin moccasins. The trail meandered around the bluff back to his original split.

He muttered under his breath, "I took the wrong fork. I'm going to run into my own tracks. That might not be too bad if they've already passed this point. I can mingle my tracks with theirs then take the low fork out. It'll take them some time to unravel that. Maybe by then, we'll have rain."

Gregor and Josef found the spot where Jonas watched them talking to Toklat and pointed it out to Toklat.

"How do you know he watched us from here? I don't see anything."

"See those little scuff marks in the rocks? That little rock was moved. You can see where the rock was as it's a little darker right there. See this? It's a little bit of leather. We think he changed to some kind of soft slippers. He wore boots on his way here. Boots would make more distinct marks in the rocks than he's been making. This makes Josef and I both believe he knew we were tracking him the other day. We lost his trail in those other rocks because it rained. From what I can see this is going to be a real tough man to track down."

"You can tell all this from just those little marks?" asked Toklat.

Gregor replied, "Not all of it for sure, but it's a good guess."

Jonas came to the fork of the two ridges. The many tracks told him they had passed this point. He walked in their tracks to take the low ridge out. He hoped to gain some time as it would take them longer to unravel this one. He prayed for rain to come before they could figure it out.

Jonas made a very careful exit from their tracks, returning to the low ridge. They would continue around the circle again to find out where he left their tracks.

"I can delay no longer. They'll come back this way soon. I see a few clouds building. I may get that rain in time to exit from here with safety. If it does rain, I'm going to town to see Emma and the resistance group. I have an idea how to stop the trackers without resorting to violence."

The trackers, with their Cossacks in tow, came back to their original starting place. Gregor and Josef stood there looking at each other when

Toklat came up. "What is it this time?" he asked.

"Don't you recognize this place? We were here once today. We're back on our own track. He led us in a full circle. We're really going to have a tough job trying to find out where he left our trail. Possibly, he's behind us laughing, taking us in another circle. Send some of your men back around so he doesn't circle us again. Space your men out so they can see each other until they come back full circle to us. Make sure they do not get off the main trail where we could get confused as to Jonas' exit. The rest of your group is going to have to stay put until we sort this one out."

"Did you know he was making a circle?"

"We suspected but still had to follow the trail to find out for sure."

"How long will it take to find his track now?"

"We might find it yet today if we hit it lucky or he makes some kind of mistake. We might not unravel it for days."

"Days!" screamed Toklat. "We don't have rations for that long. It could rain any day and wash out everything."

Gregor gave Toklat a disgusted look, saying, "Then you'd better send a detail back for a relief group or more rations. Even if we unravel this before it rains, he'll probably pull a maneuver like this again."

"What assurance do I have that you can continue tracking him if I get a relief column or more rations?"

"None if it rains; we're all through until next time. Only luck would let us find his track after the rain."

"On that basis, we better hold for one more day on short rations. If it rains, we'll have to go back. If it doesn't, I'll send for more rations. I want to be in on the capture of this man."

"You need to keep your men at this spot and not let them wander around too much. Jonas could have left this path anywhere."

Josef cut two short staffs of wood from some saplings.

"What are you going to do with those sticks?"

"We'll take turns looking for sign. It's tedious work, so we will spell each other. We use the sticks to mark our last place. If we miss something, we'll have a marked starting place."

Jonas left the main track where someone had stepped off to urinate. He stepped over the area, hoping they would not look closely at that particular spot. He made a wide swing on the rocks to get up on the lower ridge where it was solid rock. Following the low ridge for a long way, he found hard ground. The hard ground would show very little imprint where he left the ridge. They would track him, but it would be slow. The combination of darkness and the chance of rain made him hopeful that he would lose them.

A mile away from the rock bluffs, he made a dry camp to get some rest. They couldn't track him after dark.

"If the rains come, I can go to town; if not I'll have to keep trying to stay ahead of the them."

Toward morning Jonas woke to rain splattering his face. "Good," he said, "this looks like it'll last for a while. I'm going to go directly into town."

Toklat woke, hearing the rain on his tent. "That man must lead a charmed life!" he said. "Every time we get close, he gets some kind of break and we lose him." He got up, giving orders to break camp. Toklat knew this was the only move he could make. Rykov would not see it that way. He would call it another failure. Toklat wasn't looking forward to meeting with Rykov when they got back. He racked his brain to find a good excuse for failure but none came.

Jonas reached the hill above town early, too early to chance crossing the open ground to reach Emma's house. He watched the activities up and down the road, fidgeting, awaiting darkness so he could see Emma.

The rain let up a little. He saw someone come out of the house and go into the sauna. It looked like Emma. He got out his telescope to see who it was on the return trip from the sauna. It was Emma. She looked toward the hill as she went into the house as if she knew he watched her.

At full dark, Jonas went down the hill. He stopped abruptly when he heard sounds of the all too familiar pursuers. Bedraggled and wet, they plodded on to their compound. Jonas watched with a wary eye until the troop, led by the trackers, were well past. They weren't in a very good mood as they trudged toward town.

Jonas gave them ample time before following their trail, leaving it at the road to Emma's house.

Emma greeted him at the door with her usual squeal of delight at seeing him. Anna knew by the squeal and silence as they kissed who it was without having to look.

Anna busied herself around the kitchen getting something to eat for the ever-hungry Jonas. Matt came down the stairs, and Jonas greeted him warmly.

Jonas asked, "Matt, would you mind getting Vilho for me right away? I need to talk to him."

Matt teasingly said, "I know you're sending me on an errand just so you can be alone with my sister."

Emma said, "He can do anything anytime he wants with you here or not. I'm a very willing person with Jonas."

All that banter made Jonas blush slightly, delighting Emma even further. She said, "Just stick around Matt, maybe you'll learn something and be a little more successful in finding yourself a girlfriend."

This time it was Matt's turn to blush. He rushed out the door to find Vilho without making any more comments.

Matt and Vilho showed up as Jonas sat down to eat. Vilho and Jonas greeted each other warmly.

Anna said, "Vilho, you might as well sit down and eat as stand there looking dumb. Jonas isn't going to say much with his mouth stuffed full of food anyway."

Vilho pulled up a chair, saying, "I thought sure they were going to catch you this time with those Russian trackers out there."

"Oh, ye of little faith," chided Jonas.

"How did you get away from them? I heard they're really good."

Jonas answered, "I've seen them several times and, yes, they are really good. They're going to be tough. I seriously doubt that I can continue to live in the forest with them around. They're so good, they'd track me anywhere I went. The only reason I got away this time was the heavy rains came, washing out all sign. I know they'll be back."

"Just kill them," said Vilho.

"It entered my mind, but there has been so much killing, I'm getting sick of it. I don't feel the trackers are my enemy. They're two men doing their job. The high-level officers ordered them to track me down."

"I still say kill them! That's the only deed the Russians understand."

"I don't want to kill them. I admire them very much. I watched them work and really respect someone that's good at his job."

"Even if it kills you?" queried Vilho in disgust.

Jonas nodded. "It won't come to that. I'll figure out something first."

"Well, you better do it fast. The word is out that they're going to hound you until they kill or capture you. They don't care which."

Emma interrupted, saying, "All this talk of killing makes me ill. Let's talk about something else. We just heated the sauna. I'm sure you could use a good bath."

"Do I smell that bad?" asked Jonas.

Emma grew flustered and stammered, "Ah, ah, well, no, but I thought being out in the woods and all . . ." her voice trailed off to nothing.

Jonas said, "I was just fooling, but that sauna does sound good. Does any one want to join me?"

Matt said, "I just had one."

"Count me in," said Vilho.

Anna got towels for the two of them. Emma produced clean clothes for Jonas, ones he had left dirty on his last trip. They were all washed, neatly folded, ready to go, done with love by Emma.

In the sauna, Jonas and Vilho had a long, serious talk about the trackers and how they were affecting Jonas' ability to move about.

Vilho said, "We can't afford to lose you to the Russians. You're our hope. You're the backbone making our people resist the Russian yoke. They see you, one man, foiling the Russians, and that gives everyone heart."

"I hope I'm doing some good besides keeping myself alive."

"You are!" said Vilho. "Everyone looks forward to your latest run-ins with the patrols and how you make fools of them."

"I'm sure that some of the stories get exaggerated in the retelling."

"That's good. It makes you more of a hero in their eyes. If those trackers are going to put a stop to that, I'll kill them myself."

"No, at least not yet. I told you, I'm tired of killing. I'm going to stay one more day even though I know I should be getting back to the forest. It's dangerous for me, and I'm putting the entire Lehtinen family in jeopardy. There's something I want you to find out for me, if you can."

"Anything in my power, I'll do," replied Vilho.

"Find out if the trackers can read either Finnish or Russian."

"What do you have in mind?"

"I'm not sure yet. I have a plan that may solve the whole problem of the trackers without bloodshed."

"Jonas," said Vilho, disgusted, "You're too squeamish about killing those damn Russians. I wouldn't hesitate for a minute to kill them both."

"I know. You're a bit more bloodthirsty than I. We can't stoop to their level. Our enemy isn't the common soldier, it's the ruling forces."

"Yes, but that's the only way we're going to get their attention."

"Maybe," replied Jonas, "but they'll make reprisals on innocent people if we get too enthusiastic in our killing. I'm surprised they haven't made the townspeople pay because of the Russians I've killed."

"I guess we'll never see eye to eye on this," Vilho said.

"I suppose not."

"I'll find out about those trackers and get back to you as soon as possible. Maybe someone's seen them get some letters from home."

"If at least one of them can read, it would help my plan, at least the first part of it. If that doesn't work, we may have to do it your way."

"Off the subject for a little bit," said Vilho. "The trackers got me to thinking—what if we needed to get in touch with you?"

"I've thought about that. I don't want anyone to know where I'm hiding. The Russians might resort to torture to get the secret. That has been the main reason I have kept my location secret from everyone. But there's possibly a way without putting anyone in jeopardy. The only fly in that ointment is the Russian ban on forest travel. Do you remember the little waterfall on Rock Creek and that pool where we camped out a few years ago?"

"I remember the place well, what about it?"

"Well, just below that pool, on the north side, is a big hollow tree hanging over the water. It stands out like a sore thumb because there's nothing else near it. I can check that every few days to see if you left a message in there. I like it because it's out in the open so I can watch it from cover before going near. There's a big rock next to the tree. If you put a message in the tree, place a small rock on top of the big rock. That will save useless trips to the tree to see if there's a message. Secondly, there's a big swamp near so I could escape before anyone could get close."

"Sounds good to me," replied Vilho thinking to himself how thorough Jonas was about everything.

They got out of the sauna to cool off in the dressing room before drying off and putting on their clothes. "You don't know how much I miss this out in the bush," said Jonas. "When I'm back here, I take simple pleasures like this for granted."

Emma greeted them at the kitchen door with, "Well, both of you really do smell better."

Jonas replied with a grin, "I feel better, too."

Anna said, "I have coffee and fresh cinnamon rolls in the kitchen." They sat at the table while Anna poured coffee. The cinnamon rolls gave off a yeasty, tantalizing fragrance, causing Jonas' mouth to water. This was a treat, indeed, from his own cooking in the bush. The conversation ended as they got busy stuffing fresh cinnamon rolls into their mouth.

Jonas bolted one down, saying, "Anna, those are the best rolls in the world."

Anna beamed appreciation.

Emma pouted, saying, "What about my rolls?"

"Yours are good," said Jonas affectionately, but added, "You can still learn a little from your mother."

"Oh, she'll do just fine," said Anna, "after she's baked as many as I have over the past years."

The mood turned festive, especially, after Jonas told Emma, he was going to stay overnight.

Later Vilho said a reluctant good night. Anna and the rest of the family retired upstairs. Emma and Jonas went into the living room.

Much later Jonas said, "I could stay with you all night, but I have to get some sleep. If those trackers get on my trail, I'll need all my faculties working."

"I know," said Emma, "but I get to see so little of you and for such short periods. Your visits are shorter each time. I worry about something happening to you when you're gone."

Emma kissed him good night and went upstairs. Jonas stripped off his clothes, pulled a blanket over himself and fell asleep immediately.

The next morning Emma woke him up with a kiss on the forehead saying, "Up, up, sleepy head. Breakfast is on the table, and mother will be angry if you let it get cold."

Jonas stirred, still half asleep, kissing her and then stretching his full frame out over the end of the too-short couch.

"Well, get out of here so a fellow can get dressed."

Vilho came in when they were halfway through breakfast. He said, "You asked me if the trackers could read. It sounded important, so I was up bright and early to do some snooping round. I heard one of them read a letter or something to his partner."

"That's good, Vilho. I appreciate it," said Jonas.

"What are you going to do with this information?"

"You're going to the Boar's Head and get Mika to translate these notes for me. You told me Mika could read and write Russian. I wish I could meet him and ask him myself, but I don't think it wise right now."

Jonas scribbled the notes, while Vilho shrugged into his coat. Jonas finished them quickly and handed them to Vilho.

"You can read them if you like."

"Oh, I'll get to read them when Mika translates them into Russian," said Vilho as he went out the door.

Mika greeted Vilho with his usual exuberance, embracing him in his big bear hug as if he had not seen him for years, though Vilho had been there the day before. Vilho sat down at a table, noting a few Russian officers in the place. He didn't want to be obvious in passing the notes to Mika for rewrite. He waited until Mika brought him his usual cold beer. Vilho said softly as Mika sat the beer down, "I need to talk to you in private."

"All right, just give me a few minutes to think of some excuse for you to come into the kitchen."

Mika came back booming out in his full, deep voice so everyone could hear, "Vilho, you always complain about my steaks. I want you to come back into the kitchen and pick out your own. I might even make you cook it yourself, and then you can really complain to the cook. Come on."

Vilho followed Mika into the kitchen and was steered to the back pantry for privacy.

"What do you need that's so urgent and secret?" asked Mika.

"Jonas is here, and he wants you to translate some notes into Russian. He's going to leave them for the trackers. He doesn't want to kill them, which is contrary to anything I would do, but that's what he wants."

Mika quickly scanned the notes then reached into a drawer for pen, ink, and paper.

"I heard about those trackers and how good they are," said Mika. "I also heard how Jonas has given them the slip several times. I hear a lot in here. Those Russians don't know I understand everything they're saying. They just think of me as a dumb Finn."

"Well, I hope this works for him," said Mika as he finished. "I'm sure

138

Jonas is under a lot of strain with them being a constant threat to his well-being," said Mika folding the notes and handing them to Vilho.

"Oh, Jonas is enjoying this game of hounds and the hare. I know he would enjoy it a lot more if it weren't so deadly serious. Of even that I'm not sure as it would take all the spice out of the game if it were just for fun."

"Vilho, you're going to have to eat one of my steaks. We have to keep the Russians from getting suspicious, after all the noise I made. I know it'd just break your heart to have to force down one of my steaks."

"Yes, it'll be a really tough job, but I believe I can handle it." said Vilho laughing as he went back into the dining room.

Mika said, "I'll have that steak cooked and out to you in a little bit."

"Good, I'm hungry. Just make sure you don't switch one of those old tough ones for the one I just picked."

Mika feigned anger as he went back into the kitchen.

Mika brought out the steak with all the trimmings plus a small bottle of red wine. He sat down opposite Vilho. "I'm going to sit here and watch you eat every bit of that meat. If you don't, I'll stuff it down your throat."

The Russians looked their way momentarily and then went back to their drinking.

Mika soon tired of watching Vilho wolfing down the steak. He went back into the kitchen saying, "I'll be back to check on you."

Vilho finished the steak and went back to the kitchen to pay and say thanks. He was anxious to get back to Jonas.

Mika said under his breath, "Let me know as soon as you hear."

Vilho nodded, saying loudly, "Good steak but too damn expensive."

Mika feigned anger again, shouting, "Get out of here, you bum. If I can't satisfy you, why do you keep coming back?"

"I just like to hear you yell and scream, Mika," retorted Vilho as he went out the door.

Vilho hurried back to give Jonas the translated notes. He was anxious to relay the news about the trackers not being able to catch him.

At the sound of Vilho's knock, Jonas slipped quietly upstairs, not wanting to take any chances. He knew it probably was Vilho. He heard him enter and Emma talking to him.

Emma called softly, "It's all right to come down. It's Vilho."

Vilho handed Jonas the notes. Even though Jonas couldn't read Russian, he knew by the length of the contents which note was which.

The two of them talked in the living room, while Emma busied herself getting them coffee. They talked in soft tones even though it wasn't necessary. They felt if they talked louder the Russians would hear them.

That night Jonas said his reluctant good-byes as he left for the forest. It was a clear, moonlit night. He wanted to get well away before the

Russians started their morning patrol. A specific place came to mind where he was going to leave the notes for the trackers to find.

He enjoyed being out at night listening to the different night sounds, marveling at the quiet and yet noisy night. It was such a contrast to his trained ears. Not a breath of air stirred, making all the sounds sharper.

Jonas knew the search patterns well, so he put himself directly in their path. The trackers would find plenty of sign to follow to his rendezvous. If their answer to the notes was no, he would have an escape route that would be extremely difficult to follow.

He reached the rock outcroppings on a ridge that ran for several miles. The ridge had many branches running from it. The trackers would be a long time unravelling his trail from there if they decided to keep tracking him. He climbed to a high spot on the ridge to watch his back trail. The patrol was not long in coming.

As soon as he saw that they were on his trail, he moved out among the rocks. Making the trail harder to find, he gave himself the time needed to get to where he wanted to leave the first note, which read:

> Trackers: As you read this note, be aware that I am watching you from a short distance away. I could easily kill you. I know that you realize I could have killed both of you easily in the past, but I do not choose to do so if it can be avoided. There will be a second note as you go around the first rock outcropping. One of you can read the note and talk while the other watches the back trail. Just tell your commander that you want the troops to stay farther back so they will not destroy the trail. If you agree to this put the note in your pocket and wait for the commander and his troop to catch up. Then pick up trail again. You will find the second note in plain sight, weighted down by a rock.

Jonas didn't have long to wait before the trackers ran toward him. Even though he had been careful with his trail, they followed him easily.

The first tracker picked up the note and started to read. After reading the first sentence, he quickly swiveled his head around trying to see where Jonas might be watching. He said something to his partner who also started looking around. The first one went back to his reading but now was doing it out loud while his partner kept a vigilant watch all around. There was a quick discussion between them. The first one put the note in his pocket indicating compliance. They both sat down to await the coming of the rest of the group.

Jonas breathed a sigh of relief, "So far, so good."

Captain Toklat was again leading the group. He rode up to see what

140

the delay was. He had sense enough to hold the other troops back at a further distance so they would not destroy sign left by Jonas.

"What's the problem this time?" asked Toklat, dismounting.

Gregor said slowly, "He has gone into this rock pile ahead of us. It looks like this ridge is all rock to the west with many branches running off the main stem. We're gong to have to ask you to stay quite far back to make sure he doesn't double back or circle us like he did last time. We'll let you know when it's safe for you to come up. One of us will come back to get you. Jonas has a good start, but he has to get off this ridge before long. There isn't much of a place to hide, and it doesn't look like there is any water near. From here, he's going to have to head for the open, and we'll have him. The only problem would be another bad storm washing out all his sign. Right now the weather looks good."

"What do you want me to do with the troops right now?"

"Just hold them there for now."

Toklat mounted his horse, spurring him to go to the rear, while the trackers resumed the trail.

Gregor said to Josef, "What do you think of this mess?"

"I don't know, but I would as soon not be killed. I have a lot of living to do in my life. Let's see what's in the other note."

They carefully tracked around the corner of the bluff. They saw the second note weighted down by a rock. They both hurried to it. Gregor picked it up and read aloud to Josef.

Trackers: You have come this far, so I have to assume that you have elected to stay alive. The rest now comes easy. Just track me down this ridge slowly until we get some rain, which should be in a day or two. After that you will lose my trail. When you resume the search, tell them you can find no sign of me. Hopefully they will assume that I've left the country. I will mark my trail with arrows of grass or small twigs so you will know it's me you are tracking and get off. I'm sure there will be some townspeople who will ignore the ban on entering the forest. You should be able to track several of them down to allay any suspicions. If you're agreeable to all of this, please put this note in the pocket opposite the first note. Destroy them both at your earliest convenience. Good luck to both of you. You men are really good at your job. I wish we could meet under better circumstances. Over the weeks I have come to admire both of you, and this is the main reason I choose not to kill you as long as you are willing to abide by the terms in this note.

141

Gregor and Josef looked at each other for a minute. Josef said, "I think we should do this. I have come to admire this Jonas. I don't want to see him destroyed. Not by us. What do you say, Gregor?"

"I agree, Josef," said Gregor stuffing the paper in his other pocket as a signal of compliance. They both looked around and nodded to reinforce their agreement.

Josef said, "We don't have to follow him now if we do not choose. No one in that troop that would know if we are really on his track or not."

"I know, but I think we should follow him to get used to seeing the signs he'll be leaving. Besides, we're still not so good that we can't use the practice in following a real master woodsman such as this one. We thought we were really good until we ran up against this man."

"True, but I'll be a little nervous about his changing his mind about killing us."

"Oh, hell. He could have killed us before this if he wanted."

Josef went back to the troop, while Gregor continued on the track.

They wandered the ridge for two and a half days before the rains came. This forced the tracking crew to give up and go home.

Back at headquarters, Toklat got his usual tirade from Rykov. Toklat complained, "It looks like God is on his side. Every time we get close, down comes the rain to wash out all the sign, and we have to start all over."

The weather cleared and the search resumed. The trackers crossed Jonas' sign several times but chose to ignore it. They did track down several townspeople in the forest illegally, but this didn't satisfy anyone. After two weeks of running down false leads, Rykov called the search off. Gregor and Josef went back to Russia, and the forest settled down again.

Chapter 16

Vilho and Aimo

THE SEASONS WORE ON with Jonas managing to stay ahead of patrols. Whenever the Russians came back to the compound without Jonas, the Finnish people of Kiivijarvi rejoiced. Jonas was their hero, a legend larger than life and almost super human. Vilho knew that as long as Jonas remained at large, the ranks of the resistance group would continue to fill. Jonas was also Vilho's best friend. For these reasons, he worked covertly at his end to do whatever was necessary to insure Jonas' freedom. He saw Aimo as a direct threat to that freedom and tried to think of a way to prove that the man was a spy and, if he was, to do something about it. The fact that Aimo gained more favors from the Russians than other soldiers was enough proof for him, but he knew Jonas would have other ideas.

Vilho pondered the problem and decided he had to trap Aimo into giving himself away. After much deliberation, he hit upon a plan that might work. "If I feed Aimo some information, and the Russians tried to use it to trap Jonas, it would prove his guilt."

He thought of someplace that he could send the Russians on a wild goose chase that would not risk Jonas. The head of Rock Creek fit the bill. Jonas had lost his favorite dog to a pack of wild dogs there three years before and vowed he would never go back into that area. "If the Russians mount a search of that area, it will prove that Aimo is the informer."

Vilho formulated this plan and began to talk about Jonas during lunch break. Everyone laughed and joked about the inability of the Russians to catch Jonas. Vilho nonchalantly said, "Well, I know one area where they haven't looked. Jonas and I used to hunt there. I remember Jonas commenting once that it would make a good place to hide."

He let the subject drop there, both to avoid others suspecting that he planted the information and to limit who might give the location to the Russians. Vilho had to be sure it was Aimo.

"If anyone else knows, it will defeat my purpose. Even if someone else isn't a spy they might say something in idle conversation the Russians would overhear," he said to himself.

After lunch Aimo approached Vilho, casually saying, "You think you know where Jonas is hiding?"

Vilho said nonchalantly, "I don't know for sure. I was just guessing that he's up around Rock Creek because he knows that area, and he has to be somewhere. The old fox may have gone in there thinking that the Russians wouldn't bother searching it because it's so small. I mean, it's almost too small; the Russians could box it in and search it foot by foot."

Vilho knew by the gleam in Aimo's eye he was the man and had taken the bait. He watched Aimo closely all day. Late in the afternoon, he thought he saw Aimo give the sergeant a signal. Not long afterward, the sergeant sent Aimo to headquarters on an errand.

While Aimo was gone, Vilho mentioned to the rest of the group he thought Jonas might be hiding around Sand Lake. They looked at him like he was a fool. No one would hole up in that area; it was too wide open. Vilho wanted that other seed planted just in case someone else in the group was passing information. If they mounted a search to Rock Creek, it was Aimo. If they went to Sand Lake, someone else was to blame.

The next morning, they mounted a double patrol for Rock Creek, which they searched for three days to no avail. They never did mount a patrol for Sand Lake. Aimo was the Judas in their midst.

But having that information did not satisfy Vilho. "What do I do now? Use Aimo by feeding him more false information? What good would that do? How much more false information would the Russians swallow? How long before they would catch on?"

Vilho had to ponder all the variables. What if Aimo really was innocent and the patrols had gone to Rock Creek by chance? Did Aimo just make some dumb remark that the Russians picked up? Vilho felt that he had to give Aimo, a fellow Finn, every benefit of doubt, but, the more he thought about it, the more he became convinced Aimo was the spy.

The problem bothered Vilho more and more until he became obsessed with it. He had to neutralize Aimo somehow. He contemplated killing him but rejected that idea as too drastic. After all, Aimo's reporting hadn't gotten Jonas caught. The one point that bothered Vilho was that Aimo lived next door to Emma. That was a risk. There would be the devil to pay if the Russians caught Jonas there. They would execute him and imprison the entire Lehtinen family.

All these problems were on Vilho's mind as he trudged home from his daily soldiering duties. The cold snow squeaked beneath his boots, and the stars gleamed like diamond chips in the black night sky.

Vilho marvelled to himself, "Look at this beautiful night. Here I am fretting about a nonentity like Aimo. What is the matter with me?"

He speeded up his walking to vent off some of the excess energy his anger pumped into his system. His steamy breath blew back in his face as he increased his pace. He almost ran into Aimo coming from the other direction. Aimo scampered to one side like a scared rabbit.

Vilho's pent up feelings vented as he snarled, "Aimo, you damn traitor. You're the one that turned in Jonas about the ice rink. You're the one feeding the Russians information about all of us!"

Aimo shouted back, "I really haven't hurt anyone, and the Russians pay me well for practically nothing."

"You call betraying my best friend and a fellow Finn nothing?"

"It didn't hurt a thing. Jonas is still alive and free."

"Free! You call that free? The Russians are hunting him down like an animal because of you. He doesn't have a life that he can call his own."

"It's still nothing," retorted Aimo.

"No thanks to you, he's still on the run. You told the Russians what I said about Rock Creek. That was a trap, and you fell for it. If Jonas had really been there, they would have him in custody or worse, dead. And I don't call his whipping and being jailed nothing!"

"I didn't have anything to do with his killing the captain."

"If he hadn't been in trouble the first time, the killing wouldn't have happened."

"Jonas had it coming, trying to make the captain look bad!"

With that Vilho's temper got the better of him, and he hit Aimo square on the nose. Aimo tumbled backwards, blood spewing from his nose, staining the snow and the front of his coat a bright crimson.

Aimo got to his hands and knees, blood still streaming. As he came up, his knife flashed in his hand, taking Vilho by surprise. The first slash cut through Vilho's heavy coat and into his fore arm. He felt the sting of the blade. He jumped back instinctively to avoid the next vicious slash.

Vilho said, "Back off, Aimo. I don't want to have a knife fight with you. I found out what I wanted to know. I'll make you ineffective by telling everyone that you're the spy. At least you'll still be alive."

"Damn you, Vilho. You aren't going to tell anyone about me. I'm going to leave you right here, holding your guts in your hands, wondering what happened."

Aimo slashed wildly at Vilho again. Vilho sidestepped, pulling his own knife.

"Aimo, stop! You know you can't beat me in a knife fight. Quit while you're still ahead."

By way of answering him, Aimo spat blood at him from his bleeding nose and lunged again.

Vilho sidestepped again, trying to get Aimo to calm down and be reasonable. He felt that Aimo would soon see the light and quit.

Vilho said, "It won't be all that bad. Losing a little face isn't as bad as losing your life. You're young, you could move away and start a new life. No one would know about you in a big city like Helsinki."

That angered Aimo even more. He slashed and flailed at Vilho, who kept stepping out of harm's way. Vilho could feel warm blood run down into his mitten from his cut arm. He wondered, as if in a dream, how bad it was. He began to feel detached as though the fight happened to someone else.

There was no way out. He knew if he ran or turned his back, Aimo would stab him or, at the least, throw his knife. Vilho knew he was good at throwing a knife; he had seen him practice.

Vilho tried again to stop the fight, "Aimo I don't want to hurt you. Stop and we'll forget the whole incident."

"No, I won't forget. Fight, you yellow bastard!"

With that, Aimo lunged for Vilho's mid section again. Vilho's survival instinct took over. He sidestepped, knocking Aimo's knife arm down with his left hand, driving his right hand with knife into Aimo's heart.

Aimo stood stock still for a moment with a look of disbelief on his face. The only thing holding him up was Vilho's knife still in his hand. Vilho pulled the knife free, and Aimo tumbled forward onto his left shoulder, folding into a big heap. Blood gushed from the wound, melting the snow and turning it crimson black in the moonlight. Steam rose from the blood.

A long shudder came over Vilho as he realized what he had done. Even though it had been unavoidable, waves of remorse flooded over him.

He shook himself back to reality, remembering his own cut. He pulled up his sleeve to examine the wound. It was a long diagonal cut, bleeding profusely. He needed help soon or he would bleed to death himself.

His mind raced madly. "I must get away and get help. I must not leave a blood trail in the snow for some one to follow."

He knew the Lehtinen family would help him. He bound up his wound as tightly as he could with his scarf and left at a fast trot. He knew if he ran too fast his heart would beat faster, and he would lose more blood. The urgent need for help struggled with the need to slow down.

It felt like it took a long time to get there. He looked down at the wounded arm. Blood was beginning to soak through the scarf. He opened his coat and shirt putting his arm inside so he wouldn't leave telltale drops of blood. The lights of the Lehtinen house in the distance told him he would make it.

Emma answered his knock. Her face went ashen when she saw his pallor and the blood soaking through his coat.

She said, "Come in before you fall down. Mother, come help!"

Anna hurried down the stairs, alarmed at the urgency of her daughter's voice. Emma had Vilho's arm on the table and the sleeve pulled back.

She and her mother gently slid Vilho out of his coat and shirt. Emma quickly pressed a clean towel on the wound to stop the bleeding. Anna heated water and got more clean cloths plus a needle and thread. They would have to sew this one up or it wouldn't heal right. Vilho sat stoically while the two women worked on him. They still hadn't asked him what happened. They knew he would tell them in his own good time.

Vilho asked, "Has Jonas been around lately, or is he due?"

Emma said, "He hasn't been here for a while. I never know for sure when to expect him, but I think he'll show up any day soon. Why?"

"I'll probably have to join him, if he'll have me. I just killed Aimo tonight on the road and may have to hide like Jonas."

Emma and Anna exchanged glances but said nothing.

"It was unavoidable. I found out he was the informer for sure. I faced him with it. A fight followed, and I killed him. I tried everything I knew to talk him out of it, but he was intent on killing me to keep his secret."

Anna asked, "How is anyone going to find out you did it? Did anyone see you?"

"No," replied Vilho, "But how am I going to explain this cut. They'll add two and two and know it was me that did the job."

Emma paused and said, "I'm sure Jonas would welcome you as you're his best friend. I'm sure he would welcome the company. I don't know how you'll find him when he's never told anyone where he's hiding. He keeps saying the less we know the better."

"I'm going to have to do something quick."

Emma said, "Maybe they'll leave it up to the local authorities. After all, he wasn't on the post or officially on duty. The Russians don't know the reason he was killed. It could have been over a bad gambling debt or a woman."

"All that's true," replied Vilho, "but how am I going to hide this arm?"

Anna said, "I don't know. We'll think of something. The men'll be home soon, and we'll see what they have to say. I don't condone killing, but it sounds like you couldn't help it. Besides, I never liked Aimo, even though he was our next door neighbor."

They cleaned the wound, and Anna sewed it up, after boiling the needle and thread.

"It's a clean cut," said Anna. "It should heal quickly. You're young and healthy, which will help a lot."

The men came home surprised to see the kitchen table covered with bloody rags. Toi asked, "What in the world happened to you, Vilho?"

Vilho related the whole story to them again, ending up with dilemma he was in. They discussed many plans, but nothing seemed worthy of

147

consideration.

Emma said, "There's been a lot of winter sickness going around. Matt could tell the Russians that Vilho came down with it early last evening, which would give him an alibi for the time Aimo was killed."

Everyone agreed that was as good a beginning as any.

Matt said, "Let's hope the Russian doctor doesn't come to examine him."

Toivo said, "I doubt he'd come. The Russian officers can hardly get him to look after them, let alone tend a lowly Finnish enlisted man."

Anna fed Vilho some hot soup left from supper to help him start building his blood loss back. Toivo and Matt helped him upstairs to a bedroom. There he would have some warning if a stranger came to the house.

The next morning Matt would tell the Russians that Vilho was sick. He wouldn't tell them where he was in case they decided to send the doctor. Matt was going to try to find out if they had found the body and what they were going to do about it.

A farmer discovered Aimo's body early that morning. The farmer didn't recognize him. He reported the discovery to the Russians.

Gerchenoff called an emergency meeting with lieutenants Barloff, Brezinski, Toklat, and Chekok after they had retrieved the body to discuss the incident and its effect on them and the community.

"Help yourselves to the tea and rolls," Gerchenoff said as an orderly wheeled in a large samovar of tea and a tray of rolls, "and then we will get down to the meeting."

Brezinski fixed the captain a plate of rolls and his tea.

"As some of you may know," Gerchenoff started, "Aimo Hakala's body was found on the road to town this morning. He'd been dead for some time, stabbed in the heart by party or parties unknown. I'm sure all of you are aware that Aimo was an informant for us on affairs in the community or anything else he could pick up. At this point, we're in a dilemma about investigating. While he was one of our enlisted men, he wasn't killed while under our direct jurisdiction. I would like to know if he was killed because someone found out he was an informant or for some other reason. If we investigate too closely, the Finns will wonders why we're so concerned. I would like some of your input on this."

Barloff was the first to speak, "Sir, I would tend to suspect some civilian did him in. He wasn't liked in the community and was a gambler and womanizer. Rumor has it that he was having an affair with a married woman. You know how these Finns are about their women. I wouldn't be surprised if that's what happened."

There were nods of agreement and several comments from the others that they had heard the same rumors.

"Toklat, what's your input?"

"Well sir, I think we should just ignore the whole episode and let the civilian authorities handle it."

Gerchenoff replied, "That's somewhat my opinion also, but I would like to know who killed him and why. There's one possibility that comes to mind. We just got back from a wild goose chase to the Rock Creek area to look for Jonas. This tip came from Aimo via Vilho. This may have been a way to trap Aimo, and Vilho did him in for being a spy. I think we might have to take a hard, close look at Vilho as he's also Jonas' best friend."

Toklat came back with, "I doubt we will ever know. These Finns are close-mouthed. I suspect that, even if they did know, they wouldn't do anything about it. I doubt they'll spend much effort to find the culprit."

"Very well," said Gerchenoff, "We'll let it drop for now. I want everyone to keep eyes and ears open for anything that might shed light on the reason for his killing. I also want all of you to keep your eyes open for a replacement for Aimo. We need to know more of what goes on in the community. Let me know if you see anything unusual about Vilho's activities. Right now our primary job is to track down the rebel, Jonas. There has to be some people helping him. We suspect the Lehtinen family as Emma is his fiance. We had a good spy in Aimo living next door, but he's gone. He saw Jonas come out of their house, and we chased him. He could have been visiting Emma, or he could have been getting supplies or both. The Lehtinen family interrogation produced nothing."

Matt happened to be in the orderly room when Toklat came in as the duty officer. Matt got the gist of the meeting as Toklat related it to the first sergeant. Matt breathed a sigh of relief for Vilho.

Chapter 17

Marriage Proposal

SIX WEEKS HAD GONE BY and winter still dragged on. Jonas woke up feeling vaguely depressed, lethargic and reluctant to get out from under the warm covers to rekindle the fire. Not getting up at all crossed his mind; the cold was too much. The fire was nearly out, and it would take a long time to get the cabin warm. He felt like staying in bed until spring came to warm his chilly bones.

Knowing he couldn't lie abed all day, he threw off the covers, leaped out of bed and headed for the fireplace. He stirred the coals until he had a small heap glowing. Some shavings and birch bark curls piled on the coals, started a flame. They ignited quickly with a few curls of smoke and shooting sparks. The flames threw eerie shadows on the walls of the still dark cabin. Larger and larger pieces caught fire as Jonas added them. The fire was going good. Shivering, he pattered back to bed in his bare feet to stay warm until the cabin heated.

Laying there thinking of Emma, he knew the reason for his depression. He hadn't seen the love of his life for a long time.

"Can we ever get back together again like normal people?" he asked himself. "Will I keep on running and hiding until they catch and kill me? How much more of this nomadic life can I stand?" The more he thought about his circumstances, the more depressed he became.

"Those Russians have messed up my life. Nothing I really wanted has worked out. Maybe I could have acted a little differently, but then I would have felt less like a man."

The fire had warmed the cabin by then, so he got up and fixed breakfast. Emma flooded back into his thoughts as he sat down to eat. A warm glow came over him, just thinking about her. She was his beacon, his guiding light, his main reason for being alive.

"What's she doing right now?" he mused. "She's probably getting up to have breakfast with her family. I can see her moving around the kitchen, helping her mother. I have to see her."

In that instant, he made up his mind to go to her. Making a quick sandwich to take along was the only delay. The adrenalin started to flow with the excitement of seeing Emma.

Quickly throwing his gear together, he grabbed his rifle from the pegs as he started for the door. He retrieved his skis from their hiding place behind the big spruce tree. It felt good gliding on his skis through the soft snow. The familiar *shush shush* relaxed him as he pushed toward Emma.

The Russian camp and its activities crossed his mind. No doubt they still looked for him. Their last grid patterns indicated that they had not given up. Jonas knew the Russian mind too well to think they would give up. They would lose too much face.

Jonas daydreamed about something big happening in Russia. All the Russians would go home. He wondered what freedom would be like in a land where it had not been known for a long time.

"Quit daydreaming!" he told himself. "Think of what you can do despite their being here. Think what you can do to get them to move out."

He shushed on through the snow, still thinking of freeing his people from the yoke of Russian tyranny.

Time passed quickly on his familiar route to town. Cautious as ever, he stopped often to check his back trail and peer ahead intently to see if he could discern any movement. There was none.

He arrived at the hilltop overlooking town. No unusual activity caught his attention. He lingered a little longer, savoring the delight of seeing Emma. Just looking at her house from afar gave him a tingle.

Once more he resumed the journey. Darkness settled with the short, winter days still hanging on. Seeing Emma's all clear window shade signal, he moved in. Carrying his skis over his shoulder, he would look like anyone else coming in from an outing.

Putting his skis in the corner of the rear entry, he knocked. Anna answered the door. Jonas put his finger to his lips and walked in.

Emma asked, "Who is it mother?"

"Just an old friend," Anna replied.

Jonas walked into the living room. Emma looked up, saw him and gave a squeal of delight as she bounced up to kiss him.

He held her for a long time, savoring the moment before he spoke, "Oh, God, how I missed you."

They held the embrace, content to be in each other's arms.

Anna interrupted, "Jonas, are you hungry for some good home-cooked food?"

"Am I ever? I sure get tired of my own cooking."

"That's all you ever think about," laughed Emma. "You'd give me up in an instant for food."

"Yes, but, oh, what food! One would almost kill for your mother's

151

cooking."

"Seriously," asked Anna, "what would you like to eat?"

"Anything would be just fine," said Jonas going back to Emma.

Anna retired to the kitchen. Emma and Jonas sat on the couch holding hands. Emma brought him up to date on the latest news about the Russians including Vilho killing Aimo.

Jonas didn't have much to say when she asked him about events in his life. "Same old routine—eat, sleep, wonder about the Russians and think about you. Mostly I think about you."

Anna announced that food was on the table. It was a repast fit for a king—sausage, eggs, fried potatoes, buttermilk biscuits, good strong coffee laced with heavy cream, home made jam, and wild honey.

Emma and Anna sat, watching Jonas eat. Both of them urged him to eat more until he felt he was to the point of bursting.

"I don't know if I could stand being around the two of you for long. I'd get fat as a hog. I feel like one right now as much as I ate."

Anna shooed them back into the living room while she cleaned the kitchen.

Jonas asked, "Where's Toivo and Matt?"

"They're at a secret meeting of the resistance group," said Emma. "They're planning ways to get relief from the Russian oppression. Mother's afraid father will get into trouble."

"Oh, don't worry about the old buzzard. He can take care of himself. Besides, what trouble can he get into if it's a secret meeting?"

"I know he's tough," said Emma, "but I still worry about him. Matt's younger, but he's more level headed."

In a comfortably quiet moment between them, Emma said, "Jonas, I think we should get married no matter what. Who knows how long this occupation will go on. I'll soon be a wrinkled old hag, and you won't want me any more."

Jonas laughed and said, "That'll be the day when I don't want you."

"I'm serious, Jonas!"

Jonas stopped laughing and held her hand. "I know. I've given it a lot of thought, too. I've been hiding out for nearly two years, and I think we need some kind of life together. I found a place that might do for us to live. I found it quite by accident last summer when I was looking for a place to stock emergency food and water. It's a plateau, a flat place on top of a large bluff with spruce trees surrounding a clearing. It has its own spring. It's mostly sandstone up there, and that can hold a lot of water. I couldn't figure why everything was so green until I discovered the spring. I immediately thought of it as a good place to hide as it has all the elements needed for survival. One man could hold off an army up there. You could have an escape path down the other side. There's only one way you can get to it. You have to climb a small, narrow path. Up there you could spot anyone a mile away and hold them off. I thought of building us a cabin there."

Emma said, "It sounds idyllic. I wish you could take me there soon."

"I can build us a cabin out of spruce logs. It wouldn't be our permanent home, but it would do for now and until we get out of this mess with the Russians."

"Oh, Jonas, we could get started on it right away."

"Whoa, what's with this 'we,' thing? You can't go up there with me yet. I'll start the cabin. When we're married, we'll go there together."

Emma brightened. "Then you agree we should get married?"

"Yes, but I thought it was the man who proposed the marriage. What happened to that quaint old custom?"

"If I waited for you to get around to proposing," she said with a toss of her head, "it would never get done."

"I keep hoping our situation will get back to normal so we could live like ordinary people."

Suddenly, they were both talking and getting excited about the real possibility of getting married and having a life together.

Jonas dampened it by saying, "What are we going to do for money? We can't take money from your parents. I feel bad about not paying them for what they've done for me so far. I still have some money left from my savings, but that won't last long. Your parents are always giving me food from the garden and such, but we can't lean on them forever."

"They don't mind a bit. It doesn't amount to that much anyway. Besides, you always bring in game or fish that offsets what little they give you. Father would give you anything in return for fresh fish and game."

"My brother could pay me something for my share of the farm," Jonas said. "I doubt I'll ever go back to the old homestead. He loves the old place and probably would like to buy my half. That money would last a while. I'll write and see if we can get Matt to deliver it. I don't trust the postal service. The Russians might be watching his mail."

They discussed plans of when and where they would get married.

Anna came in and asked, "Why have you two got your heads so close together? What are you hatching up?"

"Oh, mother, Jonas just proposed. We're going to get married!"

Anna said, "I never thought you would get around to proposing, Jonas. Are you sure it wasn't Emma that proposed?"

Emma and Jonas looked at each other. Emma laughed and said, "Well, I guess it was kind of mutual."

"I thought so," said Anna.

Jonas said, "I still have to have your father's permission."

153

"I think he'll give us his blessing," said Emma.

Anna asked, "When and where is this event going to take place?"

"We're not that far along in our thinking," Emma said. "Jonas wants to build us a place to live first."

Anna retired to the kitchen to let them make plans.

"First I'll have to build the house where we'll live, and that takes time," said Jonas. "I'll go up as soon as I can. The logs need to be cut so they'll dry before I build. The weather is going to be the big factor for my trips to the site. I need snow storms to cover my tracks."

"How long," asked Emma, "before you finish it and we move in?"

"I don't know. Probably late spring or early summer. Why?"

"We need to set the wedding date. There's a lot a bride has to do."

"Don't plan on a big, fancy wedding with a lot of guests," said Jonas. "The Russians could show up and spoil our honeymoon."

"Oh my, I completely forgot about that. We'll have to plan it private and quiet."

Jonas thought of all the tools and supplies he was going to need to build the cabin. Emma thought of all the furnishings needed to make the house a home.

"Do you trust the minister enough to tell him ahead of time?"

"I think so, but you never know," answered Emma.

"How could we not tell him until the last minute?"

"You could hide in the church on Sunday when we're sure he'll be there. He greets people outside after service and then goes back to close up. We could wait until he went back in and explain the situation. We'd have a quiet wedding with family and a few friends. Before anyone was the wiser, we'd be gone."

"Vilho'll be my best man. Who would you get for maid of honor?"

"I don't know. I'll have to think about it."

"For now, we'll let the immediate family and Vilho know our plans. No one else needs to know until the last minute."

"Jonas, do you think you could have the house finished by June? I would like a June wedding. Then we would have the rest of the beautiful summer together."

"I'll try my best to get it done by then."

Emma let out a small sigh, knowing full well Jonas would have the cabin ready in June because she wished it.

Jonas said, "Contact Vilho and tell him the wedding'll be around the middle of June. The only reason I want him to know is that he takes time off to go fishing in June. I want him here."

"I don't know if he'll get time off then. The Russians are trying to get all enlisted men to stay and help hunt you down. A lot of soldiers are mad that they can't get time off to help with the spring planting at home. There are a few, not many, that are saying they wish they could catch you so everything would get back to normal."

"Those cowards," Jonas growled. "Are they willing to call living under the Russian tyranny normal? Who said that anyway?"

"I don't know, Jonas. You know how rumors float around."

"I know, but it still makes me mad."

Matt and Toivo came home from the meeting. Toivo didn't bother saying hello but went into a tirade related to the meeting. "Some people around here can't see the nose on their own face. Several people said it wasn't bad living under Russian rule. We had a knock-down, dragged-out fight. Fortunately, only a few thought that way, but it still makes me mad. I don't know if they'll come around to our way of thinking. A few might bear watching."

Jonas asked, "How many were at the meeting?"

"About thirty."

"How many were for the Russians?"

"Three to be exact," replied Toivo. "I guess that's not bad for that big a group. You have to expect a few to go along with the line of least resistance regardless of the consequences for the future."

Toivo began to calm down.

Jonas said, "We have some good news. Emma has consented to marry me if you'll give your blessing."

"It's about time," said Toivo. "You have problems right now, but they'll work out, especially with a good woman behind you all the way. I don't know what I would have done with my life without Anna here."

Anna smiled, putting her arm around Toivo's waist, saying, "I wish you two all the happiness in the world. Toi and I have had a good life together, and I hope you two can have the same."

"I know we will," said Emma.

Matt came from upstairs just in time to hear the news.

Matt said, "Congratulations Jonas. I couldn't ask for a better brother-in-law. I'm glad for you, sister."

They all said good night and went off to bed. Emma lingered a little while to talk and kiss Jonas good night.

"Another bit of news is that John Barloff is probably available as an accomplice of sorts to the resistance movement. I talk with Elsa a lot, and she tells me how much John admires you and is in your debt for saving his life. I don't know how we could use him and still be safe, but he's there."

"I'll have to think about that some. I know he could be invaluable to us if I can think of some safe way to use him without exposing us or him."

"See you in the morning, Jonas," said Emma giving him another little peck on the cheek as she went on to bed.

"Good night, Sweetheart."

Jonas slept fitfully that night. He woke up dreaming about the Russians chasing him and Emma. He was having a hard time protecting her. He got back to sleep and dreamed they were running again, but this time they were carrying a baby.

He woke up, saying to himself, "No babies until we're safe. It's going to be bad enough to bring Emma into this mess, but a baby!"

Jonas got up the next morning, feeling out of sorts from lack of sleep. Emma met him in the kitchen. She said, "You look glum this morning, Jonas. Have a change of heart during the night?"

"No, but I dreamed the Russians chased us all over the country."

"Well, remember that they're just dreams," said Emma kissing him on the cheek and turning back to her breakfast chores.

After breakfast, Jonas put together a list of tools needed to build the cabin. Toivo looked over his shoulder. He said, "I've got most of those tools. You're welcome to them. I don't do much carpenter work anymore."

"I hate to take your tools, Toi."

"That's all right, Jonas. You're practically one of the family now, and I know you'll take good care of them."

Jonas assembled the most essential tools. The rest would wait for a later trip. The tools along with his regular supplies made quite a load.

Jonas said, "I'll get them there, even if it breaks my back."

"It looks like it might do just that," said Toivo. "I thought you weren't going to the site until after the snow melted?"

"I'm not going there right now. There's a cave close by where I can leave the tools. Later, I'm going up there to cut trees before warm weather makes the sap rise.

With marriage and the cabin on his mind, Jonas spent the night like a caged bear. He was anxious to get to work. Even though he couldn't work on the cabin, he could make some furniture.

Early the next morning, he bolted breakfast, kissed Emma good-bye and was out the door. On his way home, he would detour to drop the tools in the cave, keeping the ones needed for furniture making. A practiced weather eye told him snow would fall in a few hours. It would hide his trail, but he worried the storm might hit full force before he reached his cabin.

The snow came even quicker than he thought. Within the hour, a few big, wet flakes began floating down, clinging to his clothes. He looked up into the sky and had to blink as flakes hit his eyes. He didn't like the looks of the oncoming storm.

He hurried on, hoping to beat the brunt of the storm. The snow would cover his tracks, but it was more important to get to cover. This looked to Jonas like a bad, wet, late winter storm. Wet snow clinging to trees would make traveling through the woods miserable.

He skied on, noting where he was in relation to the cabin. He thought about where he could take cover, but no place came to mind.

Visibility deteriorated; he couldn't recognize landmarks a few feet away. He tried to stick to the ridgetop, but several times he felt the ground drop away before he realized he was going off the slope. Every time he returned up slope, he feared getting turned around. To keep some sense of direction, he watched the snow flakes. He knew the wind probably was out of the west, but it could change and thoroughly confuse him.

He shushed along with his clothes getting wetter and wetter. Each time he brushed a bush or tree more wet snow fell on him. With the snow and perspiration, he was getting soaked. Even if he could find shelter, he would probably freeze, unless he could build a fire and get dry.

Landmarks got less distinct. Jonas had to admit defeat. He had to stop and find shelter, but where, how? He had to keep warm. He feared blundering off into one of the steep ravines, breaking a leg or worse and no one would ever know. He thought of the irony of it, just when life was looking so bright for him and Emma.

He stumbled into a big spruce windfall. Snow had drifted along it from previous storms, creating a big drift. He went to the deepest drift near the upturned trunk to see if it could shelter him. Using his ski as a shovel, he dug a large hole in the drift. When the hole was big enough, he crawled in, enlarging it with his mittened hands. It was warm and cozy inside. When he got it large enough, he dragged his pack and skis in after him.

Rummaging through his pack, he found Emma's fresh bread, along with some cheese. He felt better after he ate.

He mused, "Well maybe I can sit this one out right here. A fire, I do need a fire or these clothes will freeze me to death."

Digging down with his mittened hands, he broke off a few dry twigs. He scraped a bare place inside the snow cave to lay out his fire makings. The small twigs caught fire immediately, warming up his snow cave. He broke off more twigs to keep it going. The small amount of smoke drifted out the hole. The warmth seeped into his body, he stretched out his legs and was soon fast asleep.

Several hours later he woke with his teeth chattering. He was numb. He blinked several times trying to clear his mind and remembered where he was. Every muscle in his body ached. He looked for his fire. Snow had fallen off the roof of the snow cave, putting it out.

Realizing hypothermia might be setting in, he knew he had to get a fire started or get moving to get circulation going, but he just lay unable to move.

From somewhere, he heard Emmas's voice gently chiding him. "Jonas, get up and get out of there!"

He still didn't stir. It was much easier to go back to sleep.

The voice came again, more insistent. "Jonas, move!"

Finally, he stirred enough to look out the snow cave opening. It was still snowing but not as hard.

He crawled out with great effort. He felt like some one had beat him all over his body. He pulled his pack out, shouldered it, then bent over to put on his skis. It took great effort to get this done. Finally, he got his skis moving. The effort restored his circulation, and he started to feel better.

He recognized where he was in relation to the cabin. This gave him renewed strength and hope. Blood circulation increased, and he was back to his old self. His stiffness disappeared.

While it was still snowing quite hard, he could make out a few familiar landmarks. A long time later, his old, familiar cabin came into sight. He breathed a sigh of relief as he walked in and threw down his pack. It was good to be home.

Jonas immediately built a roaring fire. He stripped to the buff and rubbed himself down with a rough towel to warm himself, then put on dry clothes. He added wood to the fire and lay down on the bed. Several hours later, he woke up, looked about and remembered the voice telling him to get moving. "Was it really Emma's voice or delirium? I must remember to ask Emma if she felt anything about then." He lay thinking about it but came to no conclusion. He was happy to be safe and sound in his cabin.

Chapter 18

The Cabin

SPRING, FINALLY CAME. The snow melted quickly, turning the ground into a soft carpet. Jonas was extra careful not to leave foot prints.

Several hard trips into town saw his cache of tools grow. Everything he needed to start his project he stored in the cave. Inbetween time, he made furniture. Two straight-back chairs and a rocker made from willow wood and rawhide turned out to be quite handsome pieces. He planned to take them to the cabin as soon as the roof was in place.

He enlarged the lean-to, built earlier, for more comfort as he planned to stay at the site as much as possible. The logs were cut, limbed and the bark peeled. They weren't quite as dry as he would have liked, but they would have to do. He let the trees lay where they fell. He had to measure what he needed and skid it to the building site. Ax work he saved for rainy or windy days when the sound wouldn't carry.

The foundation dug and built of rock was sturdy. It had to be made extra thick as he had no cement. Bound together with mud and grass, once dry, it worked well.

But all of it was back-breaking work. At night he fixed a small supper, fell into bed exhausted to wake up at dawn stiff and sore but ready to go. After all, the cabin was the labor of love. The notches he cut on a stick each morning to keep track of days told him he was behind in his timetable for June. He pondered how to speed up the work.

At first he shrugged and said to himself. "Work harder."

Ax work delayed the project. The weather didn't cooperate. The ringing of his ax did not carry on windy days, and on rainy days the Russians wouldn't be out. But, as fine weather held, he had to content himself with chores like carrying rock for his fireplace and chimney. He wanted Emma to have both a cook stove and fireplace. For this he would have to have cement. He wasn't looking forward to back packing cement all the way to the remote site.

The logs went together well, each fitted and notched to mate with the one below it. Not even a piece of paper fit between the logs when he had snugged them into place. Sphagnum moss provided added insulation between the logs and would take up any future shrinkage. It would be a cozy, tight cabin.

One night, the wind died completely. Jonas knew it would probably stay that way for several days. He dressed and headed for town to get cement. With cement he could work on the fireplace on quiet days and on the logs when the wind blew enough to dissipate the ax noise.

The thought of seeing Emma cheered him, but he knew he couldn't stay. The work had to get done. But he would enjoy telling Emma about the progress he was making on the cabin.

When he arrived, it was still dark enough to negotiate the open stretch to Emma's house without being seen. No light in the house told him no one was up yet. He had to knock several times before Toivo called through the door, "Who is it?"

Jonas answered, "Your future son-in-law."

Toivo quickly threw open the door and called for Emma.

Emma ran down the stairs in her night gown to throw herself into Jonas' arms with wild abandon. She tilted her face up for a kiss.

Toivo said, "I got you two sacks of cement. How many do you think you'll need?"

"Just one more if I fit the rocks up real close. Don't buy any more yet, I may not need the third bag if I do some really close rock fitting.

"I have to get some more anyway as I told them down at the store that I was doing some cement work in the sauna and barn. I have to do some of that to keep them from knowing about you."

"I'm sorry this is creating additional work for you"

"That's all right, I needed to get some of these projects done a long time ago. This is making me do them now."

Anna had breakfast ready quickly and bade them sit down and eat.

Jonas waited until dark before he packed to leave. The cement and a few other items went into his rucksack. The cement's weight limited how much extra he could carry.

Vilho had made him a fireplace grate and swing for kettles. Toivo had made two windows from scratch, but Jonas could only carry one of them at a time. A pack animal would help, but that was out of the question. Jonas was going to have to be his own mule.

A small cast iron cook stove with oven was picked up by Vilho. Dismantled, it had taken two trips getting it to the cabin site. Furnishing a home was turning out to be a big job.

All the trips from town to the new cabin site and back to his old cabin made Jonas nervous. The Russians hadn't given up their search. Their predictable patterns made it fairly safe, but they might change patterns. A

160

random patrol—like the one returning for the birthday party of the Cossack Hetman—might catch him any time.

Packed and ready to go, Jonas delayed leaving, wanting to stay with Emma a few more minutes. They sat by the fire talking and making plans. The wedding date was now set for June 15. Jonas knew he would have the cabin done by then. The waiting was unbearable.

It was late before he said good-bye. Emma finally said, "I hate your having to leave, but I know you have a long trek. I don't want you out there when the patrols start. Remember we'll have the rest of our lives together."

"You're right my love. I'll get on my way."

Emma kissed him good-bye as he went out the door.

It was a long, arduous journey back to the cabin site; he didn't arrive until the next evening. The heavy pack forced him to rest more often. On the way, he vowed not to waste one drop of cement. He reached the cabin site tired and hungry. After a cold meal, he fell into his lean-to and slept.

Most days he wasn't sure what job to do first. The next morning, the wind blew hard, dictating ax work. The wind was welcome, as his ax work was falling behind and it had to keep pace with the other work. For two days it blew, allowing him to get much done on the main structure.

When the wind died, he went to work on the fireplace. He would lay up a few tiers of rock and let them set while he carried more rock from the surrounding area. He chipped many stones to get them to fit closely. The pinging of the rock hammer didn't carry like the ring of ax on wood.

Dead tired at night but too keyed up to sleep, he sat by his small fire whittling wooden pegs. Jonas drove the pegs into drilled holes on each corner log to hold them in place. He even made pegs for each log at window and door openings. He wanted this cabin to be secure.

For a while the wind blew hard every day, allowing Jonas to choose which task to do on the building. It progressed rapidly. All the logs were up, most of the chimney and fireplace done. Cedar shakes were split for the roof. Most of this was done at night by firelight. With the roof on he would have shelter for himself and could work inside when the inevitable spring rains came.

He had just put the last shakes in place when the rains moved in. He said to himself, "This will be a good test to see if I built a good tight roof."

It rained for several days. No leaks.

Though he had no windows or doors in yet, Jonas was out of the weather and could work inside whenever it rained.

The floor was in and smoothed. It would not do for his Emma to walk on a floor full of splinters. Windows and doors came next, neatly closing the cabin. It was beginning to look like a home.

Jonas diverted the spring so it would run directly into the cabin. He made a large hole and lined it with rock so the water would stay clear. He built rock shelves above the spring to keep food cool.

The fireplace and chimney were complete. Another two trips into town brought out the cook stove and pipe. Jonas liked the cook stove. Meals over an open fire were eliminated, and the stove stayed warm most of the night to keep the interior of the cabin comfortable. The visibility of rising smoke ruled out a fire on calm days.

Then he cut and split wood so Emma would have good dry wood for cooking. Dry wood would not give off much smoke, so they could have a fire on days with just a little wind.

By the first of June, the cabin was nearly done, except for a few finishing touches. The hard work was done and well worth the effort. His hands had gone from tender, to blisters, to heavy callouses. His body had new trim, not that he was ever out of shape. A little weight loss he attributed to work and not taking time to fix proper meals.

He needed one more trip into town to stock the cabin with staples. All other items they needed would he brought to the cabin after they were married. Emma would want to bring many items of her own.

A small-boy excitement welled up in him to see Emma and tell her the cabin was finished. Swinging his rucksack to his back, picking up his rifle, he was on his way. At the edge of the clearing, he paused to look back and admire his work. The new spruce logs—all peeled and shining in the morning sun—contrasted with the dark green background. The door and the kitchen faced east to get the first morning sun. Nestled against the back drop of green spruce trees, the cabin looked like someone had just painted it on canvas. "I hope Emma will like it," Jonas said to himself as he started down the trail. "One more trip into town after this, and I'll be bringing her back with me."

He chose a new route to town, and he had to be extra careful. His old way was so familiar that, if anything were amiss, he would spot it immediately. Not so on this new path.

Out of the corner of his eye, he caught some movement. He stopped immediately, his brain working all the possibilities of hide, fight, or run. Then he saw a doe with two fawns that didn't sense he was near. The fawns had wintered well. It was always the young that suffered the most in the long, hard winters. The deer saw him, raising their white flags to jump away gracefully.

Jonas realized how much he liked living in the forest. He saw nature as God intended, free and wild. An inner peace came over him. Tension about building the cabin, making the extra trips to town and preparing for the wedding had weighed on him. The small incident with the deer did wonders to bring him peace of mind.

Thinking of the deer and all that nature had brought to him had sharpened his senses. Without the experience with the deer, he would not have become alert as quickly. His mind said, "Smoke! Wood smoke!"

He stopped, looking around carefully. He couldn't see a thing.

"There, there it is again. I smell smoke. "The wind is in my face or nearly so. The smoke is coming from in front of me. I'm too far from town to be picking up that smoke, and no lakes or streams are close where someone might be fishing. It's too early for hunting or berry picking. A wood cutter wouldn't be out this far, and he wouldn't have a fire at this time of day."

Jonas moved behind a large tree. Gently shrugging off his pack, he retrieved his telescope. Maneuvering his telescope around the tree trunk, he scanned the area. An occasional whiff of smoke drifted back to him. Directly in front of him stood a small hill. Possibly, the fire was somewhere over the brow of the hill. It wouldn't do to walk over the hill to see where it was coming from, though. Better to go around. He scanned the whole area again to make sure he wasn't being watched covertly from some vantage point. Everything looked normal and in place.

A long circle to the right moved him to heavy cover between himself and the brow of the hill. Slowly, he circled it. Now he saw the tell-tale smoke of a camp fire. At first he could discern no movement or people, but, when he glassed the area, he saw three people lounging around the fire. They were soldiers with their field uniforms of grey-brown that blended well into the back ground, one a Russian officer and the other two enlisted men. At first he couldn't tell if they were Finnish enlisted men or Russian. Finally, he saw the yellow crescent on their collars indicating they were Russian. The Finns were not allowed to wear the yellow crescent. He studied them for a long time and could not come to any logical conclusion other than that they were on a random watch for him. It was cool, so they had a fire going, more than likely against orders. He was glad they built the fire, otherwise he might have stumbled into them. If this was going to be their practice, he was going to have to be extra careful. Random watches could be anywhere.

Jonas eased back below the brow of the hill to skirt the operation. He hoped there wasn't a line of observation posts. He moved carefully and cautiously all the way to town. At the edge of town he had to wait until total darkness before crossing the open ground. He saw several groups of three and four Russians come out of the forest and head back to camp. Now he was sure they were setting up random forest watches for him. He vowed to be extra careful or else travel only at night. After dark, he swung his pack up to walk across the field to his beloved Emma.

Chapter 19

Marriage

ON HIS LAST TRIP INTO TOWN before he and Emma were to be married, Jonas had a hard time keeping up with all the details. The old axiom that the most useless person at a wedding was the groom seemed to be holding true.

Jonas arrived at the Lehtinen house to discuss ways to keep problems to a minimum. The Russians didn't pose any new threat, but the house was under scrutiny since they lost their spy, Aimo.

"There's a possible problem with my being in the church ahead of time," Jonas said. "Emma, I know you want a church wedding, but there are some problems with that plan that I hadn't thought of until now."

"You mean we can't have a church wedding?" asked Emma.

"I know how badly you want that, but think about this. One, I have to break into the church. Two, we get married, but I have to stay there until after dark or risk someone seeing me. We're not altogether sure of the minister, who could accidentally or purposely tip someone that I was there. The safest course is to invite the minister and his wife for Sunday morning breakfast. Then we can get married here at the house and take off immediately for our cabin. The only danger will be when we cross from the house into the woods. Even if someone gets the word, we will be long gone."

"I see your point," said Emma.

"Well," said Anna, "I'll have to clean the house from top to bottom."

"Why?" asked Emma, "The only ones not here now are the minister, his wife, and the maid of honor."

"You're right," said Anna, "What am I getting upset about? All I care about is seeing you two get married."

They scheduled the wedding for Sunday two weeks hence.

"Well, that's settled. Let's go into the kitchen for some coffee and fresh baked rolls," said Anna.

They moved into the kitchen to sample Anna's rolls. The talk still centered around the wedding and the reason for holding it in the house.

Toivo said, "Someday we'll get back to normal where we can have a simple church wedding without having to worry about the Russians."

"That can't come too soon to suit me," said Emma, "I'm getting tired of their domineering arrogance."

Jonas said, "One more person I would like to see at the wedding is John Barloff and his new wife. I know it's a bit dangerous, but, from what Vilho has told me, he's been helping our movement a lot. We did become close friends while his leg was healing. We were kindred souls, so to speak, with me talking about my love for Emma and he of his love for Elsa.

Vilho replied, "I think we can solve that problem without any danger to you. I've talked to both of them several times, and they've been a big help on the movement. I'll ask him and Elsa if I can come over to discuss the movement. I'll go to his house early Sunday morning and invite him over here at the last minute.

"Vilho, you've solved that problem well. I'll look forward to seeing John and meeting his wife, Elsa, for the first time. He told me so much about her, I feel like I already know her."

After much talk and almost as much eating, the family disbursed, leaving Emma and Jonas alone.

"I know you really wanted that church wedding," Jonas said. "We'll get remarried in the church when life returns to normal. In a way, I'm glad that we're marrying here. If we got married in the church, we would have to stay here the first night. It'd be too late to start for the cabin. This way we can leave right after the ceremony and arrive at the cabin with a little day left. I really want you to see that place for the first time in the daylight."

"I thought of that too," Emma said, "and I'm glad it's going this way. I want our first night together to be just the two of us."

"The only thing keeping me going is that we'll soon be together. If I don't keep telling myself that, I'll go out of my mind with the waiting."

"When you go back to the cabin tomorrow, would you mind taking some of my things with you? I know we'll have a lot to carry when we go in after the marriage."

"I don't mind at all," said Jonas with a smile.

"Mostly curtains and such, little things to make the place homey."

"With you there it'll be home regardless," said Jonas with passion.

They talked on into the night, neither wanting to leave.

Anna called from the top of the stairs. "Emma let Jonas go to sleep or he'll fall asleep on his feet going back."

With one more good night kiss, Emma left reluctantly for bed.

Jonas tossed and turned, thinking about what problems might confront them in the wilderness.

"I wouldn't care about myself, but I could never forgive myself if something happened to her."

Jonas had barely fallen asleep when he felt Emma gently shaking him awake. He opened one eye to see Emma bending down to kiss him.

"Good morning, sleepy head. It's time for you to be up and on your way."

"Would you be trying to get rid of me?"

She giggled. "Your breakfast will be ready as soon as you get dressed and wash up. I was going to say shaved, but you're still wearing that winter beard. Would you shave it off for the wedding?"

"If you want it off, it will come off. It did help keep my face warm this winter. The beard might help disguise my identity. The only identification they have of me is an artists drawing with my moustache. Not many Russians looking for me now have seen me in person."

"That's something to think about, but I like you better without the beard. Right now you look like a big woolly bear."

"The beard will come off for the wedding," he promised.

She tickled his lip. "Keep the moustache. I kind of liked that."

"From an identification stand point, it might be better if I took it off. What the heck. They aren't going to catch me, so why worry about it?"

With that Emma went back into the kitchen. Jonas dressed.

Jonas sat down to a loaded breakfast table, saying, "You put out a big breakfast, Anna. I'm hungry, but I don't know if I can put it all away."

"You'll need all the energy you can get," said Emma. "Wait until you see the load you're going to have to take back to the cabin for me. It's really not all that much, but it's things I need."

"You always said I was as stubborn as a mule and now you're going to load me up like one."

Emma laughed, saying, "Oh, it's not that heavy, just kind of bulky, curtains and the like."

It was bulky. Even stuffed tightly into his rucksack plus an extra roll tied to the outside. Jonas said, "It looks like I might have to make two trips if it gets any bigger. Do you really need all this stuff?"

"Yes, silly, a woman needs all that and more to make a house a home."

Jonas shouldered the pack, gave Emma a big hug and kiss and was out the door.

Emma called after him, "See you about the fourteenth. Don't leave me standing at the altar."

"No way would I do that to you," he threw back.

Jonas entered the woods admiring the beautiful spring day.

"Maybe it's just because I'm so full of love," he told himself. "It's pleasant to be off skis and even better not having to worry about leaving tracks in the snow."

He walked on, enjoying the heady smell of spring and all the new plants growing. The forest floor felt soft, carpeted with new grass and spring flowers. The tree buds burst open showing their new, bright green colors.

"I hope the flowers last until after the marriage," he said. "Emma would like that. There should be lots of flowers to welcome her to our mountain-top retreat. It's right for it to be that way, and I'm sure it will be."

He came to the cabin almost before he knew it and couldn't remember details of the trip with his head in the clouds, enjoying the spring.

It was a joy to come into the clearing to see the cabin that was going to be his and Emma's home. Jonas was proud of the job he had done building it. He paused a moment, taking it all in. With the sun about to set, the cabin was shadowed by the tall spruce trees behind it. Long tapered shadows of the trees reached over the lawnlike clearing. A few fresh-cut stumps still showed. Jonas had been selective in choosing which trees to cut so not to disturb the overall appearance of the stand. All the debris of building had long since been cleared away. The cabin was all that remained of his long, hard labors. It only awaited the approval of his Emma.

He put everything away, laying out Emma's curtains carefully so they would not wrinkle. After supper he cleaned up to keep the kitchen spotless for Emma. The small fire in the cook stove took the slight chill off the cabin, making it feel cozy.

Jonas lit one of the kerosene lamps. It threw flickering shadows on the walls until it steadied down to a regular, even burn. Jonas kept looking for something he might have missed doing, but nothing came to him. He sat dreaming about the future before he blew out the lamp and went to bed.

The next two weeks dragged by for Jonas. He kept busy fishing and then smoking the fish for future use. The wind obliged by blowing steadily for several days, allowing him to run his smoker until the fish were done to perfection. He split more wood, giving them a plentiful supply of dry wood for the coming winter. He puttered around, stewed and fretted about everything being right for his bride.

The day came for him to leave. He packed his best clothes in his rucksack. He scrubbed the cabin down and straightened everything for the hundredth time. He really was the proverbial nervous bridegroom.

He looked back at the cabin just before he entered the trees to assure himself that it was still all right.

He said to himself, "Jonas, old boy, the next time you stand here it will be with your bride."

With that he set out with long, purposeful, distance-eating strides.

He thought, *I'll have to cut back my pace when Emma is with me. Right now she'd have to run to keep up with me. There are lots of changes I'm going to have to make when she gets here.*

At the hill overlooking the Lehtinen house, he stopped to make sure it was safe. It looked fine. The window shade was in the all-clear position. He waited impatiently for darkness to cover his movements.

Emma answered his knock immediately. She had probably waited impatiently for him. She kissed him quickly and led him into the house.

"Everyone's here for the big day tomorrow except John and Elsa. Vilho has contacted them and will fetch them before the ceremony tomorrow," said Emma, looking radiant. "The minister's coming for breakfast. He still doesn't know he's going to perform a marriage ceremony."

Mary Lahti, one of Emma's closest friend and the maid of honor, came out to greet Jonas. She was pert and lively with reddish-blond hair and the greenest eyes Jonas had ever seen. She had a habit of talking non-stop. Even when she wasn't excited she dominated the conversation.

She said, "You lucky man, you just don't know what a jewel you're getting in Emma."

"Oh, yes I do!" said Jonas.

"Mary is going to stay the night and help me to get ready in the morning," said Emma.

Jonas had shaved off his beard at the cabin. Emma kept looking at him strangely and said, "I just realized you shaved off the beard. I almost forgot what you looked like underneath that bunch of hair."

Mary said, "I never saw you with the beard. I'm sorry you shaved it off before I got a chance to see it. I'm partial to men with beards. No, I'm kind of partial to men in particular."

Everyone was jovial. Anna had outdone herself baking all kinds of sweets for the occasion. The kitchen table fairly groaned with the food she heaped on it for the occasion.

Matt said, "Mother has baked enough to feed the whole town. She's still thinking of a big wedding."

Jonas and Emma were in the living room. Toivo built a small fire to take off the evening chill.

Emma whispered to Jonas, "Vilho is paying a lot of attention to Mary. I have never seen him attracted to anyone before. Do you suppose he's catching love fever, seeing us getting married?"

"I hope so, that old reprobate ought to be thinking about getting married."

"Look who's talking! Vilho is twenty two, that's two years younger than you. You still wouldn't be here if I hadn't forced your hand a bit."

"A little bit!" said Jonas jokingly.

"Seriously Jonas, I think they would make a great couple."

"You can't push Vilho into anything. If he thinks you are, he has a tendency to get stubborn and go in the opposite direction."

"Mary'll get him to do what's right if that's what she wants."

"I know, I think she's even more devious than you."

"Devious, I'm not devious!" Emma said with a toss of her head. "I told you right from the start I was going to marry you!"

"You better tell Mary not to be too direct, or Vilho will bolt like a scared rabbit."

"Mary knows what she's doing. Even if Vilho is against marriage, he has yet to see Mary's determination if she really wants something."

Mary and Vilho came into the living room, carrying coffee and talking quietly. Jonas eyed his old friend covertly, wondering just what was going through his mind in relation to Mary.

Vilho came up to the two of them saying, "Well, old buddy, hunting and fishing friend, you're really going to take the big step in the morning?"

"Yes, I guess so," said Jonas somewhat embarrassed, "That coffee smells good. I'll get me a cup."

"No, let me get it for you," said Emma, "I'm going to start spoiling you right now."

When she was out of earshot, Vilho said, "I may not get a chance to talk to you later. I need a way to get in touch with you. The resistance movement is growing, and we may have to contact you. From what you told me, this place is far enough from your old cabin that our other message center may not do."

"It would be far. Do you remember that big hollow tree by Rock Creek where we got that honey several years ago?"

Vilho chuckled. "You got stung several times and looked like a stuffed toad."

"Well, we did get a lot of honey. Anyway we could use that tree like the other message center. There's a hole in the base of the tree where you could leave a message. Set a rock up on another rock just like we did before. I can see this tree from a long way off before I go in to retrieve the message. There's a small cave just north of it a few hundred yards if you have to hide or wait for me."

"Sounds like as good a plan as any."

Emma came back bearing coffee for Jonas. She looked from one to another and asked, "What are you talking about so seriously?"

"Just activities of the Russians," said Jonas not wanting her to start worrying about the resistance movement. "Mmm. This is good coffee."

Mary, maybe sensing that Jonas and Vilho needed more time to talk, said to Emma, "Let's go upstairs to make sure we have it all ready for the big event tomorrow." They skipped up the stairs.

Vilho picked up the thread of their conversation about the resistance movement. "Right now we have about a hundred men in the group. All of them have some reason to hate the Russians. They can make a good cadre to form other groups in this area and elsewhere."

"What about weapons?" asked Jonas.

"That's our biggest problem. They have a few old rifles. Weapons are our first priority. I heard rumors about new American-made Winchester repeating rifles that might be coming. If we could get our hands on them, it would go a long way towards equipping our men. We really need more guns if we're to expand. What we have now is inadequate. I am going to see if John has any information on the shipment while he is here."

"It sounds good," said Jonas somewhat distractedly, thinking more about the wedding than anything else.

Vilho let the subject drop but vowed to get Jonas more involved. He could think of no better leader for their group.

The women came downstairs and talked for a little while but that soon died down. Vilho went home and the rest went to bed, leaving Emma and Jonas alone. As she started for bed, she said, "This is your last day of freedom, Jonas. In the morning it'll be too late."

"I'll be right here in the morning," he assured her, "waiting for the minister to show up so we can get on with it."

Emma blew him a kiss as she went up the stairs.

Jonas woke early to a quiet house wondering what time it was. He lolled in bed, feeling lazy, enjoying the warmth and thinking about the coming day. He didn't know how long he had been awake when Anna came down to start breakfast. Anna hummed happily as she went about her chores, waiting for everyone else to come downstairs.

Anna planned a light, early breakfast before the minister got there for the big wedding breakfast. She knew the men would not want to wait that long to eat something.

Matt came down next and had a cup of coffee before he went out to heat the sauna, saying,"I suppose everyone will want a sauna before the wedding. It should be hot in about an hour."

Anna said, "That's good. Sit down and have some more coffee and rolls. It will be a couple of hours before we have the main meal."

Jonas got up and dressed, joining Anna and Matt in the kitchen. He said to Anna, "I need some of your good strong coffee to get me awake this morning. I've been awake for at least an hour but was too lazy to get up. I didn't sleep well last night."

"We have plenty of coffee and anything else you want. Are you having pre-marital jitters?"

"Well, maybe, just a little," he said laughing.

Emma and Mary came downstairs giggling about something one of them had said. Mary was animated and chattering like a magpie as usual.

Anna said, "You're giggling like a couple of young school girls."

"Oh mother, we don't get together that often. We're a bit excited and acting a little silly."

"Well, come sit down and have a bite to eat."

Just then Vilho came in with John and Elsa in tow.

Vilho said, "Let's go into the living room, John, I want you to see an old friend of ours."

As they entered the living room, Jonas stood up to greet John. John was so surprised, he couldn't say anything for a minute. He said quietly, "Jonas, I've been wondering if we would ever see each other again. I can't tell you how much I've thought about our time together in the wilderness and what a profound effect you've made on my life. And here is the light of my life, Elsa. Elsa, meet the fabulous Jonas I told you so much about."

"I'm so glad I got to meet you," Elsa said shyly.

"Great to meet you. John talked about you constantly while we were together and his leg was healing."

John said, "Speaking of my leg, it's perfect, thanks to your care."

Jonas said, "I've very glad. Besides breakfast, do you know why you're here today?"

John shook his head, looking from Jonas to Vilho.

Jonas grinned. "You and Elsa are special guests for my wedding with Emma this very morning."

John and Elsa both looked shocked. "When and where is this wedding going to be?" John said.

"This morning, here and now. The minister will be here shortly."

"Oh, Jonas, I feel so honored that you thought enough of me to have Elsa and me in on this important moment in your life."

"My pleasure. I appreciate the help you've given our movement."

"You were instrumental in that. If it weren't for the accident and our talks, I'd still be one of those looking for you under every bush and behind every tree. I still have to do that, but my heart isn't in it, and I know we're not coming close to catching you. They don't make me go on many of the search missions anymore. Maybe they're not sure where my loyalty lies."

"I am glad for all of it. Let's have some of Anna's light breakfast."

After a bite to eat, they went through the sauna to get refreshed before dressing for the occasion. Emma and Mary went upstairs to primp.

Jonas and Emma had packed and were ready to leave. As soon as the ceremony and breakfast were over, they would change clothes and be off, preferably before the minister left, so there would be no way anyone could pass word that Jonas was in the area.

There was no need to worry about the minister. He was as anti-Russian as anyone. They didn't know it at the time. They would learn later of his intense loyalty to his flock. For now, they weren't taking any chances.

Matt was looking out the window when he saw the minister and his wife pulling up in his horse and buggy. "Here comes the man of the hour."

Everyone stood up while Anna went to the front door to let them in.

"Good morning, Reverend and Mrs. Koski," Anna said in formal greeting. "I'm glad you could make it this morning."

Everything looked normal to Reverend Koski except that everyone was dressed better than usual.

When Jonas came downstairs all dressed up, he might have suspected something. Jonas said, "Reverend Koski, we would like you to perform the marriage ceremony for Emma and me."

The full impact didn't sink in as he said, "Well, Jonas, I didn't expect to see you here, what with all the rumors about where you are or that you might be dead. Yes, I'd be glad to marry you. When's the happy date?"

"Today. Right now," said Jonas.

He blinked rapidly. "Ah, yes, we can do that."

"Good," said Jonas, "Let's get on with it. Anna will you tell Emma and Mary that we're ready to start. We'll begin as soon as they come down."

The minister said, "I guess I'll go out to the buggy and get my Bible."

Anna said, "Here's our family Bible, if you don't mind. We would be honored if you would say the words from it."

"I would be glad to do that, and I understand completely."

Everyone assembled in the living room. Jonas and Vilho stood by the fireplace awaiting Emma's arrival so Toivo could give the bride away.

Emma came down the stairs all dressed in white, floating as if she were a cloud. Her hair shone like spun gold. Her face radiated happiness like Jonas had never seen before. It took his breath away.

He said softly to Vilho, "She is unbelievably beautiful. I have never seen her shine so in my life."

Vilho nudged him in the ribs and said, "Well this is her big day and yours too, of course."

Toivo took her arm at the stairs, escorting her into the living room.

Toivo brought Emma to stand beside Jonas and stepped back.

The ceremony was simple and over quickly, and Anna wiped tears from her eyes. Toivo smiled bravely, but a few small tears gave him away. Jonas kissed Emma tenderly after they were pronounced husband and wife.

The guests all patted the happy couple on the backs and wished them good luck and a long, happy marriage. Anna bustled about, telling everyone to sit down and eat before it went to waste. They sat down to enjoy Anna's efforts.

The minister said, "I wish this could have been in the church, but, under the circumstances, this is about the only way it could be done. Church

172

or no church, you're still husband and wife in the eyes of God."

"Thank you, Reverend," said Jonas, "Maybe, someday, when life gets back to normal, Emma and I will get remarried in the church."

Minister Koski said, "I would like to see that happen some day. I have been preaching peaceful coexistence with the Russians, but, recently, I have changed my mind. I don't think any strategy will work with these people. I hate violence, but, if that's what it's going to take, maybe we'll have to resort to that. Jonas, I really admire the way you have been fooling the Russians. You have purposely not gone out of your way to get them and yet you resist. I think all of us can resist, at least passively. If we don't cooperate in any way, they'll have a hard time existing in such a hostile environment."

"I'm glad to hear you say that, Reverend. We must all resist or we'll never be free," said Jonas.

"Are you and Emma going back into the wilderness?"

"Yes, it's still not safe for me here, and I have built a place out there for Emma and me to live."

"If you need help of any kind, let Toivo or Vilho know. I'll do anything short of disobeying God's laws."

"Thank you. Emma and I appreciate that. Right now we have to get on our way, or we'll not reach our destination before dark. We want to thank you, and I appreciate your confidence. I have often wondered how the people of this town felt about my actions against the Russians."

"You need not worry. The people are solidly behind you."

Emma changed her clothes and readied to leave. Jonas went upstairs and did the same. The family kissed them good-bye. They shouldered their packs and headed for the door. Matt, watching out the window, reported all clear for them to cross from house to wood.

As soon as they were in the woods, they stopped. Emma looked back at her house one more time.

Jonas gave her a light kiss, saying, "It's not as though we were leaving here forever. We'll be back from time to time, and maybe someday we'll be back for good when we get rid of the Russians."

"I hope it's soon."

Jonas asked jokingly, "What's in this pack? I may need a horse to pack it for me."

Emma laughed. "All the goods a woman needs for housekeeping. Besides I'm carrying a pack myself, a little smaller and lighter perhaps."

The trip back to the cabin went quickly. Jonas was more on the alert than ever with Emma with him. As they neared the cabin, Jonas stopped to examine the trail carefully in front of him.

"What are you doing?" asked Emma.

"Every time I leave, I tie this twig across the trail with light thread. If anyone went in ahead of us they would have broken the thread and not noticed it, but I would know immediately and be on the alert. I tie it high enough so no animal would break it. Further on I have three rocks set so no one can get by them easily without disturbing them. So far it looks good. If the rocks get disturbed, they'll go clattering down amongst those rocks below, telling us at the cabin that some one is coming. A little further on we have another alarm."

Down the trail, a hawk began screaming and diving at them.

Emma asked, "What's the matter with that bird?"

Jonas replied, "That's our other alarm. We're close to her nest in that dead tree. She screams that way whenever I come by here. Of course, when she goes south in the winter, we won't be able to rely on her."

As they got nearer the cabin Jonas stopped and took his telescope out of his pack. He approached a small clearing to glass both sides.

Again Emma asked, "What are you doing now?"

"This small area in front of us is our biggest danger. It's completely open and observable from both sides of the main land. Someone could see us going across, and we wouldn't know it. Right now it looks good. Over on the right is a doe and two fawns browsing. If anyone were around, they wouldn't be in that area or they would be on the alert."

"And on the left?" asked Emma.

"See those two crows in that dead tree? They wouldn't be there either. At least they would be giving some kind of alarm call."

They crossed the open area quickly and entered the spruce trees surrounding the cabin. Jonas gave a sigh of relief. He didn't realize how tense he had been.

He guided Emma to the edge of the clearing, pointed and said, "Emma there's our home."

"Oh, Jonas, it looks better than I ever imagined. I just love it."

They both half walked, half ran to the cabin, their packs keeping them from running fast. When they reached the door Jonas slid his pack to the ground and took Emma's pack from her. He opened the door and carried her over the threshold into their new home.

Emma said, "I'm proud of the way it looks. It's just wonderful."

"I'm so glad you like it," said Jonas gratefully.

"Who couldn't like it?" said Emma giving Jonas a big hug and kiss.

"Welcome home, Sweetheart," said Jonas returning her kiss.

They retrieved their packs from outside the door. Jonas lit one of the lamps, then the kindling in the cook stove that he had laid ready before he left for town. Emma prowled the cabin, ooing and ahing over all Jonas' handiwork. Jonas was pleased that she liked his efforts.

They were both slightly embarrassed at being alone for the first time. Each wondered what the other thought and how to proceed. They just stood there, looking into each other's eyes.

Emma spoke first. "Should we eat?"

"Are you hungry?" he asked not taking his eyes off her face.

"Not really. What about you?"

"Not yet."

With that Jonas picked her up and carried her to the bed. When he stood her on her feet again she looked at him, a little scared and doe-eyed. She stood stock still as Jonas started to undress her. He was slow and deliberate as he unbuttoned her blouse and slipped it from her shoulders.

She whispered, "I wanted to get into something soft and flimsy, but it's too late now."

"You're right," said Jonas nervously.

He kissed her on the neck and shoulders and then kissed her again full on the mouth. They were oblivious to everything else but each other.

Emma stepped back a little and unbuttoned Jonas' shirt, letting it fall to the floor.

Jonas stripped her undershirt from her to reveal her full, pointed breasts. He blushed slightly and the blood raced to his temples. Emma pushed her hard breasts into his bare chest and laid her head tightly under his chin holding him for a moment. She pulled away slightly to make him let go so she could sit down on the edge of the bed and remove her short boots. She stood up after she unlaced them and kicked them off. Then she reached up and kissed Jonas gently, softly, enjoying herself. Jonas reached down to unfasten her belt and push her underclothes over her hips. As they slid to the floor, Emma stepped forward to reveal her glistening white body to Jonas. He just stood back to drink in her beauty.

Emma stepped forward to undo Jonas' belt and get him undressed. The pace quickened as Emma fumbled with the unfamiliarity of men's clothing. She finally got his buttons undone to let his clothes drop to the floor only to discover that he still had his boots on. Emma stared and blushed at his nakedness. She had seen her brother when they were little but had never seen a mature male in full erection. She watched fascinated for a minute as it throbbed and pulsed with each heartbeat. She quivered inside and didn't quite know why.

Jonas sat down at the edge of the bed and pulled his clothes back over his knees so he could unlace his boots. He laid back on the bed to kick everything off. Emma couldn't believe the erection standing up straight as he lay there.

He stood up to take Emma in his arms. He hesitated for a moment not knowing where his maleness was going. It kind of went to one side as

175

he pulled her close. She could still feel the hardness of him and the hot throbbing against her cool body. He kissed her long and hard and then picked her up and laid her gently on the bed. He leaned over her, kissing her neck and shoulders. He worked down to her breasts kissing both. The nipples rose erect to meet him. Emma squirmed with a passion unfamiliar to her.

Emma reached over and tentatively touched his maleness. She shivered deliciously, feeling her own juices start to flow in anticipation.

Jonas reached down and laid the flat of his hand between her thighs covering the small patch of hair. He knew she was ready, he felt like he was more than ready.

Jonas gently spread her legs and got between them. He lay there a moment resting his weight on his elbows. His erection barely touched her, but he could feel the intense heat radiating to him. He gently eased forward. He didn't want to hurry or frighten her, even as much as his male eagerness told him to push as hard as he could.

Gentle, short strokes moved him farther and farther in. After an eternity, he was all the way in. He just lay there for a few minutes, holding tight with the realization that he was there.

Emma said, "It hurts a little, but it hurts good."

"Just tell me anytime, and I'll stop."

"No, it is all right," she said as she gave a little tentative push back.

Jonas gently worked back and forth. Both of them were beginning to lose their shyness and enjoy the connection between them.

Emma could feel something happening to her but was not sure what. She felt different all over. Jonas could feel the new throbbing of her from within and knew. Emma began to twist and moan when Jonas let go. They both writhed and squirmed in sweet ecstasy. The marriage was consummated.

They lay in each other's arms for a long time, totally spent.

Chapter 20

Summer

THEIR FIRST DAY TOGETHER as husband and wife turned out to be more wonderful than expected. They lay in bed feeling great, but exhausted.

"In all my wildest dreams," said Emma, "I never thought it would be as good as this is between us."

"It'll get even better as we get to know each other better."

"I don't see how."

"I can't think of anything that's greater between two people in love."

"I won't mind practicing to make it better."

They both laughed, and Jonas said, "I hope we'll get plenty of time to do that this summer."

"Me too. Are you hungry now?" asked Emma.

"Now that you ask, yes. I could stand a little something to eat."

They both got up. Jonas put on his pants and shirt with a pair of moccasins he had made. Rummaging through some gear stacked in a corner he found the pair of moccasins he made for Emma, lined with sheepskin he had brought from town to keep her feet warm. The moccasins delighted her. She curled her toes back and forth in the soft wool lining. She found a light house dress, which she put on with nothing underneath.

Jonas looked at her, her body showing through the dress and said, "We just got through, and I look at you, and I'm ready to go again."

"Why not?" said Emma pulling the dress off over her head and kicking off her moccasins.

They headed for the bed again. This time Emma knew a little more of what to expect and really enjoyed it.

They finished and Emma said, "You're right, it does get better."

Jonas laughed and said, "Well, I meant later and a lot better."

"I don't know if I can stand it if it gets any better."

Jonas laughed and held her close in his happiness. Warmth and satisfaction flooded over him like a great tide.

"I was worried. You've led such a sheltered life that I was a little worried about how you would react to my touch. It's turning out just great."

Emma said, "We better fix ourselves something to eat. We can't keep going unless we eat to keep our strength up."

"You're right. I'm absolutely famished."

With that they both got up and put their same clothes back on.

Jonas had to rekindle the fire, and they busied themselves with food.

Emma prepared supper while Jonas tidied up the cabin. Emma's personal belongings he left alone so she could put them away where she could find them. "Tomorrow I'll show you around the place and what to do in case of an emergency," he said.

"I almost forget about the Russians," she said.

They had supper, and Jonas asked if she would like a sauna.

Emma raised her eyebrows. "It's an awful long way back into town."

Jonas grinned. "No, right here. Come on."

He led her by the hand to the back of the cabin, opened a door, showing her a small sauna with bathroom built in.

"See, you'll never have to go outside."

"What about water?"

Jonas showed her the spring that fed the kitchen water and the sauna both. She marvelled at his ingenuity.

"I'll heat it up to show you that it does work. In the cold winter months we can heat that, the fireplace, and the cook stove. On days with no wind, the three of them should hold enough heat until night when we can build a fire again. The only days we could have a problem is on clear, calm days when the smoke rises straight up to give away our position. Even then, if we're careful to use nothing but dry wood and a little at time I know we'll be all right. If it gets real cold and we can't build a fire, we can go to bed and get under the covers for the day."

"That might not be so bad," Emma said with a twinkle in her eye.

"Here we are, married for one day and you're turning into a harlot for me," he teased, "but I like it."

They both laughed and hugged each other.

Emma got busy cleaning up the supper dishes while Jonas went out to get more wood and kindling.

Jonas checked the sauna and announced that it was hot. They undressed and went in, still not accustomed to seeing each other naked.

"Up to the top bench," said Jonas.

"I don't know if I can stand that much heat. I'll try it."

Jonas filled a bucket with cold water and climbed to the top bench with Emma. He threw the first dipper of water on the hot rocks. It hissed and steam rose momentarily to disappear into the super-heated air. The heat rolled over them enveloping them in warmth like a giant hand. It was difficult to breath, beads of perspiration glistened on their bodies. Jonas threw more water on the rocks. Emma stayed for a while but then announced, "I have to move down at least one level."

"While you're down there, check the water in the tank. It's attached to the sauna stove, see if it's hot."

Emma checked the water and said with surprise, "It just dawned on me that you packed all this in from town on your back!"

"Vilho made the sauna stove and water heater plus the fireplace swing, grates, and tools. It was quite a load packing it in. The fireplace stuff was one load and the sauna two. It isn't hard when you're doing it for love."

"Oh, you asked me to check the water. It's hot."

Jonas climbed down and put water into one of the buckets he had made, and Emma filled the other. They soaped each other up enjoying the total sensuality of touching each other and the slickness of the soap.

Jonas was ready again and Emma too. Jonas sat down on the bottom bench pulling Emma to him and facing him. As she sat down on his lap he penetrated her. Their own juices and the soap helped.

Emma said, "Ooh, that's good and different. I like it but then this is only the third time and I liked it every time."

They finished and washed up. Jonas sluiced the sauna down with fresh water and went back into the cabin part. They sat and talked for a long time about the future of Finland and its relationship to themselves. Finally, they decided to go to bed.

When they got into bed, Emma said, "This feather tick is so soft to lay on. I am glad mother made it and you packed it in."

Jonas said, "That was the worst item I hauled in here. Even rolled up tight, it was still so bulky that it caught on every branch and twig between here and town. I'm glad it had a tough cover. A thinner one would have torn to shreds before I got here. The Russians could have followed the feather trail all the way here. It did get a couple of small tears that I sewed up."

"Oh, what a talented husband I have," said Emma, laughing, "he can even sew."

"I have to admit that my sewing isn't the greatest in the world."

They went to sleep in each others arms content with the world.

Jonas woke up early to look at his wife sleeping in his arms. He swelled with pride just looking at her. She was so beautiful. He lay for a long time enjoying watching her in sleep. She stirred and opened one eye to look at Jonas quizzically and say, "Good morning."

Jonas bent down and kissed her gently. She stirred and stretched like a long, lithe cat, enjoying the warmth of the bed and her husband next to her. They were up and dressed in no time. Emma fixed breakfast.

Jonas asked. "What would you like to do today, my love?

"You mentioned you would show me the emergency procedures. I should learn about that first."

"You're right. I'll show you the safety items I've built."

Breakfast over, Jonas led Emma back to the sauna area. He showed her a small, hidden trap door in the back wall. He pushed his finger into an innocent looking knot hole to trip a catch holding the door. It swung open to reveal the outside behind the cabin. Jonas led her through. It was like a tunnel through the thick spruce trees to the edge of the bluff. At the edge was a coil of stout rope tied to the bole of one of the bigger trees. There was a pair of heavy leather gloves weighted down with a big rock.

"If we ever have to get out we can go this way. We can be gone before they know it. If I'm not here and you have to get out, make sure you use the gloves. You don't want to get rope burns on the way down."

"I hope I never have to use it."

"If you do, just go down the rope and then up that small ravine. At the top of the hill from that ravine, follow the ridge to the right until it forks. At the fork is a blown down tree. Go the way the top of the tree is pointing until the trail forks again. You will see a small rock against a big rock part way down the left fork. Go that way until you see where three spruce trees blew into a big pine tree. At that point you head away from the pine tree. Look back often to make sure you can see two of the spruce trees, one on each side of the pine. This will keep you in a straight line. It's a little longer this way, but it would be hard for you to get lost. As long as you keep that line, it'll take you to the lake at the edge of town. From there you won't have any trouble getting to your parents' house. I'll write all of this down, and we'll put it inside one of the gloves. I'll also make you repeat the directions from time to time. If you lose the paper, you'll remember the way.

"The first time we go into town, we'll go that way so you'll be thoroughly familiar with it. If you have to use this route, you'd have an hour's head start. They might not know that you were in here as long as you remembered to close the trap door."

Jonas took her around to the other side. He showed her that she was completely hidden at the back of the cabin.

"I built it this way on purpose. It was a little hard building this close to the trees, but it was worth it. I planted some small spruce trees to give additional screening to the tunnel."

"You thought of everything for our safety," she said with awe.

"I hope so, I lie awake at night thinking of what could happen and make plans in case this or that happens."

"I hope none of it happens,"said Emma.

"If we take every precaution we can think of, we might, just might, avoid a lot of trouble. Do you remember the rock alarm I showed you?

"Yes, I remember."

"If you ever hear those rocks go clattering down, you would still have time. Go to the edge of the clearing to make sure it wasn't an animal that knocked them down. If that hawk starts screaming, you know for sure someone's coming. It still might be an animal, but it's not me. I won't knock the rocks down. In any case you could see anyone starting across the clearing. It would still give you plenty of time to exit through the trap door. Never worry about me. If I come in and see the thread broken or the rocks gone, I'll take all precautions. I can come up from the other side and approach unseen. But I have to know that you're safe."

The two of them wandered around the clearing arm in arm taking in all the natural beauty of the place.

Emma asked. "Could we start a small garden up here? The soil looks good, and we have plenty of water. We're up high enough where we will be out of a lot of frost danger."

"I don't see any reason why we couldn't. The next time we're in town, we will get some seeds and give it a try."

"I already thought of it and brought a few seeds with me. When could we start?"

"In a few days. We've got a few other jobs to do around here."

"It would be wonderful if we could become self-sufficient."

"We could never become totally self-sufficient," said Jonas. "We need a few staples—flour, sugar, gun powder, and components for reloading. But we could trade furs for the items we can't produce."

"That sounds good," said Emma. "Let's get some lunch."

They went back in and had lunch. Jonas suggested they take the rest of the day off to go fishing.

Emma said, "Great! I haven't been fishing for such a long time." She paused and frowned slightly asking, "Do you think it's safe? I mean, from the Russians."

"Yes, it's safe, but we do have to take a few precautions. There are safety measures we have to take all the time if we're going to live out here."

Jonas picked up a small musette bag and went out the door. Emma asked, "Where are our fishing poles?"

"They are growing out there on the stream bank."

Emma grabbed her shawl and went running after Jonas as he was already striding away from the cabin. Jonas remembered to slow down and let her shorter legs catch up.

They walked arm in arm to a small stream. Jonas parted some thick brush and saplings to get into this particular part of the stream. He proceeded to cut some long willow poles and tied the hook and line to the end. He then turned over a few rocks to find worms to bait the hooks.

Emma said, "Jonas, that looks like a better place to fish down below, not so much brush and a big pool. There ought to be some big fish in there. Let's go down there."

"No, this is one of many lessons you have to learn. The fishing may be a little better down there, but that's out in the open, and the Russians can see you from a long way off. They could be down here before you knew it. Right here we would hear them coming long before they saw us."

"I guess I have a lot to learn."

"It will come in time. You'll get tuned to the forest and know by the sounds when everything is all right or something is amiss. You'll get so tuned that any little disturbance perks up your attention."

They sat on the stream bank, effectively hidden from prying eyes. Emma caught two fish almost immediately, and she ribbed Jonas, "Looks like I'm going to have fish for supper, but I don't know what you'll eat."

Jonas said, "If I didn't have to keep your hook baited and take your fish off the line, I'd have time to catch my own."

The spring sunshine was bright and warm. They caught a few more fish and lolled around talking, when Jonas said quietly and urgently, "Set your pole down and come with me quickly."

Jonas led her up the stream and into some large boulders interspersed with spruce trees and willows. He got the two of them behind some rocks and trees where they could barely see the trail.

"Don't move no matter what you see or what you think until I tell you it's all right," Jonas whispered.

They sat quietly. A mosquito buzzed insistently in her ear but she dared not do anything about it. She could feel the mosquito on her neck, helping itself to a free meal. She wanted to swat it. Then she heard a faint clicking, jingling noise she hadn't heard before. They came into view shortly, six Cossack cavalry men on their horses. The last one in line stopped as he got abreast of them and stared at the spot where they were hiding. Emma's heart was in her throat, her mouth was dry, she couldn't swallow. She was petrified. Jonas sat still and gently squeezed her hand for assurance. The rider rode on. Emma breathed a sigh of relief and whispered, "That was close, I was scared to death."

Jonas admonished her with a, "Shush!"

Emma froze again. Ten minutes later, Emma was not sure of the time, a lone rider came down the trail like a ghost. He didn't make a sound. He rode bareback. The horse and rider were a uniform grey-brown color that blended well with the surroundings. He eased on down to the stream crossing, following the path of the other riders. He stopped often to look around the area closely.

When he disappeared from sight Jonas said, "It's all right now. Let's pick up our fish and go home."

Emma was ready to go in seconds. She wanted to get back to the relative safety of their cabin. Jonas broke the ends of their poles to wind the line around the stubs. The fish went into the musette bag, and they were on their way. Jonas didn't worry about anyone at the cabin. They were close enough that they would have heard the hawk screaming as it did at their approach.

When they were safely back in the cabin Emma started chattering like a magpie, "How did you know those horsemen were coming? I didn't hear anything for a long time after we were in the rocks. That last horseman in the group—I was sure he saw us, he stared right at us. That lone horseman, how did you know he was coming?"

"Whoa, whoa, one question at a time. First, I didn't hear the horsemen any sooner than you did. This is what you learn living in the woods all the time. The forest noises changed ever so slightly. I heard some crows give a different call. I saw the flash of some deer running on that far ridge. That wouldn't be normal unless someone or something disturbed them. I knew from experience they often have a silent trail rider following the main body to catch someone who thinks it's safe. The first time it happened to me, I almost got caught. I started out of my hiding place to get a better look at the group with my telescope. A squirrel chattering an alarm told me to hide again. I barely got hidden when a rider ghosted by me just like that one did. I could see something on the horse's hooves but wasn't sure what they were until I found one on the trail. It's a soft leather boot ingeniously made with cross strips for traction, yet it makes no noise as they walk."

"I was scared when that rider looked at us so close. I thought for sure he would hear my heart pounding."

"The rider knew something was wrong. He wasn't sure enough to take the time to investigate. I imagine they see hundreds of objects a day that don't look just right to them. I'm glad they're a little lazy about getting off their horse to look at something. This has happened to me several times where they thought something was wrong but didn't take the time to investigate. You don't move; even the slightest movement will catch the eye. I got many a deer because I caught the movement of an ear, leg or turn of head."

"All I know is I was as scared as I've ever been in my whole life."

"Now you know what I mean when I say you get tuned in to the woods. It'll come to you after a while. It's an almost imperceptible difference in the sound of the woods when something is wrong. I've learned the hard way to move slowly and listen. Stay mostly in the heavy cover of trees and brush. Movement is what catches the eye. You need to wear a cap to break up the white oval of your face. Any time you suspect anyone in the area, you need to keep your hands and face in shadow. A quick movement of your bare hand will bring immediate attention to your position."

"There's so much to learn," said Emma.

"Not to worry. Just do as I say, and we'll be all right."

Jonas cleaned the fish while Emma prepared the rest of the supper. Jonas said. "We better delay cooking supper until after it gets good and dark. With the Russians in the area, we better not take a chance on them seeing smoke from our chimney."

The next day Jonas spaded up the spot for the garden. He heard the faint jingling of horse gear coming from the valley below and behind the cabin. He looked up to make sure their chimney was not giving off tell-tale smoke. It was not. He went inside to take Emma with him through the back trap door. They crept to the edge of the bluff to look down and see the troop. The troop went right below them, oblivious of their presence. A few minutes later the silent rider came, bringing up the rear as he did the day before. They were heading back into town. Experience told Jonas that it would be quite some time before a patrol came back into the area. He learned long before that the Russians were predictable creatures of habit. He was not fool enough, however, to rely on this assumption completely.

"It sure gives me a funny feeling just watching them and knowing they are out to do us in," Emma said.

"I doubt seriously if they would do anything to you. You haven't committed any crimes."

"I never want them to have that chance."

"I have managed to survive all this time, and I think I can keep on doing it. I learn more every day about survival out here, and I learn more about the Russians."

The summer slipped away quickly. Their garden grew. They harvested a few vegetables from it early and the rest were doing well.

They did have one encounter with a Russian patrol. They were picking berries when Emma looked up at Jonas quizzically. Jonas nodded and they both moved to a large thicket to lie down. The patrol rode by.

After the patrol and ghost rider passed, Jonas said. "You're catching on. You heard the change in forest tempo about the same time I did."

"I wasn't sure what I heard or didn't hear other than that little difference in the sounds. I'm beginning to see what you mean about learning the forest. I'm really beginning to like the feeling of awareness."

"I don't know of anything to compare it with, the oneness with nature or whatever you want to call it."

They made one trip into town for supplies around the middle of summer. Jonas took Emma via the escape route so she would be familiar with it if she ever had to use it by herself.

The family was glad to see the both of them again. Anna marvelled at how marriage agreed with Emma. She looked positively radiant. Anna wondered if Emma were pregnant. "No," she thought, "She would tell me."

Jonas, Vilho, and Toivo had a long discussion about the resistance movement and how it progressed.

Early the next morning Jonas and Emma were up and gone. On the trail, Emma said, "I used to wonder what was the matter with you. Most of the time you got so edgy, wanting to get back into the forest. Now I'm beginning to see. I was getting nervous. I had a cooped up feeling or something. I felt hemmed in with no place to run."

"It's hard for someone to understand who hasn't been there and experienced the freedom. It's like freedom in life. We, against the Russians. You have to experience freedom and really know it before you miss it."

They were soon back at the cabin and their familiar routine.

Emma said, "I missed the privacy of our place when we were in town. I'm glad our first night was right here. I don't know if I could have coped with making love in my mother's house."

"Is that why you were kind of cold and standoffish last night?"

"I guess so, I kept thinking that other people were in the house."

"Well, what about now?"

She smiled. "I'm ready."

Emma had shed her clothes and was in bed before Jonas could get started taking his off.

"Come on slow poke," she giggled. "What're you waiting for?"

Jonas jumped into bed, and they made love. Afterwards, Emma said, "Now that was worth waiting for. I couldn't have given it that kind of effort back in town."

"Neither could I!"

They dressed slowly, and Jonas said his thoughts out loud. "I'll have to get started stocking our meat larder for the winter. We'll smoke some deer and dry some into jerky. When it gets a little colder, I'll kill some more and hang them up outside in our own natural freezer. I know how you hate killing deer, so I'll go out alone. You'll be all right by yourself."

"I'll be a little nervous, but I've been living out here long enough, I'll be fine. You'll be back before dark won't you?"

"Of course. See you then. Plan on having fresh liver for dinner."

Jonas started out, not knowing for sure where he was going as this was basically new hunting country for him. A few places where he had seen deer came to mind. The place first in his mind would be safe and a short pack to the cabin. He planned to kill the deer and bone it out on the spot to eliminate extra trips.

Thinking to himself. "It will be good to have fresh meat, especially good having fresh liver for supper if I'm lucky."

The wind blew hard. Jonas had mixed emotions about being out in the wind. It made getting a feel for the woods more difficult than on calm days. He understood why animals didn't like to move in the wind. But a windy day would make it difficult to locate his shot if someone heard it.

One-shot kills were essential for several reasons. Tracking a wounded animal could take a lot of time, and, if a patrol were within earshot, locating a single shot in the wind was difficult. Also, he needed to conserve bullets.

Jonas remembered a small grove of trees situated in a hollow. Deer would go there on a windy day for the protection from the wind. It was difficult to approach without the deer seeing him. He eased into the grove and sat down among some rocks to blend in well. He pulled his cap down over his eyes and laid his rifle across his knees.

The wind blew hard in the tree tops above his head, while down in the valley the grass barely rippled. It wasn't long before a doe and two fawns came into sight. It amazed him how deer could materialize out of nowhere. He watched the trio for a long time. The fawns gamboled around their mother, suckled and ran on again.

"That's a good sign when does have twin fawns. That means they have wintered well, and we'll have a good crop coming up next year."

The doe and fawns melted into the forest. Shortly, a big buck came stepping along cautiously, testing the air and looking all around before he moved again. Jonas watched and marvelled at how much more wary the buck was than the doe and fawns. Clearly he was the hunted animal and had learned caution. The buck sensed something wrong but didn't know what. He was unaware that Jonas sat and watched him. Jonas waited for a clear shot. The buck stepped from behind some bushes when Jonas squeezed the trigger. The buck fell in his tracks. Jonas sat for a few minutes to make sure no one heard the shot before he went to the deer.

He eased down to the deer. Always a little sad when he killed an animal, Jonas made short work of the processing. He had a heavy pack when he got through. He rolled the hide tight and tied it to the outside of his rucksack, picked up his rifle and was on his way. He was back at the cabin within three hours from leaving. He and Emma would have another full day's work preparing the meat for the smoker and drying it into jerky.

Emma met him as the edge of the clearing. The screaming hawk had alerted her to his approach.

"I can tell by the size of your pack that you had some good luck."

"I got a prime buck. The heart and liver are on top in the pack. Let's have some to eat now and get to work on the rest afterwards."

Their simple repast over, Jonas sharpened knives, and they went to work, cutting up the meat. The wind still blew hard, so Jonas lit the smoker and filled it full. Jonas didn't like jerky as well as smoked meat.

The wind stopped in a few days, and the weather warmed. Even on the hilltop no breezes stirred.

Emma said, "I wish there was something we could do to cool off."

"Well, maybe there is," said Jonas mysteriously. "Put on your shoes, barefoot girl, and come with me."

"Where are we going?"

"Just wait and see. You know curiosity once killed a cat."

They walked several hills away when Jonas said, "Take my hand and close your eyes. No peeking now."

Jonas led her a short distance further through some trees and told her to open her eyes. She opened them, looked around and said, "Oh, Jonas, this is a beautiful spot."

They were in the middle of a green glade with a small waterfall tumbling down into an oval pool below. Trees, mostly willows, surrounded the whole area. Even the splash of the waterfall did not penetrate the wall of trees. The crystal water was the prettiest blue Emma had ever seen.

"How in the world did you ever find this place?"

"I stumbled on it one day. When they hunt you all the time, you're always on the lookout for good hiding places. This grove looked thick, and I decided to investigate. I didn't know the stream and water fall were here until after I broke through the tree line. I considered building the cabin here, but it wasn't defensible and didn't have a good escape route. It's a beautiful spot though. I thought we might swim for the rest of the day."

"Last one in is a rotten egg," said Emma, peeling off her clothes and heading for the water.

Jonas dashed after her and caught her before she dove in. He held her with his legs while he peeled off his clothes.

"Let me go, you big ox, you cheat. That's not fair," Emma wailed.

Jonas finished undressing, jumped up and gave her a shove down as he bolted for the water. Emma managed to snare his ankle and sent him sprawling. Then she jumped up and dove into the water.

"See there, I beat you anyway," she said when her wet head emerged. "Cheaters never win!"

They laughed, swam, and splashed in the water like children. But the spring-fed pool was quite cool, so they soon climbed out to bask in the sun. Lying on the rocks in the hot sun, looking up at the blue sky with white clouds like woolly sheep, Emma said, "This is what God meant Eden to be."

"Summer has been like heaven to me," Jonas said lazily.

"I hate to think of winter coming, but I love big roaring fires, too."

Jonas said, "I like the fall when leaves turn the whole world different colors. Game is mature and fat. Fishing is good."

After a few moment of pleasant quiet, Emma said, "We're going to have to go into town soon to get some more staples. We're getting low on flour, sugar, and salt."

"I know," said Jonas. "We'll have to make several trips before the snow flies."

The sun was setting below the trees, and the willow pool cooled rapidly.

"I'm starting to get chilly and hungry. Let's go home," Emma said.

They dressed and walked arm in arm back to the cabin, enjoying the last part of summer.

Chapter 21

Winter

SUMMER AND FALL CAME AND WENT all too quickly. Jonas woke up early one morning, feeling troubled. All he noticed was an eery silence. Walking to the window, he discovered that snow had fallen during the night. It's soft covering muffled all the sounds of the forest. Snow would complicate their life in the cabin. They needed supplies from town, and snow would make it easy for someone to track him back to the cabin.

While he looked out the window, Emma tip-toed up behind him, grasping him around the waist with a big hug, asking, "What are you looking at so seriously, my love."

"We have snow earlier than I expected."

"So? We can stay here and enjoy it. I just love snow."

"We need supplies. Snow makes it easy for someone to track me."

"You? You mean--"

"You're not going. It'll be hard enough for me, but if the Russians got on the track, I don't know what I'd do with you along. It's better that I go alone."

Emma pouted, wanting to visit with her family, but knew Jonas was right. In an emergency, she would be a hinderance rather than a help. She wasn't sure she could handle a rigorous chase. "Let me make you a list," she said, "so you'll remember everything."

"There you go, typical housewife, nag, nag, nag."

"I was just teasing," said Emma kissing him lightly on the nose.

"So was I," said Jonas kissing her back.

Emma started her list while Jonas prepared for the trip.

He said, "I could make it without my skis, but we might get more snow before I get back. I would need them with deeper snow. Anyway, I'll make better time with them."

Jonas gave his skis a good waxing, as this would be their first use that fall. They packed venison and trout for Toivo. Jonas kissed Emma good-bye. "I'll see you in a couple of days. Don't worry unless I'm over a week late. If I'm that late, you'll need to go back home. You know the way

189

now. Use your skis."

"I know sweetheart. You be careful."

Jonas carried his skis out to the mainland before he put them on. The narrow trail to the cabin was difficult to negotiate on skis, especially since the wind kept it clear of snow.

"It feels good to have skis on with new snow under them," Jonas said as he sped along.

Skiing toward town, his thoughts went to Emma and the wonderful summer they had had together. Winter would be even better. He could picture them staying close to the cabin with a roaring fire going. Before he knew it, he was at the edge of town, looking at the Lehtinen house. All signals were good, but it wasn't quite dark enough to cross the open ground. Waiting for dark, he squatted on his skis under a large spruce tree.

He said out loud. "If Emma was in there, I'd really be getting impatient to see her."

Darkness came, and he crossed to the house. Anna greeted his knock, looking quizzically past him for Emma.

Jonas anticipated her question saying, "I thought it better she stay behind because of the snow."

Anna said, "I understand. Come in before someone sees you."

Jonas gave them the list of supplies he needed and sent Matt to get Vilho so they could talk. Anna put the list of groceries together with no problem. She had expected them coming for supplies.

Jonas and Vilho talked far into the night about worsening problems with the Russians. They formulated plans for the resistance movement and talked over the passive resistance already in progress.

Jonas was up early the next morning anxious to be on his way back to Emma. Emma was a capable woman, but he didn't like leaving her alone.

The Russian patrols were in another area. He wasn't worried about them. It would snow in a few days to cover his tracks before the patrols operated in that area again. This was accurate information but didn't take into consideration that a careless ski patrol man had broken his leg. The patrol had aborted their mission and started back along the shortest route.

Jonas saw them the same time they saw him. He cursed himself for being complacent about their schedule and had not stayed alert.

At the distance he was from them, they couldn't know it was Jonas. But, a travel ban was in effect for the area, and the Russians knew he shouldn't be there. They yelled for him to stop, but he kept going. By the time they had unslung their rifles and got ready to shoot, he was out of sight in the trees. Still, they fired several shots after him.

The patrol leader yelled, "Hold your fire! We'll track him down. That may not be Jonas, but we'll soon find out."

Jonas knew he couldn't lead them anywhere near the cabin. The fired shots told him that they were serious.

The patrol leader pointed and said, "You two men get the injured man back to camp. Report to Rykov that we are possibly on Jonas' track."

This reduced the chase patrol from the usual eight troopers to five tired men. They were on their last search grid when the accident happened.

Jonas was sure he could stay ahead of them for a day or two. He was thankful he had food stuffs in his pack from Anna. If this had happened on his way to town he would have had only raw venison and fish and no way to cook them. Still, if snow didn't come to hide his tracks, they would keep patrols on him day after day until they wore him down completely.

He stayed ahead of them all that day. Crossing back across his pursuers tracks several times, he left them to unravel his true direction. He made a loop close to dark that night so he could watch the Russians make camp. After they bedded down, he made a rough shelter to get a little sleep himself. It was difficult sleeping sitting up, so, if he slept too soundly, he would fall over, waking himself.

Jonas dozed fitfully, waking himself several times as he fell over. Toward morning he gave up trying to sleep and started a new trail in the dark. The stars shining on the snow gave him some light but travel was difficult. The patrol would be on his trail at first light. He went quietly past their camp where he could see the first stirring of the men. He crossed the back trail several times to confuse them. The delay would give him more time. He had a plan in mind, but it would have to wait for more such trail crossings while he watched the head tracker. After the third such crossing, he decided the plan had a good chance to work.

As if talking to the head tracker directly, Jonas said, "This time I'm going to give you a real problem. Don't solve it the right way."

Jonas made a big wide loop again. He waited for the patrol to pass him. As soon as they were out of sight, he made another loop. This time he put his skis in their track, backed up past his track that intersected their trail. He made several ski marks making it look like he was not going on their track. The tracker would think he was not following them. Before he left, he threw several small pellets of snow in his own back track. His ruse checked out the way he wanted. Back he went to his original vantage point so he could watch the patrol from cover. Would the tracker take the bait? Screened by a huge spruce tree, he watched the patrol come to the intersection of the two trails.

"A-ha, head tracker," he whispered, "you have not deciphered the trail yet. I hope you decide my way. If you don't, I'm no worse off than before. If you go the way I want you to go, you'll never figure it out. The snow will be here before you can back track enough to solve it."

191

Jonas watched as the patrol leader and head tracker talked, pointing and examining the tracks he made.

The head tracker said "This is good. I believe he wants us to think he took the loop a second time. He really went back along the old trail."

"What makes you think that?"

"See the slight bevel in the snow as he turned one of his skis to the left. That bevel means he was swinging that ski toward the return trail. Secondly, there are some small snow pellets in the track of the loop. If he went that way, he would have mashed the pellets. I believe he kicked those small pellets in the track as he started down our back trail. I really think he wants us to start around the loop again. If it wasn't for those two subtle points, I would say that's the way he went. I have tracked him enough to know he's a sly old fox. This time he did go down our back trail. I've been right every time."

"All right we'll go back that way," said the patrol leader. "We'll have him this time. He doesn't know our relief patrol is following our trail. He'll run right into them or have to jump off the trail, making new tracks. In that case we'll have a fresh trail to follow and fresh men to push him hard. I'll give our patrol a little rest and then follow the fresh patrol. I'd like to be in on the kill."

Jonas watched with satisfaction as the patrol started down their own back trail. From the top of the loop he turned in his track for home. It would be dark and snowing before they found their error. Jonas was sure another patrol was coming to relieve them.

It happened as Jonas predicted. The first patrol leader questioned the new patrol about tracks leaving the main trail. No one remembered any.

The new leader said, "We were following your tracks and assumed you were following him closely. We did heed your signs where he crossed your tracks a second time and did not take the loop."

"I'm sure he's down the track somewhere," said the first leader. "Our tracker thinks he came this way, and so far he has been right. He may have gone on one of the loops you bypassed, let you by and got on your track going back. We should back track and follow the loops out to see if he jumped off them somewhere. With two patrols we can cover a lot more ground. My people are tired but they can go a little longer. It looks like snow, so, if we don't catch him soon, it will be too late. Tracker, how much of a head start do you think he has on us?"

"He's a good skier, but I doubt if he could have gained over an hour on us from the crossing back there," said the tracker getting a little niggling feeling that Jonas had outwitted him. He didn't dare voice that opinion to the leaders. He hoped silently that the dark clouds gathering would bring snow to cover his blunder, if indeed, he had blundered.

After several fruitless runs down the back trail, following all the loops, the leaders decided to camp for the night. In the morning they would split, with one following the back trail and the other going to the original intersection. After supper, they discussed the situation with both their trackers. One sat hoping for snow before morning.

He said with as much conviction as he could muster, "I really believe he came this way. He has out-distanced us or jumped the trail somewhere that we missed."

"I hope, for your sake, you're right," said his patrol leader.

Jonas headed for home on a circuitous route. He did not want tracks pointing to his lair if he read the weather wrong and it didn't snow. Yet, he knew by the looks of the sky that it would be a bad storm. Early storms could be fierce if short lived. He was hoping for a hard storm but not so bad he couldn't see landmarks to find his way home.

It started to snow shortly before he got to the point where he must head directly for the cabin. He waited for about an hour, watching his back tracks fill with snow before heading home. This was his third day out without a hot meal. Anna's bread and cheese had been eaten to keep up his strength. He was just beginning to realize how homesick, tired and hungry he had become. As he reached the edge of the clearing near the cabin, he paused to watch with satisfaction how well the snow was filling his tracks. No one could follow him to the cabin now.

Jonas opened the door, half stumbling into Emma's arms. She supported him to a chair, saying, "I've worried myself sick about you. I expected you the day before yesterday."

"I know, sweetheart. I've been playing hide and seek with a Russian patrol for three days. If this snow hadn't come, I don't know what I would have done, I was getting so tired and hungry."

"You mean you went without food all that time?"

"I ate your mother's bread and cheese, but I'm hungry now."

"I'll fix you something to eat right now."

"If you don't mind, light the sauna. I smell bad and need the heat to penetrate these cold and weary bones."

Emma hurried to the sauna. Jonas stripped off his clothes, put on a clean shirt and pants, lay down on the bed and fell asleep immediately.

Emma came back to find him asleep. She didn't know if he needed sleep, food, or the sauna the most. She decided he needed the food first and went to fix it. When it was ready, she shook him gently. He jumped up with a start saying, "I thought I was still running from the Russians and had fallen asleep and it was one of them waking me."

She looked concerned. " That's past now. Your food is ready. Come eat. By the time you're through, the sauna will be hot."

Jonas bolted his food down, he was so ravenously hungry.

Emma admonished him, "Jonas, slow down. You'll get cramps."

When he finished eating, Emma took him into the sauna and threw water on the rocks to bring the temperature up.

"You don't know how good this feels on my tired, old body."

"You just lie down there on that top bench while I get some oil to rub you down. I don't want your muscles to cramp up during the night."

Emma came back with mineral oil that she warmed by the fire before she rubbed him down. She rubbed him down all over paying particular attention to his legs. They could cramp easily, having skied for the first time that winter. After rubbing him down, she washed him. He fell asleep several times. She had to wake him to get him to turn over so she could finish. She got him up, dried him off and put him to bed.

He woke up cheerful and said, "Good morning, nursemaid! Thanks for the tender, loving care. How long did I sleep?"

"You're welcome, and you slept fourteen hours."

"I wonder how those Russians made out in this storm? They had no shelter to amount to anything if they didn't go back. And they didn't have a pretty nurse like you to rub the kinks out of their tired bodies."

The Russians hadn't fared well. They had waited out the storm without enough provisions for both patrols. Their small tents and sleeping bags weren't adequate. The heavy snow weighted their tents down to the point where they collapsed. Only a few tired men had had the foresight to get up and brush the snow off to keep the tents from falling in on them.

The only one glad to see the snow other than Jonas was the tracker who had made the mistake. He vowed secretly that it wouldn't happen again.

By morning, the troops were miserable from either having their tents collapse on them or getting up every little while to brush them off. Fires helped their spirits, as did the meager breakfast.

The two patrol leaders conferred, deciding that there was no point in further pursuit with the blanketing snow. It still snowed, but the visibility had improved only slightly. They could see all of twenty or thirty feet. The leaders knew the direction of their compound, and both men had compasses, but neither was adept at navigation.

The patrol started back slowly in single file, fearful of going over a cliff in the near-zero visibility.

One of the men said, "I would just as soon sit this storm out. My belly can go without food for a few days, but I can't fly if I go over a cliff unless it's after I'm dead at the bottom."

They fought their way through the storm, with the leaders listening to the men's fears. To minimize the dangers, they lashed everyone together with rope. This produced different grumblings. Now the men feared that the leaders might go over a cliff pulling everyone after them.

The leaders saw they were getting nowhere with the men. They camped in a grove of spruce trees that gave them some protection from the storm and a plentiful supply of dry wood. The short rations became a sore point, even though the men had said they would rather suffer with short rations than take a chance on going over a cliff. Several men voiced the doubtful intelligence of chasing one Finn all over the woods.

The storm let up the next day, and they pulled out for the compound, tired and hungry. Finally, they could see where they were going.

The Russians didn't appreciate the beauty of the forest after this snow storm, though it was truly beautiful, with the new snow weighing the tree limbs down and softening the harsh lines of the woods to a fairytale look. The sun shining on the new snow sparkled like diamonds. The Russians skied on through it with heads bowed, too tired to care. Upon reaching town, the two leaders dismissed the men and reported to Rykov and Gerchenoff.

When Rykov heard the news, he exploded in his usual furious harangue, "Of all the incompetents in this outfit, you two are the worst. You can't track one damn Finlander in the snow! What the hell does it take to get some men that can get the job done in the field?"

"It really wasn't all our fault," said the leader of Patrol One, "We tracked him all over and never lost him once. It took a little time to untangle the trail each time he doubled over our tracks, but we unravelled it right every time. What stopped us this time was the snow storm."

"Snow storm be damned! If you had pushed him harder, you would have had him before it stormed."

"I don't see how, sir. We had to decipher his tracks so many times. We could have gone on chasing tracks all over and maybe not been on the right set. I have to hand it to my tracker, he never missed a thing. But Jonas was doing his utmost to fool us."

"Which way was he heading when you lost him in the snow storm?"

"Generally west, sir."

"Well, he has to be holed up somewhere in that damn country. We'll concentrate our efforts in that western zone. He had to know this storm was coming. He had to be heading for his hideout. He surely wouldn't have gone back east after the storm hit."

"That's right," said the patrol leader, glad to be off the hot seat.

In truth, of course, Jonas *had* headed east and was that very minute toasting his feet by a big roaring fire with Emma at his side.

This would be an easy winter. The Russians would concentrate their efforts far to the west of the cabin.

Chapter 22

Change in Plans

TWO INCIDENTS OCCURRED IN TOWN that seriously polarized opinions against the Russians. One was the killing of a slightly retarded Finnish man whom John Maki allowed to live in his barn and care for his horses. Known for his slowness and great size, this man, Jake, often suffered teasing and ridicule at the hands of the Russians, and, after he had been drinking some, he could strike out with surprising strength. Six Russians—a young officer and five troopers—had teased Jake in the Boar's Head. Jake had pounded them bloody. In retaliation, the poor slow man was found a few days later, beaten and stabbed to death. The Finns were incensed. The second incident involved Emma's maid of honor, Mary. A Russian officer caught her walking alone one evening. He grabbed her, dragged her into the woods and raped her.

These were just two more in a growing list of grievances that the Finns had against the Russians, yet the Russians couldn't understand why the Finns were mad at them all the time. Resentment fed the resistance movement.

Vilho decided to take some time off to get over the killing of Jake and deal with his outrage over Mary. The post was not busy at the moment and granted him a week's leave. Vilho felt he needed to talk to Jonas about the senseless killing and violence and how best to avenge it.

He took a circuitous route to the message tree and camped on his own trail for a day, watching his back trail to make sure he was not being followed. It looked safe enough to proceed to the message tree.

Vilho scratched a message on a piece of birch bark and put it in the hollow tree. He set the message rock on top of the big rock. Moving to the nearby cave, he could watch for Jonas and not be seen.

Vilho had just settled down for a long wait when he heard crows giving an alarm call. His eye caught movement. At first, he wasn't sure it was Jonas, but as the visitor neared, Vilho recognized Jonas' cat-like walk. He sat still, waiting for Jonas to give him a sign. Jonas read the message, gave the sign and headed for the cave to meet him. They embraced momentarily and both started talking at once.

Jonas said, "Tell me your story first."

Vilho related the events of the last three days briefly while Jonas listened without comment until he was through.

"Well, you're here, safe and sound, and I'm glad you're here."

"I didn't want to put you and Emma in any kind of jeopardy."

"I don't think you've done that. I know you took all the precautions. Let's go to the cabin. Emma will be glad to see you. We have some good news, but I'll let Emma tell you about that."

With that they left, checking their back trail every few minutes. Vilho followed Jonas, wending his way through the forest. He gasped when they broke through the trees and saw Jonas' cabin for the first time. "Jonas, it's just beautiful," Vilho said appreciatively, "I never imagined anything like this out here. It's so safe and isolated."

"Wait until you see the inside," beamed Jonas, "There's some of your handiwork in there."

"If you have that sauna working, I sure would like to try it out."

"It works great, and we'll heat it for you. I better announce to Emma that we're having company. Sometimes, because we have no one else around, she runs around naked or wears nothing more than an apron."

Vilho intoned, "Newlyweds!"

Jonas called through the door, "Emma, dear, we have some company. I hope you're decent."

"Come in. Come in. Who's with you?"

Emma saw Vilho and rushed to give him a big hug and kiss before asking. "What are you doing here?"

Jonas laughed and said, "Hurry and fix him something to eat. All he's had to eat for several days is a fish and berries."

"Yes, yes. We don't get any company here, Vilho, as you know. It's wonderful to have you as our first guest. What would you like to eat? We have some cured ham or fresh venison. We have fresh fish, but if that's all you ate last, you probably would like something else."

"The venison sounds good. I haven't had venison for a long time."

Emma busied herself around the kitchen while Jonas and Vilho sat down to talk. They talked about the death of crazy Jake and current happenings in town.

Vilho said, "We're getting more and more people to join the resistance. Some are active with our group, and some just support us with food, money, clothes, and sometimes weapons and ammunition. The ghost symbol we use has paid off. They can't understand how you can be in so many different places or how you always get away. I know the officers suspect there's more than one person involved. The rank and file still believe you're a ghost with supernatural powers. You can't believe how much fear and superstition is associated with your name. Killing Jake brought some more to our side."

"This is serious stuff," said Jonas. "It's getting more and more dangerous getting supplies from town. As you probably noticed, Emma is pregnant. When her time comes, I'd like to take her into town, but it's so dangerous that I hesitate."

"I noticed her condition. I hoped she'd spill the good news."

"I probably should have let her do that, too. Act like I hadn't said a word."

Vilho grinned, then grew serious again. "I've had talks with several in the group, and the consensus is that we can't take the chance of your being captured. We think the movement would lose a lot of momentum if you were caught and killed or put in prison."

Jonas scoffed. "You know they're not going to catch me. I've eluded them too long and know too much about how they operate."

Vilho didn't back down. "There's always that chance that they'd get lucky. Then our main symbol of resistance is gone."

Jonas looked toward the kitchen, his face filling with concern for Emma. "But where would I go with Emma the way she is and all?"

Having gotten that far, Vilho took a deep breath and plunged. "We've given that some thought. We thought of Sweden, but that might be a bit close. The Russians could set up a raid to get you back. Sweden does have a few Russians sympathizers that might turn you in, especially for the reward money. Our best solution is to send you to America where there's no way they can touch you. We have some friends that have immigrated there. I'm sure they'd be willing to help you get started in farming or whatever else you might like to do."

This was a lot to consider. Jonas sat back. "I must admit it does sound appealing. I'm getting a little tired of constantly looking over my shoulder. With the baby coming, I'm getting more apprehensive about our position here in the wilderness."

"Lieutenant Barloff and Elsa might be able to help. Elsa used to work for a shipping company in Helsinki, and she still has connections. She can book you and Emma secretly on one of their ships bound for America."

Jonas called Emma from the kitchen and briefly filled her in. "It would mean leaving all our family," she said, "but when I married you, I agreed to go where you went, forsaking all others. It would be hard, but I think I would like America from everything I've heard."

Vilho said, "I think you should make up your minds to go as soon as possible for several reasons. Right now it's the height of the shipping season. Two, Emma is still able to travel with no problems. Three, we don't want to wait for cold weather and the difficulties that would bring."

Jonas looked about the comfortable cabin. "I sure hate leaving this idyllic spot. It has a lot of good memories for both of us."

"I've been thinking of that, too," replied Vilho, "I would like to buy this place from you, and I know Mary would like it. Ever since the incident with the Russian officer—"

"What incident?" Emma asked quickly, concerned.

Vilho drew in a long breath. "She was raped, Emma. The bastard raped her. Since then, she's withdrawn into herself. She thinks she's tainted somehow. Spending some time here in the wilderness with me might be good for her."

Emma's mouth hung open in horror. She said, "What happened? Did you find out who it was and do anything?"

"All I know is that it was late afternoon, and she was going to my house to wait for me. This Russian officer grabbed her and dragged her into the woods and raped her. She made it to my house, but she's been depressed ever since. I assured her it wasn't her fault. I told her it made no difference about my loving her. We know who it was, but I haven't been able to get at him. Rest assured, I will kill him and carve 'Vilho and Mary' on his chest!"

Emma said, "I'm so sorry. I wish I could be there to comfort her. She needs a woman to talk to about it."

"I think I would like her to come out here while you're still here."

"Oh, yes! Please bring her as soon as you can."

Jonas said, "Forget about buying the cabin. I'll just give it to you."

"No, you'll need the money in America."

Jonas knew this made good sense. He would need every cent he could get to tide him over until he could get started in America.

Emma set out venison, fried potatoes, and onions. She then brought out some fresh-baked bread, saying, "You'll have to eat the bread with jam or cheese as we're out of butter. We're due to go back for supplies soon."

"Don't apologize. Everything looks great, and I'm hungry."

Vilho dug in with gusto. Emma looked pleased that he liked her cooking. The tense atmosphere began to relax enough to allow them to talk of old times, old friends, and all they would miss leaving their beloved land.

They bedded Vilho down on a pallet on the floor as there was but the one bed. When Jonas built the cabin, he hadn't planned on guests.

Emma awakened early to the chirping of birds in the trees surrounding the cabin. One old blue jay used to eating out of Emma's hand was especially raucous. She went out to feed him to shut him up so the two men could sleep awhile longer.

Vilho woke, stretched leisurely on his pallet and watched Emma bustle about the kitchen. He thought of how wonderful it would be to get Mary to such an idyllic place. Then she would have time to heal.

Emma called them to table, admonishing them to eat before the food got cold. The men got up, washed in the sauna and joined her at the table.

"I ate like a horse last night," said Vilho, "and thought I'd never want to eat again. Looking at this fine food, I'm starving again."

"Help yourself," said Emma. "There's plenty."

After breakfast, Vilho offered to do the dishes to repay their hospitality. Emma would have none of that. "I like doing them myself. Besides, I might not get many more times at it before we have to leave this lovely place. If it wasn't for the baby coming, I could be happy here forever."

Jonas busied himself getting his pack ready to go to town. He put in smoked and fresh fish for Toivo. His father-in-law looked forward to the fish and game they brought almost as much as seeing them.

He said, "I hope America has good hunting and fishing. If not, I might have to come back and take my chances with the Russians."

Emma eyes him, hearing regret in his voice. "It's probably better there. It's truly wild country with plenty of fish and game."

"I know you're right, Emma, dear." Jonas said. "I guess I just felt a little sad about leaving here."

The walk into town was leisurely and nostalgic. Jonas pointed out good places to watch for deer, several good fishing spots, and berry patches. He also pointed out the trails usually used by the Russian patrols. Earlier Jonas showed Vilho his alarm system on the trail to tell if he had visitors.

They arrived at the hill overlooking the town before it was dark enough to cross. They sat down among the pine needles, and Emma passed out the remnants of lunch.

They talked in hushed tones as though they could be heard in town and watched the coming and going of Russians and townspeople alike. They recognized a few people by their particular walk or garb. Every time one of them thought they recognized someone, Jonas put up the telescope to see if they were right or wrong. Emma had the best score in recognition and teased the two men about ignoring people's little mannerisms.

After dark, they eased quietly into town like ghosts, wearing dark clothing to better blend with the night. With Aimo gone, the danger of someone spying on them had lessened.

Anna answered the knock, her eyes lighting up at the sight of her daughter. She called softly to Toivo, "Toi we have some unexpected company. Come see who it is."

Toivo was cat napping and came to the door with a dour expression on his face. It lighted up immediately when he saw the three of them.

Hugs and kisses were exchanged all around.

"We wondered if you caught up with Jonas or not, Vilho," said Toivo. "We heard about your going into the forest and thought you would try to contact Jonas. I can see you did that, and I'm glad."

"Come," said Anna, "I'll put on the coffee pot. I just baked some fresh cinnamon rolls, and I was thinking about you when I baked them."

The consensus around the table was that none of them should leave the house. They were going to get Matt to contact Barloff and Elsa about making arrangements in Helsinki for their passage to America.

Vilho said, "The fewer people who know about this, the better for safety's sake. We want everyone to think Jonas is still out there wreaking havoc with the Russian forces."

Matt came in, surprised and delighted to see them all but left immediately to contact John and Elsa Barloff.

One element in their favor was that Barloff was in charge of the monthly trips to Helsinki for supplies. Elsa often accompanied him. This would look less suspicious when she went to make the arrangements for their passage. Barloff was due to leave on one of his regular trips the next week, so the timing was good.

Matt came back with Barloff and Elsa in tow. Barloff was glad to see Jonas. "Matt told me a little of your plans. I'm glad that I can return the debt I owe you in some small way. I know I can never repay you in full for saving my life. Between you and Elsa, I've come around to your way of thinking. Elsa and I have thought about going to America ourselves to get away from a job that I hate."

"Why don't you make arrangements to go with us? All you have to do is make both arrangements to coincide with your next trip to Helsinki."

Barloff said, "It's a thought. Elsa and I will have to talk it over."

Elsa said, "There's nothing to talk over as far as I'm concerned. I'd like to get us away from here."

Barloff looked at her in surprise and said, "Our biggest obstacle is that we don't have the money."

Jonas said, "You're going to leave the Russian Army and the country forever. You could sell all the Russian horses and wagons to some crook in Helsinki just before we left. It would do my heart good to stick another needle in the Russian hide."

"That's a thought, it would compensate me for the mustering out and retirement pay I won't get for the time I've served," said Barloff.

Everything was settled as to what was going to be done in Helsinki. Their departure would be determined by the availability of space on any ship bound for America. Barloff wouldn't be back for two weeks, so Jonas put supplies together to go back to the wilderness. The plan was to return to the cabin immediately. They wanted to avoid any danger of snooping Russians.

"I want you to bring Mary to the cabin," Emma said. "I want to help her get started. I know I can be a big help to get her over feeling the shame of being raped."

"Mary would love it if you're sure she won't be in your way with your packing and all," said Vilho. "I wish I could come with you, too, but I have to report back for duty, and I want to try to find out who killed Jake."

Matt left to get Mary. Everything else was soon ready, and it was still dark enough for them to melt back into the forest. Good-byes were said all around as they slipped out the back door and into the night.

Matt and Mary waited for them on the lake trail.

The two women followed Jonas closely. He had made the trip many times before in the dark and could read the way by the stars and skyline.

Chapter 23

Raid

JONAS STIRRED TO NOISES IN THE CABIN. Emma was up early fixing his breakfast. He rolled to the side of the bed and said, "You're an early riser this morning."

"I was restless," she said, "and was wondering what was going on about our trip to America."

Jonas thought he heard something else. He came into the kitchen and gave her a hug. "It wouldn't be because you want to see your family again, would it?" he said gently. "Are you getting a little lonesome and worried about leaving them ?"

"Well, a little," she said. "We're so close and I'll miss them."

"All right. I'll get everything ready. I want to see Vilho to see how they're doing with the resistance movement. Where's Mary?" he said, seeing her pallet empty.

"She went out to get a little kindling. She'll be back in a minute," she said. "That resistance movement worries me a little. It could get out of hand. Vilho can be so reckless and headstrong sometimes. He scares me with his intensity for freedom.

"He believes in freedom so strongly that he acts a little dangerous at times," Jonas said, "but that's what makes a good leader. He does have the courage of his own convictions. He is a bit more ruthless than I think necessary. We have never agreed on all this killing he wants to do, and it has caused a rift in our relationship."

Mary came in with the kindling. She greeted Jonas cheerfully. He was pleased that she had perked up so well since coming to the cabin. She and Emma had had long talks together, many, especially in the beginning, accompanied with tears.

The three of them had breakfast outside. It was a beautiful summer day, and the sun crept over the spruce trees, giving everything a warm, golden glow. The grass shimmered emerald green. Dew drops glistened on the grass, and the spruce needles gave back an occasional flash of light as though someone was signalling.

Jonas said, "I can't believe how just one dew drop can reflect so much light back at you."

"I was just thinking the same thing," said Emma, "It's funny how we think the same so many times."

"I suppose it's because we're so much in love that we communicate with each other silently without knowing it."

"I think you're right," Emma said.

"It's so peaceful and quiet here," Mary said. "I just love it. I'm anxious to go into town to see everyone, but I know it's not a good idea. You two go, and I'll keep the cabin safe. It might be nice to get a feel of how my life will be when you two leave for America."

It was agreed, Jonas and Emma would go to town, and Mary would stay behind. She offered to clean up from breakfast to let them get an early start.

They loafed for a few more minutes before Jonas got up to get their packs ready to go. He said, "We'll take our fish lines and see if we can get a few fresh fish to take to your father."

"Oh, he would like that."

In a few minutes, they had shouldered their packs to head for the fishing hole and then town. The grass was still wet from the dew. Their feet got slightly damp in their soft moccasins, but they knew they left fewer traces by wearing them.

Their favorite fishing hole, secluded from prying eyes, was calm and serene. It was so still the water's images made telling up from down difficult. Trout finned lazily below the crystal clear surface.

Jonas cut two willow poles and strung hook and line to them. He turned over a few rocks to get worms. He baited Emma's hook out of courtesy as she was still a bit squeamish about putting the worm on the hook.

Emma flipped her baited hook into the pond to disturb the mirror surface. It broke the upside down image, making larger and larger circles toward shore. The ripples barely stopped when the line when taut and started cutting through the water. Emma squealed with delight as she fought the fish. She had it almost to the bank when it got away.

She said, "I lost that one, and it was a great big one."

"That's the way it is," said Jonas. "The big ones always get away."

Shortly, they had a large stringer of fish and Jonas said, "We'd better clean these and get on our way."

Emma was lying on her back, her pole propped up on a rock while she looked up at the fleecy white clouds in the azure sky.

She said, "It's so beautiful. I could just lie here and do nothing."

Jonas, busy cleaning the fish, said, "We don't have to go in today. The trip could wait another day or two."

"No, we better go. Besides, I want to get a pair of pants."

"Pants?"

"Yes, pants, trousers just like I'm wearing to travel to town. I only have this one pair, but I like them a whole lot better than dresses. I think I'll wear them all the time."

Jonas looked at her quizzically, saying nothing. With her slender build and recently shortened hair she could pass for a young boy.

The hike into town was pleasant. Warm and windless, the day was as Jonas described it, "soft."

Emma asked, "What do you mean, soft?"

"Just that. The air and warmth feel soft on your skin."

They walked arm in arm whenever the trail permitted. Before they knew it, they were at the edge of the woods looking at Emma's house. The long summer day was coming to an end, and Jonas sat and watched the Lehtinen house and the one next door with his telescope. Everything looked good, the window shade signal was right. They waited a little longer for more darkness before they crossed the open ground.

Anna was glad to see them both, giving each of them a hug and kiss. She held Emma at arms length and looked at her with love.

"You look so well, Emma, married life is really agreeing with you. You cut your hair short. I kind of like it. Toi and Matt just went into the woods to look for timbers for the barn. They weren't going to do any cutting today, just looking. They needed an excuse to get out of the house for a little while, but I don't understand what's keeping them after dark."

Anna talked rapidly as though she had to hurry to get everything said about all the recent happenings. All the while she was setting the table with baked goods and putting a fresh pot of coffee on the stove.

Jonas was pleased to hear about the raid for the new guns. He asked more questions of Anna but she could only tell him a small bit.

"All I know is that the Russians are missing two wagon loads of guns and ammunition. I assume Vilho and his bunch were the ones that did it, but I don't know for sure. Oh, yes, there is some speculation that their own people might have done the job as the leader spoke fluent Russian."

"That's Vilho," said Jonas. "Mika's been teaching him Russian."

Just then Matt and Toi came back from their trip to the woods.

Toi said as he came into the entry, "Anna must have known we were coming because I smell coffee brewing." His eyes lit up when he saw Emma and Jonas. He rushed over to give Emma a big hug and kiss, slapped Jonas on the back saying, "It's sure good to see the two of you."

Matt came over to give both of them a hug. He asked Jonas if Anna had told them about the raid.

Jonas replied, "Yes, but I would like to know more. Can you get word to Vilho? I'd like to talk to him about that and several other ideas."

"I sure will. He's either home or at the Boar's Head. He's been spending a lot of time with Mika lately. I'll find him."

Matt left to find Vilho. An hour later he came back with Vilho. Greetings were exchanged all around. Soon Jonas and Vilho found a quiet moment to talk in low tones about the Russians. Vilho gave Jonas the details of the raid.

"Mika and I had two heavy wagons like the Russians would transport the American guns. We filled them with stones and waited just off the river road. When they came past, we stopped them, tied up the teamsters and took the wagons. Then we transferred guns to our wagons and stones to theirs. If they got trackers after us, we didn't want them to notice when the wagons got lighter. After our wagons full of their guns and ammunition had left the road and we wiped those tracks completely clear, we gradually threw off the stones and had teams of men on horses ride up to the wagons and away as if riders muscled the guns and dropped them in the woods. Trackers or no trackers, they never got close to finding the guns. Now we have a good stock of Winchester rifles."

Jonas said, "That was good planning on your part."

Vilho equivocated. "Well, we had a lot of good luck on our side. I see that now. There could have been heavy guards with the shipment, or someone could have come down the road while we were transferring the guns and stones. I've lain awake at night thinking about everything that could have gone wrong. Next time I'll plan better."

"There were no problems," Jonas said. "That's what counts."

Vilho whispered, "We're planning another raid. Would you like to join us? This might be your last chance before you and Emma leave."

"Danger or no, of course I would. What do you have planned?"

"John Barloff told us of a shipment of American-made revolvers, .45 caliber, made by Colt Firearms just for the Russians. I saw one of them, and it looks like a formidable weapon. They're in the warehouse now, but the Russians are going to issue them next week. We want to take them before then."

"How many guns are there, and how are they packed?"

"There are one hundred of them. They're packed ten to a box, which will make them easy to carry away. There's a lot of ammunition for them and those boxes are heavy. John said there are reloading tools too, but he didn't know the location in the warehouse. I thought we would steal anything useable and then set the warehouse afire."

"Sounds like serious business," said Jonas.

"I would have part of our group stampede the horses. All of us would be in town by then. By stampeding the horses, they would think we scattered to the forest and were trying to delay pursuit."

"That's good thinking. By the time they get their horses back and organized, Emma and I should be back at our place."

"I thought we might use some of the horses to transport the guns and ammunition to a safe place. The tracks would be going everywhere in the stampede so they won't be able to follow any of our tracks."

"When?" asked Jonas.

"I thought we might try for tomorrow night. Our little group knows about it and are on alert. All I have to do is send the word. And, of course, we'd use the ghost symbol."

"Ghost symbol?" said Jonas.

Vilho snickered. "Well, as nervous as the Russians are about you being a ghost, we thought we could use a symbol of a ghost to convince them you and people associated with you took the guns. They've never had any luck finding you, and if they thought you were behind it, they wouldn't look so hard at the rest of the Finns in town. Mika made up some ghost masks, and we left a rag with holes in it as a ghost symbol in the empty wagons. And, because I spoke Russian when I ordered the teamsters out of the wagons, they think maybe a Russian might be to blame."

"Interesting," said Jonas. "I think I'm glad I'm going to America. Pretty soon they'll have the whole Russian army looking for me. It would make sense to continue to use the symbol if for no other reason than to confuse the issue."

"That was kind of my thinking, too," replied Vilho.

"Emma will be glad we're staying a little longer, but she will be upset that I'm going on the raid."

"Let's meet in the woods directly behind the warehouse tomorrow night. There's a grove of spruce trees there."

"I know right where it is," said Jonas, "I'll go a little early and scout the area to make sure we have no unwelcome guests."

Then Vilho left to alert his team to the update in their plans.

Jonas broke the news to Emma about the raid. Emma was in tears, begging him not to go, but Jonas was just as insistent about going. "After all," he said, "I'm the one that started this whole resistance movement. I'm their reason for being. I am their symbol. This will be good for the new men to see me involved to keep the legend alive after we are gone."

"I know all that, but what if you get killed or they capture you? There will be no leader or symbol or anything."

They went to bed, both very troubled. This was their first disagreement. They stayed on their own sides of the bed until Jonas took her in his arms and said, "It'll be all right. I wouldn't go if I thought otherwise."

Emma said, "I can't help worrying."

Jonas woke up the next morning to look out at a bright and beautiful day. The sun in the east made the sky look like burnished gold. Crows cawed in the distance. Still farther away a rooster crowed to announce to the world that morning was here.

Emma was sleeping quietly, like a young child, all curled up in her half of the covers.

Jonas said to himself, "Such a beautiful day to be planning violence. The world, at times, is such a controversial place to live."

Anna was rattling pots and pans for breakfast. Jonas heard the noises and quietly slipped into his clothes to go down and join her for coffee.

The rest of the day dragged for Jonas. He cleaned his rifle twice, sharpened his knife even though it was already razor sharp. He paced about the house like a caged animal.

Vilho came by to tell him everything was go for that night. They planned to wait until about midnight when it got good and dark.

Shortly after Vilho left, Jonas kissed Emma and slipped into the woods to scout the area. As soon as he was in the woods, he relaxed visibly. This was his element. Now he felt at home, safe with a feel and knowledge of everything going on around him. A short circle around the spruce grove showed no suspicious signs of anyone in the area. He slipped quietly into the grove.

The center of the grove had a small clearing not visible from the outside. It was a good place to meet. Jonas looked around, slipped his pack off and hid it in an old fallen spruce. From his pack he extracted his telescope, crawled through the trees to the edge of the grove to look over the Russian compound in front of him. An attack from this angle had been chosen because it was the only area with wire fence. The rest of the compound had a high board fence. The board fence for that last section hadn't been built yet. He sat cross legged so he could support his elbows on his knees to steady the telescope. He was effectively screened by low spruce branches. Swinging the telescope back and forth, he observed everything going on. This brought back memories of his soldiering days in the same compound. He saw many changes in the place since he left, most of them due to the Russians hunting him so hard.

He noted all the changes so he would remember where everything was in case of an emergency during the raid. After several more sweeps of his telescope and intensive study, he was satisfied. He eased back into the center of the grove to await the rest of the raiders.

Vilho was the first to arrive, but Jonas knew someone was coming long before he got there. The almost imperceptible change in forest sounds alerted him. He then saw Vilho slipping quietly through the trees. Jonas slipped quietly around to come up behind him saying, "You're dead."

Vilho spun, drawing his knife. Then he recognized Jonas.

"My God man how did you get behind me? I just came through that way, and I doubt if a mouse could have hidden from me."

"Practice and a long time living like a hunted animal."

"It scared the hell out of me. I had no idea there was anyone around even though you told me you were going to scout the area ahead of us."

"I did scout the area and didn't find a thing out of the ordinary. I watched the compound for a long time with the telescope, and everything looks very normal."

The rest of the raiders trickled in by two and threes. Each time, long before they got there, Jonas told Vilho how many were in the party and from what direction they would come. Vilho was absolutely flabbergasted at Jonas' ability to detect intruders.

As each of the men got there, Vilho said to them, "Sit quietly, watch and listen."

Shortly Jonas said, "Two coming from the northwest." A little later, "Two coming directly from the north."

The men looked at him in awe. No one heard the newcomers until they were practically on top of them. They could hardly believe what was happening, but they were seeing it with their own eyes.

With the arrival of the last men Vilho said, "Jonas and I outlined the plan last night. If you will listen closely, I'll give each of you your assignments. I want you to listen to it all, so you will be aware of the entire plan. If you see someone miss their assignment for any reason, you should be able to take it over so everything goes as planned.

First, Jacob, you pick ten men to go with you to the horse corral. Pick the best riders. One man will stay there to stampede the horses when you hear an explosion in the warehouse. The other men will ride the horses to the warehouse so we can haul guns and ammunition. There will be a total of ten horses. We made slings to go front and back with you on the horses to hold guns and ammunition. We want the pistols and ammunition to go first. We should be able to load four cases per horse. The rest will take anything else that might be useful. Individuals can pick up smaller items before we set off the explosion to torch the place.

You men with horses will tie them near the door and come inside to help carry material out. As soon as your horse is loaded, move out. We'll use the house on the rock quarry road as a dump station again until we can distribute them.

"Arne will go with us and be lookout in case someone comes this way. The rest of us will go into the warehouse and get the goods we want. Jonas and I will fix up some powder and ammunition to set the warehouse off. We want ammunition to be going off so the fire fighters will be afraid to get close. As soon as we get the last horse loaded and on its way, we'll set everything off. That will be the signal to stampede the other horses. Those of us on foot will scatter to the four winds. It will be some time before they can round up the horses to start an effective search of any kind. By then we should all be where we are supposed to be normally, and Jonas will be well on his way back into the wilderness. There are no guards, so all we have to do is be reasonably quiet. If there are no questions, we'll wait a little longer for it to get darker, and then we'll be on our way."

"What if we meet someone on the road with the horses?" asked one of the riders.

"A good point. It's not very likely that late at night and on the back roads. If it's light enough, stick to the woods adjoining the road. If you do meet someone, keep going unless they're Russian. Then you'll have to kill them to insure our safety. We better break open one of the boxes of pistols and some ammunition. Each rider will have a pistol. If you meet any Russians, they won't expect a pistol, so you should be able to shoot them at point blank range. These are single-action pistols, so you have to pull the hammer back for each shot, but you do have six shots. After tonight, we'll need to hide the pistols for a while. We need a cooling-off period on this raid before we issue them to our own people. The only one I want to have one is Jonas. He's going to be suspected of taking them, but he won't be subject to search and interrogation."

One of the other men asked, "When can we expect to get some of these new rifles and pistols?"

"We'll just have to play it by ear, but soon. The problem is, if you do happen to get caught with any of these, it will be the same as signing your own death sentence."

As soon as it was dark enough everyone looked to Jonas and Vilho for the go signal. Jonas stood up and said, "It's time. Horse riders move out first, so you'll have a head start. Good luck to everyone."

"The riders should be able to go through the woods unless the night gets a lot blacker than it is right now," said Vilho.

"Yes, it looks very good," Jonas answered quietly.

They moved toward the warehouse following Jonas and Vilho. Everyone had dressed in dark colors to better blend with the night. Vilho couldn't help notice how much quieter Jonas moved than anyone else. Each step made no sound. Vilho could hear himself and the rest of the men lumbering along like so many cows. Jonas signalled the men to stay behind the warehouse until they got a door open. Jonas and Vilho eased up to the door nearest the woods. A small pry bar, brought for the purpose, pried the lock loose. The nails screeched a bit as they pulled the lock and hasp loose. Jonas cringed, turning to survey the compound for anyone hearing the noise and coming to investigate. It remained quiet.

Vilho slid open the door while Jonas signalled the men to come forward. Once inside Vilho found some lanterns he had seen earlier. He shut the door. The only window he covered with a handy blanket before he lit the lanterns. They found the revolvers and ammunition and began moving them to the door, awaiting the horses and riders.

Jonas said urgently, "*Shush*, two people coming toward us from the compound."

Arne slipped in to tell them the same news. They put out the lanterns. It was pitch black inside the warehouse. Jonas ripped the blanket off the window to let in a little light and watch the intruders. He stationed two men at the door by which they had entered and two at the big door. He doubted anyone would be using the big door that late at night, but he did not want to take the chance. He and Vilho went to the small front door nearest to the compound. He was praying that the riders didn't come up until they could take care of this problem.

Muted voices and footsteps came from outside the small front door. One of them had a key as he was fumbling with the lock. Jonas signalled to Vilho to take the one nearest him and he would take the other. Vilho pulled his knife, Jonas saw the flash of steel and signalled use your hand swinging his fist in pantomime. Vilho slipped the knife back into its sheath.

As they came through the door, they both struck their targets. Jonas aimed for a point just behind the man's ear. The man fell like a stunned ox from Jonas' fist. Vilho had to hit his man twice before he put him down. Vilho quickly closed the door and rehung the blanket window shade before he relit the lanterns. They found a small coil of rope to tie the men and gag them. Jonas put a sack over each head so they couldn't see.

Vilho said, "Whew, that was close."

Jonas said, "Don't talk. We'll use sign language to tell everyone what to do. When we're sure they're conscious, give some orders in Russian. Some of us can answer yes and no to you in Russian. We might get away with them thinking these are Russian thieves. We'll leave a ghost symbol."

Vilho moved to one of the other men and whispered in his ear to pass along the word of no talking and then answering Vilho only in Russian. Vilho would nod his head or shake his head if the answer was to be yes or no.

One of the Russians stirred. Jonas motioned to Vilho to let him know one was conscious. Vilho nodded and gave some orders in Russian. Jonas and Aero grunted back yes in Russian.

They pried the top off one of the gun boxes with Vilho's pry bar. The guns were heavily greased. Jonas rummaged around to find rags and a rod that would suffice as a ram rod to clean the guns. He quickly ran a patch through each of the cylinders and then through the bore. He loaded the gun with six rounds showing the riders how to cock and fire the piece. He demonstrated with an unloaded gun, making the riders try it to make sure they knew how to fire it.

Riders brought their horses around to be loaded. They loaded quickly and went on their way. Two pair of men were assigned to carry the trussed Russians outside. Jonas was sure they were both conscious, but they were acting like they were still out.

When everyone had cleared the building, Jonas and Vilho broke open a couple kegs of powder. Jonas piled a quantity of ammunition on top of the spilled powder, while Vilho laid a trail of powder to the side door. Jonas checked outside and gave the all clear sign to Vilho.

Vilho threw his still-lit lantern into the powder trail. He made sure the powder caught, and then he and Jonas took off running for the woods. They barely made it to the edge of the woods when the first explosion came. It was a little muffled, but the second one was much louder. When the second one went off, everyone had reached the spruce grove again. Vilho pantomimed and gave orders in Russian to leave the two Russians in the grove. Everyone left quickly to go their separate ways.

Jonas said to Vilho as they ran, "I'm going to get Emma and start back. By midmorning these woods will be swarming with Cossacks and foot soldiers. I need a head start especially with Emma along. I would hate to have the Russians chasing the two of us. I'll be back soon and will see you then. Good luck, and God keep you well."

Vilho trotted quickly in the direction of his house. Jonas watched him go, suddenly saddened by the turn of events. He and Vilho used to have so much fun hunting and fishing, and here they were involved in a small-scale war. Then he took off at a trot with his rifle at his side. The bulge of the new pistol in his belt and four boxes of ammunition in his jacket pockets felt good. The Lehtinen house came into view shortly. Hardly any effort was expended in getting there.

Emma was up waiting for him. She seemed enormously relieved and gave him a kiss before saying anything. She said, "I'm glad you're back safe and sound. I heard some explosions over that way and assumed it was you and your men. How did it go?"

"It went well. Get your gear. We must leave right now. It's a light night, and we can get almost back to the cabin by daylight. By daybreak, there'll be Russians all over these woods."

"I thought we might have to do that," she said, "so I got everything packed and ready to go."

"Good girl, let's get on with it."

"I've written a note for mother. I told her this might happen and not to worry. I thought we would be leaving at first light anyway."

They left quickly but quietly. As they crossed the open ground, they could see a glow from the still-burning warehouse. They hurried along, often stumbling in the semi-darkness. By holding hands, they kept each other up.

Emma said in a stage whisper. "I don't see how you can tell where we're going. I'm completely lost."

"Have faith my love. We'll get there."

Jonas moved by memory and instinct. He knew to stay to the ridge tops, and every time he felt the ground sloping away he backtracked to find the right path.

He lost his way several times in heavy timber where very little light penetrated, even in daylight. He made Emma stand still while he reconnoitered the area to find the right path. Then he returned for Emma and guided her on the way again. By midmorning, somewhat later than expected, they made it to the cabin. Jonas felt they were safe, as no pursuit could be mounted that early. He was glad they decided to take off in the dark.

* * * * *

Back at the compound all was pandemonium. People were running everywhere, but no one wanted to get close to the fire because of the heat and exploding shells sending bullets whistling through the air.

Gerchenoff was jolted out of his sleep by the first muffled explosion. "What the hell was that?" he grumbled. Then the second one went off.

He leaped out of his bed screaming, "Orderly, find out what the hell is going on out there at this time of night!"

The orderly came running, "Looks like the big warehouse, sir."

"Damn. Get me a horse so I can go see what's happening."

Gerchenoff threw on some clothes while the orderly went to fetch a horse. He started walking over to Rykov's quarters only to meet him coming toward him. Rykov, as usual, was fully dressed and immaculate.

Rykov snapped, "What's going on around here?"

"I don't know," said Gerchenoff. "Looks like the big warehouse is on fire."

"I can see the warehouse is on fire you ass! I want to know why!"

Gerchenoff snapped back, "I don't know a damn thing more than you. Stop shouting and let's go see what we can find out."

The orderly came running up saying, "I'm sorry sir, the horses are all gone, stampeded, either on purpose or by the explosions. I think on purpose because the corral gate was wide open."

They got near the fire and Gerchenoff said, "I'll get a bucket brigade going to put the fire out."

Rykov said, "Forget it. It's too late to save anything, even the building is too far gone. There's no use getting men hurt around that exploding stuff. Just let it burn to the ground. I'm going back and get some sleep."

With that he turned on his heel and left Gerchenoff standing there.

The two hapless Russians that Jonas and Vilho had tied up got themselves free. They reported to Gerchenoff of their capture by the raiders who had set fire to the warehouse. They said they saw some light and went to investigate when they were slugged, trussed and gagged. In truth they were both scheduled for leave in Helsinki. They were going to help themselves to some supplies they could sell in Helsinki for extra cash.

One of the men said, "The men were Russian. The leader gave orders in Russian, and the men answered in Russian. They didn't know we had regained consciousness so soon after the slugging. We both acted like we were still out even after they took us out of the warehouse. That's the other reason we think they were Russians, as the Finns probably would have just let us burn with the warehouse."

A soldier ran up to Gerchenoff and handed him a ghost symbol he had found tacked to the corral gate. Gerchenoff was furious.

Several hours later, Gerchenoff and Rykov met to discuss what they knew. Rykov said, "If it was Russians doing this job, that's what they would do, try to blame the Finns."

"Why would they burn the warehouse?"

"Probably to hide what ever they took. I want the contents gone over after it cools to see if we can find out what's missing."

Gerchenoff made a good guess saying, "I doubt we'll have to look further for the new pistols. I'd bet on it. This was probably the same group that hit us for the new rifles."

"You're probably right," said Rykov grudgingly.

*   *   *   *   *

The next day Vilho found out what the Russians were thinking. He could hardly wait until night when he strode into the Boar's Head to see Mika saying, "It went unbelievably well. The Russians are sure it was a job done by some of their own men. They didn't bother to mount a search of any kind outside the compound."

He related the incident of the two Russians with Jonas getting the idea of giving the orders in Russian so they would hear.

"All in all, it was great," said Vilho reaching for the mug of cold beer that Mika sat in front of him.

Chapter 24

To America

ELSA ACCOMPANIED HER HUSBAND to Helsinki so she could arrange passage for Jonas, Emma, John and herself. Her ex-boss was sympathetic to the idea. He expressed resentment of the Russians and admired the exploits of Jonas.

The trip proved uneventful but tedious for Elsa, riding the big, lumbering freight wagon. She and John, had a small tent they shared at night, but, during the day, privacy was almost impossible as she was the only female on the trip.

She longed to be someplace where she and her husband could settle down. She disliked John's soldiering for the Russians.

The men on the trip made snide remarks to John about a Russian officer marrying a Finn. Barloff was going to bash in some heads. Elsa reminded him he had only a few days left. There was no point in getting into trouble now. "Patience, my dear husband," she told him. "I know you love me, and that's all that counts. Soon all this will be behind us."

"I love you, and I feel like letting them know it."

Elsa stayed quiet for a time to let John's temper cool down.

"I'm worried about what I'm going to do in America," he said sometime later. "All I have ever known is soldiering."

"I know you well enough to know that you can do anything," she assured him. They talked about everything they had heard about America. It was going to be a good life for them. For the first time since they were married, Elsa felt like they had a good future. "We can sell the house and furniture when we get back," she said, planning. "We've saved a little, but, if we find someone to buy the Russian horses and wagons then we'll have plenty of money."

"I'm a little worried about that. We'll have the teamsters to worry about. I don't know how many wagons we'll have on the next trip, but it'll probably be at least six. How do we get the teamsters to help get the wagons delivered to the buyer?"

"I don't know," Elsa admitted, "but it has to work out."

"I feel like we're doing wrong selling the horses and wagons."

"Remember, you're going to give up your mustering out pay and your retirement pay. I think my ex-boss could put us in touch with a buyer for the horses and wagons."

"We'd surely get caught."

"How could we if we waited until the last minute before the ship sailed? We would be far out to sea before they would even suspect that they were gone. It would be four or five days before word could get back to Kiivijarvi that something was wrong. The men won't care. It'd give them extra days of carousing before they could arrange for more wagons."

"We probably couldn't get much for stolen property."

"Who cares," replied Elsa. "Anything we get would be that much more help in getting started in America."

John's natural honesty worked at him, but Elsa pushed him into agreeing. Then Elsa said, "We ought to make arrangements right now for the horses and wagons. We may not have time next month."

Barloff said, "Let's think about it some more."

Elsa's impatience bent, and she chided, "You know we're going to do it, so don't waver. We'll never get an opportunity like this again."

"You're right as always," replied John.

Elsa made arrangements for the four of them to embark on a ship leaving for America in one month to coincide with John's next supply trip.

The buyer for the wagons and horses contacted them at their hotel. Young, well-dressed and sure of himself, he spoke Russian and Finnish fluently. He assured them that he dealt in stolen Russian goods all the time.

He said, "You'd be surprised at how many high-ranking Russian officers I deal with. This deal is small compared with many I put together every day. I agreed to it because my friend and your ex-boss at the shipping company asked me. I'll give you top money when you deliver. I won't cheat his friends. I went to the stables and looked over your horses and wagons. I'll give you $1000.00 when you deliver those or ones like them next month."

They were both surprised and pleased as they didn't think they could get anywhere near that kind of money for stolen merchandise. John felt more at ease when he heard there were other high-ranking officers selling stolen goods.

The dealer in stolen goods asked, "Do you know that Jonas everyone is chasing? He's my greatest living hero."

John looked a little guilty but answered, "Yes, I know him. I owe my life to him. I was the only survivor in a ski patrol disaster. This is the reason for our leaving. I can't stand to help hunt him down after what he did for me."

"Jonas represents freedom to a group I belong to here in Helsinki."

John said, "In a roundabout way he's my hero also. All the people he killed were killed out of necessity as they were trying to kill him. The one exception was Captain Karloff, and that really was an accident."

"I wondered about that. I heard so many versions of what happened I didn't know what to believe."

John said, "As a Russian, I'm supposed to be his sworn enemy. Admiration for him and his beliefs is the reason I'm leaving the Russian army. The high command did him an injustice from the very beginning."

"I'm glad," said the young man. "I'd hate to do business with someone who might wish do him harm."

The dealer took them to a warehouse that would serve as an intermediate drop-off. John would dismiss his teamsters, and the dealer would move the wagons and horses to another location.

The Barloffs returned to their hotel. Elsa was happier than she had ever been in her life. When they got to their room they made love ever so tenderly. It was like the first time for both of them. A great burden lifted from them that day. Elsa said, "I know you and I are going to have a full and happy life in America. Fate has been good to us."

"After the ski jump, it took me a long time to realize that it wasn't all my fault the men had died nor Jonas' either. He was just trying to save his own life. If we caught him or got close enough we would probably have killed him. What a loss that would have been. When my leg was healing, he and I had some long and serious talks. He made me realize the importance of freedom like no man has ever done."

Elsa checked all the arrangements for the four of them to leave in one month. There would be three ships leaving at that time. They could sell the horses and wagons and be gone before anyone was the wiser.

The loaded wagons headed back to Kiivijarvi. All the way back, John and Elsa felt jubilant at having decided to leave for America with Jonas and Emma.

Back in Kiivijarvi, they got word to the Lehtinens that all was arranged. The Lehtinens, in turn, would get word to Jonas and Emma.

Vilho had been waiting in his own house for news from Helsinki. As soon as Matt brought him word, he left for the wilderness cabin. He was anxious to see Mary as well as Jonas and Emma and was glad the symbol of Finnish freedom was leaving before anything happened to him.

Vilho reached the cabin in record time, remembering to step over the alarm rocks as he approached the cabin. When he reached the clearing he called out. "Hallo, the camp! It's Vilho, so don't shoot."

Jonas, Emma, and Mary came to meet him as he crossed the clearing. Greetings and hugs were exchanged. He gave Mary a long, hard kiss.

"It's all arranged," he told them once they got inside. "You leave in one month for America. We'll have to get you to Helsinki, but that should not be a problem. We were going to let you ride one of the wagons as an enlisted man and wife going to visit relatives in Helsinki. Then we thought someone might recognize either one of you, and there'd be trouble. We don't want anyone to know you've left, or we lose the value of you as the phantom freedom fighter no one can catch."

Emma said, "I'm glad it'll be so soon. We'll have plenty of time to get settled in America and have the baby born free in the new country."

Jonas said, "We're sad to leave this idyllic spot, but we know it's for the best. It makes it a little bit easier knowing that you and Mary will be using it. I hope you two will be as happy as Emma and I have been living here."

"I know we'll be happy," replied Vilho.

Emma said, "I'm glad we brought Mary out. I've had a chance to show her the woman's view of life here."

Jonas said, "I still need to show Vilho around the place."

"I'm planning on going with you to Helsinki to make sure you get there safe and sound," said Vilho. "That means Mary will have to stay here alone until I get back."

"Vilho, you treat me like a child," Jonas said. "Emma and I can make it to Helsinki on our own. You're needed here. The fewer people traveling together the better."

"How will I know you got on the ship?"

"We'll post a letter to Emma's parents as soon as we're sure we're going to make it safely on board."

Emma put on the coffee and they sat around talking about events in town. Jonas and Vilho talked seriously about the resistance movement.

Mary went to Vilho's pack to take out some fresh eggs and cured pork for breakfast.

"Eggs will be a treat," said Emma. "Let me make some fresh biscuits to go with them."

The month went by quickly for the four of them. They made several productive trips to their favorite fishing hole. Vilho and Jonas killed a deer for fresh meat. The four of them enjoyed each other's company even though the quarters were a little cramped.

Jonas and Emma made one trip into town with some items from the cabin and some clothes they wanted to take with them to America. They packed a large trunk and made arrangements for Barloff to haul the trunk into Helsinki on one of the freight wagons. Barloff had to smuggle Jonas' and Emmas' trunk and their own into the barns at night. He was going to say they were officers' goods to be delivered in Helsinki. He would have to wait until the last minute to load them so no questions would be asked.

When it was time to go, Jonas told Vilho, "I'm going to leave my rifle with Mika's supplier in Helsinki so you'll have it back. It's served me well."

Vilho objected, "You'll need it in America. We have a lot more like it at the Rock Quarry cabin. I'll get my own soon."

Jonas argued, "First, you gave it to me. Second, you need it more here as guns are scarce. I'm sure I can buy one just like it in America."

"I insist you keep it as a reminder of our friendship." Jonas kept the rifle.

Then came the time for Jonas and Emma to say a tearful good-bye to Vilho, Mary, and the cabin. Emma gave one last, long, farewell look and wave as they left the clearing, heading to town for the last time.

In town they had a last dinner with Emma's family. Jonas' brother took the chance to come to say good-bye. Hugs and kisses all around. Toivo, usually unemotional, had copious tears flowing down his cheeks.

Matt said, "Sister, you know how much I love you, but you do have a good man to take care of you. From that standpoint I feel good about your leaving. If I had to pick a good man for you, Jonas would be it."

Jonas shouldered his pack with most of their supplies for a week's trip to Helsinki. Emma insisted on carrying a small pack to help out. They stayed in the woods parallel to the road for several miles until they were clear of Kiivijarvi. Then they took to the road, figuring they could move into the woods if they heard someone coming. The biggest worry on the road was being recognized. Jonas knew they couldn't do much in the way of flight with Emma in her condition.

The first night, Jonas moved well off the road into a small gully for their camp. Jonas had a small canvas they used for a tent. Spruce boughs went in to make a softer bed for the night.

They planned their meals day by day, supplementing them with fish and game. That night they dined on smoked venison and potatoes baked in the coals of a small fire. A sense of excitement filled them about their adventure and what the future was going to bring.

They crawled into their lean-to tent, sleeping until the sun awakened Jonas. He eased out to start a small fire and make coffee and breakfast. Emma woke smelling the coffee and stretching like a lazy cat.

"Oh, Jonas you're doing my job."

"I don't mind. You need the rest."

"Jonas you treat me like an invalid. I'm not the first woman in the world to have a baby."

Breakfast over, Jonas packed their belongings to get them on their way again. The further they traveled from Kiivijarvi the better they both felt. Their mood of great joy and release from bondage grew with every step.

Jonas prayed with all his heart that nothing would happen to destroy their feeling of tranquility their last days in Finland.

They walked the road with relative safety. Jonas' long role as the hunted animal made him aware of approaching people long before they ever came within sight or sound. The subtle change in forest sounds warned them to get off the road to let them pass. They took no chances.

Their second night out, they had to stay near a swamp. Many exits from the road caused them to miss their planned stop. They got very little sleep because of mosquitoes. Jonas built a small smudge fire. It helped, but, by the next morning, they both came away covered with bites. Jonas vowed this would not happen again if he could help it.

Their original, planned stop had been farther down the road. They would have to make up for lost time. The stops were laid out by Barloff, based on short marches to good camp sites with good water. The delay upset the timetable. Jonas wasn't sure if Emma was up to making better time. With a little extra push, they could be back on the right schedule if they had no problems. Jonas worried about the next night forcing them into another bad camp site.

Emma sensed Jonas' apprehension and said, "Don't worry, Jonas, I can take it. I know you're capable of taking care of us under the most adverse circumstances."

"I know, but I can't help worrying about you and the baby."

"Jonas, unborn babies and newborn babies are a lot tougher than you think. Just think of all they've survived throughout history."

"I know you're right, but I can't stop worrying about what if this and what if that. In a way, it keeps me alert, but some is just worry."

Near nightfall, Jonas knew they would not make their pre-selected camp, so he started looking for an alternate without the plague of mosquitoes. He found a clump of spruce trees some distance off the road. There was no water near, but they had enough for the night and next day. The dearth of water meant no mosquitoes.

The next day, they did make up enough time to get to Barloff's recommended campsite. It was well hidden with a small, fast-running stream. No stagnant pools for mosquitoes to breed. They were far enough from the road to have a comfortable camp fire. Jonas even caught a few trout from the stream for their supper.

As they finished supper, Jonas said. "I hope you're right about fishing and hunting being as good in America as here in Finland."

"That's what I have read and heard," said Emma.

"Freedom is what I'm looking forward to in that land," said Jonas.

"I'm looking forward to our children growing up in freedom."

"Children," chided Jonas, "We haven't had the first one yet."

"I know, but I also know we're going to have a large family. We'll be free to do that, and our children will be free to do what they want."

"Freedom, such a precious commodity—I hope Vilho and the rest succeed in getting it for our homeland. I feel sad that I'm not staying to take part in it. And it will come. So many people are willing to work hard for it, and I think God is on our side as men were meant to be free."

Three more days without incident brought them to Helsinki. The Barloffs had arranged a place for them to stay near the docks until sailing time. The house was owned by some people known to be sympathetic to the cause, though they didn't know they were housing the famous Jonas. Everyone felt that the fewer people who knew they were leaving the better off they would be in keeping with the ghost-freedom-fighter concept.

Jonas paced constantly in the room, feeling cooped up and vulnerable in the city away from his beloved forest. Emma had to keep reassuring him it would turn out all right, but he still paced like a caged animal. They had three days to wait before sailing time. Time passed very slowly.

The Barloffs showed up the day before they were to sail. They sold the Russian wagons and horses. That, coupled with the money they got from selling their house and furniture in Kiivijarvi, gave them a nice nest egg.

The night before sailing, the Barloffs insisted they all go out to dinner. They went to the old Boar's Head, once owned by Mika but now owned by his chief cook. Again, Jonas was nervous about their being in public, but the dinner went without incident.

They boarded the ship the next morning. Both couples had cabins, though small and cramped. Jonas didn't expect a cabin, but Barloff insisted he pay the difference so they could both travel in some comfort.

Jonas did not really relax until the ship was well out of the harbor. He and Emma stood by the rail, arms around each other, watching the receding shoreline as the ship headed for America and a new life.

Epilogue

VILHO CONTINUED AS THE VISIBLE LEADER of the resistance movement. The cadre that moved into other areas became the basis for self-government. Unknowingly, the Russians helped by sending Finnish non-commissioned officers from Kiivijarvi to other outposts. Most of the men transferred were already in the resistance, and they set up new groups at each new location.

The ghost symbol was used continually to tie elements of the movement together into one cohesive unit.

Vilho was far more aggressive than Jonas in thwarting the Russians. He was also more blood thirsty and didn't hesitate to kill Russians that opposed him. Jonas had killed only in self-defense. But Vilho's aggessiveness helped make the resistance successful. Long before the final coupe of the Bolsheviks in Russia, the decision had been not to include Finland as part of the Communist movement. Russians already knew how costly and time consuming that kind of merger would be. Finland gained her independence in 1917.

When the Bolsheviks took over Russia, many Russians remained in Finland, forming outlaw bandit groups. The old resistance groups had a tough time fighting them. The tables had been reversed, with the Russians being hunted down. Freedom still had to be paid for in blood.

In the mean time, Jonas and Emma, along with their good friends, John Barloff and Elsa had traveled to Michigan and were exploring the wonderful woodlands there, thoroughly enjoying the hunting and fishing. They both had small farms. And, though they often thought longingly of their homeland, they had made new starts in America, and their many-childrened families thrived in freedom.

THE END

About the Author

Leslie W. Wisuri was born in Iron River, Michigan, on March 26, 1925. The first born of William and Anna Wisuri, he had one brother, Edwin, now deceased, a sister Betty, now deceased, a sister Shirley, living in Atlanta, Georgia, and sister Kathryn, living in California.

After having graduated from Iron River High School in 1943, Leslie entered the army in September of that year. He took basic training in Camp Van Dorn, Mississippi, with the 63rd Division, then joined Cannon Company 30th Infantry Regiment of the Third Division. He served in Italy, France, and Germany and was wounded near Colmar, France. Discharged in September 1945, he earned the Purple Heart, the Bronze Star, the Presidential Unit Citation, Good Conduct Medal, Combat Infantry Badge and American Theater and European Theatre ribbons.

Leslie entered Michigan State College in September of 1945 and graduated in June of 1949 with a bachelor's degree in forestry. For two years he owned and operated a sawmill in Iron River.

On January 12, 1951, in Waukegan, Illinois, Leslie married Jacqueline Brown of Sandy, Utah. They have two daughters, Karen and Kim, and one grandchild, Anna.

During his life so far, Leslie served a short hitch with the Waukegan, Illinois, Fire Department, went to work for Titan Chain Saws in 1952 as a field representative for three years, then worked for McCulloch Chain Saws in 1955 as a district manager for nine years. He later started Village Marina on Lake of the Ozarks, Missouri, in 1965, storing and selling boats, a business he owned and operated for thirteen years before selling it in 1978. He then built and operated a Scuba Diving and Salvage business where he taught diving and salvaging sunken boats. He sold this business in 1989.

Leslie started writing *Jonas of Kiivijarvi* in 1982 at the insistence of relatives who had not heard the stories told to him by his grandfather, Jonas Wisuri.